every man's marriage

Every Man's Guide to...
Winning the Heart of a Woman

Stephen Arterburn
Fred Stoeker with Mike Yorkey

WATERBROOK
PRESS

EVERY MAN'S MARRIAGE
PUBLISHED BY WATERBROOK PRESS
12265 Oracle Boulevard, Suite 200
Colorado Springs, Colorado 80921

Scripture quotations taken from the *Holy Bible, New International Version*®. NIV®. Copyright © 1973, 1978, 1984 by International Bible Society. Used by permission of Zondervan Publishing House. All rights reserved.

Italics in Scripture quotations reflect the authors' added emphasis.

Details in some anecdotes and stories have been changed to protect the identities of the persons involved.

ISBN 978-1-57856-522-1

Previously published under the title *Every Woman's Desire,* copyright © 2001 by Stephen Arterburn, Fred Stoeker, and Mike Yorkey.

Published in association with the literary agency of Alive Communications, Inc., 7680 Goddard Street, Suite 200, Colorado Springs, CO 80920.

Published in the United States by WaterBrook Multnomah, an imprint of the Crown Publishing Group, a division of Random House Inc., New York.

Library of Congress Cataloging-in-Publication Data

Arterburn, Stephen, 1953–
    Every woman's desire : every man's guide to—winning the heart of a woman / Stephen Arterburn, Fred Stoeker with Mike Yorkey.—1st ed.
        p. cm.
    ISBN 1-57856-522-7
    1. Husbands—Religious life. 2. Marriage—Religious aspects—Christianity. 3. Arterburn, Stephen, 1953– I. Stoeker, Fred. II. Yorkey, Mike. III. Title.

BV4528.2. A78 2001
248.8'425—dc21   2001046676

Printed in the United States of America
2009

20 19 18 17 16 15 14 13

Special Sales

Most WaterBrook books are available in special quantity discounts when purchased in bulk by corporations, organizations and special interest groups. Custom imprinting or excerpting can also be done to fit special needs.
For information, please e-mail SpecialMarkets@WaterBrookMultnomah.com or call 1-800-603-7051.

from Fred Stoeker:

To my heavenly Father:
All I know comes from You.

And to Brenda:
The thought that amazes is that you love me…

———————

from Stephen Arterburn:

To Nancy Simonian,
the best mother-in-law a guy could have.
You gave me a wife who is
strong, talented, funny, and gorgeous,
because you are all of those things also.

contents

have you found the keys to her heart?

(by Stephen Arterburn)

I don't know whether this is true in your part of the country, but in Southern California where I live, bagel shops and cell phone stores (and almost any business) will hire a guy to stand on the sidewalk and hold a sign advertising the store. Most signs are painted in garish red and shaped like an arrow, figuratively pointing you toward the best deal on a dozen bagels or a minutes-per-month cellular plan.

When it comes to traversing the sidewalks of life, most married guys should take turns pounding the pavement while wearing a sandwich board that says, "Work in Progress Here." I know that's been the case for me, and my cowriter of this book, Fred Stoeker, would agree in a heartbeat. No matter whether you're unpacking after the honeymoon or packing up to retire from a lifetime career, becoming the husband that your wife always desired you to be is a constant work in progress.

That's been true ever since I became a young adult. When I was a single man in my late twenties, I embarked on a new career in the counseling arena after years of rebellion, doubt, and mistakes. I finally felt that I was getting my Christian act together. My spiritual résumé looked great on paper: I was active in my church, I participated in missions work, and I sang in the choir. I thought I would make someone a nice husband.

One Sunday evening after our church service, I traveled to a nearby restaurant to eat dinner. I was alone, but that was okay. Although the restaurant was nearly deserted, a young couple was seated at the table next to me. The young woman, Sandy, recognized me from church and, from her table, commented on how much she enjoyed my solo effort that morning.

I swelled with pride for being noticed. "Thank you," I said in my best aw-shucks Texan manner (I was born in Ranger, Texas). I continued to grin as I made small talk with the couple. After a few minutes, however, even I realized that two was a party and three was a crowd, so I asked for the check and quietly excused myself.

As I walked to the car, I admitted to myself that I was attracted to Sandy. When I later learned that she was "just friends" with her date, I asked Sandy out for a date on Mother's Day. I knew what would impress her. "I'm leaving soon on the upcoming missions trip to the Marshall Islands," I mentioned as the waitress handed us our menus.

"Oh, really?" replied Sandy. "I'm going on the same trip!"

Amazing grace! Who wouldn't be convinced that we weren't a match made in heaven after a coincidence like that? To ensure that the match stuck, however, I couldn't divulge the secret compartments of my life. My continuing feelings for my old girlfriend. My various and sundry sexual experiences. The abortion. The thousands of dollars of debt fueled by maxed-out credit cards.

I rushed the relationship because I was acting out of fear that I would go through life unmarried, unloved, and an outcast in the Christian community. I only divulged the existence of my first marriage and subsequent divorce when I thought Sandy could handle that news, but I never let on regarding the desperation I felt to marry again. Sandy was a "catch"—bright, attractive, talented, and gracious—and I didn't want to mess up this courtship. I would hide who I really was.

SHATTERING THE INTIMACY

We married and immediately had problems. We didn't know it at the time, but the brick wall we ran into was named Intimacy. My secret compartments and my resistance to letting her forge her own identity kept us on opposite sides of the wall. And our inability to conceive a child added more bricks to its height.

Communication was one-sided; it flowed from my direction only, in the form of impulsive comments on topics ranging from her cooking skills to her choice of clothes. I insisted that she wear conservative plaid outfits with bows under the neck—like a Texan belle—although no one in Southern California dressed that way. The constant harping and my dominating presence suffocated Sandy. Our marriage lacked intimacy, and we were starting to live like married singles.

But was I so different from most men? Rather than connect with women and understand them, most men seem to want to command them. Many husbands use 1 Peter 3 as their official standard, for it instructs women married to nonbelievers to keep silent and win their husbands over with loving words and actions. This Scripture passage has given many men free rein in their behavior as leaders, often shattering marital oneness and intimacy to smithereens.

I know of these things because I became one of the worst offenders after I married my first wife, a fellow student at Baylor. Amazingly, I thought everything was going well until the day she said she was leaving me.

Rather than humble myself to ask what I had done to be so hurtful, I pulled out the Bible to prove to her that it was not right for her to go. I just knew that this "scriptural club" would knock some sense into her. I preached Ephesians 5 at her so often that I had it memorized. In my narrow view, this passage said that she should submit to me and that God was going to be very upset with her if she did not get in line with what He wanted for His boy Steve. But my arrogant reaction to her announcement simply proved that she was right: I was an insensitive, egotistical, self-obsessed, uncaring jerk of a husband who had no idea how to win the heart of a woman.

She left my house for the courthouse and filed for divorce. She never screamed, yelled, or asked me to change. (She probably thought change was impossible!) And although she left, I felt quite content that I had done the right thing to prove to her that I was the good guy in all this.

As I look back now, I find it ironic that I picked the fifth chapter of Ephesians to prove to her that she needed to stay. Although the passage *does* focus on a woman's need to respond to the leadership of her husband, it contains many more instructions on how a man should lead. I conveniently missed the part about dying to myself and sacrificing my life and rights as Christ did for the church.

I know what it is to be ignorant of truth and to do stupid things in the name of Jesus. I know how good it feels to be always correcting from the pinnacle rather than connecting from the pavement. I enjoyed pointing my finger more than opening up my arms. I was no husband; I was a judge. Everything in marriage had to reflect me, and God was left way behind.

So now here I was married again and doing the very same things to Sandy. My schtick wasn't playing any better this time around. How would I get our ship, the USS *Matrimony,* turned in the right direction? Or, to use another analogy we follow in the rest of this book, *How would I resurrect a relationship that had grown cold and lifeless?*

REVIVING A MARRIAGE

I can't pinpoint the time or a particular incident that started my change in course, but seeing a Christian counselor allowed me to recognize that I needed an attitude adjustment. I needed to verbally build up Sandy, focus on what a wonderful person she was, and look for opportunities to encourage her. I needed to respect her uniqueness and her viewpoints. I needed to allow her infectious personality to bubble up to the surface.

As I worked on these long-term attitudinal changes, there were also some things I could do immediately to become the husband Sandy had always desired. I limited my travel to two days per week. I came home from work by 6 P.M. and left my briefcase at the office so I wouldn't work at home. I regularly called Sandy to ask her to join me for lunch. Most of all, I decided to meet her needs by lavishing thoughtful gifts and getaway weekends on her—and by taking the trash out without being asked and by making sure my dirty laundry actually reached the clothes hamper and then by learning how to operate the washing machine.

Those seemingly small but dramatic changes revived my dying marriage. Our relationship improved when we brought our daughter, Madeline, home from the hospital in 1990. Suddenly building a career and a national reputation as an author and speaker didn't seem so important anymore.

Following this turnaround, as I talked with more husbands and wives, I heard them say that their marriages improved when the husband sought to do things to please his wife—when he began to allow her personality and convictions to find a place with his in the marriage. This is what mutual submission is all about, and that's the profound, life-changing theme Fred and I will be exploring with you in this book.

Are you ready to put this incredible concept to practical use in your own marriage? We hope you've picked up this book because you want to find the keys to a woman's heart and provide what she needs and wants in marriage. If you're willing to trust God and implement what we tell you, some amazing things are going to happen to you and the woman in your life. You'll discover a world that few men ever find because they've never considered traveling the sacrificial path where Jesus first led. But we believe you want to do just that, and we're inviting you to enter into this journey with us.

You'll notice, especially in the first half-dozen chapters, that this book centers around many lessons learned from the mistakes that Fred made with his wife, Brenda, and how he eventually turned things around. Keeping the spotlight on Fred's story is by design. First, Fred agreed to hang out his dirty laundry for the world to see if his story would help change marriages, and I can respect that. Second, the difficulties in my marriage have been the subject of other books I've written, and numerous magazine articles describe our story of hope, despair, struggle, and now renewed hope. So in this book I've given Sandy and myself a break and will allow you to immerse yourself in Fred's remarkable story, made possible by his uncommon openness and vulnerability. Those are the qualities that made me want to write with Fred, and I know you'll come to appreciate him and Brenda as you read of how their relationship was transformed. I'm confident, too, that your own marriage will change for the better as you learn from Fred's struggles.

So...ready to get started?

PART I

when love grows cold...

in the beginning: a painful revelation

I* sat across the kitchen table from my wife, Brenda, and I could tell she was waiting until she had my undivided attention.

Then she looked intently into my eyes and changed my world. "I don't know how else to say this to you, so I'll say it straight," she began. "My feelings for you are dead."

Her words arrived like a fastball pitch to the solar plexus. *Dead?* My head spun. Where was this coming from? Our marriage had begun with such promise. How could I have messed things up so badly that my wife—the love of my life—now felt totally numb to me? My mind quickly searched for answers, but it would take me some time to piece things together.

SEARCHING FOR CLUES

The seeds of my marital discord were planted four years before I met Brenda. I was attending Stanford University in the San Francisco Bay area, desperately trying to make sense of my life, seeking truth in any intellectual nook and cranny I could find (I was a non-Christian, though I'd attended church many times over the years).

---

* Because this book focuses on Fred's story (see the next-to-last paragraph in the introduction), first-person pronouns refer to Fred, unless otherwise indicated.

First, I dallied in the writings of Marx and Engels. Next I turned to Eastern religion, a fad that swept the Stanford campus in the late 1970s. I even accepted a flower and an invitation from the Moonies, who "love-bombed" me but failed to convince me to join their ranks. Meanwhile, I meandered up and down the West Coast, spending seminar weekends with enlightened gurus as they "merged" with the universe.

I hungered to find the Meaning of Life, but since I wasn't having much luck, I looked for solace and comfort in the arms of female companions. That was something I could understand. One year after graduating from Stanford, I had four girlfriends and was sleeping with three of them. Obviously, I was a busy man—too busy to notice that God was drawing a bead on my hungry soul.

Late one afternoon before leaving the office of my first real job, I settled my feet on the credenza to enjoy the beautiful California sunset bursting through my window. In this unguarded moment, God somehow interrupted the scene with the horrible revelation of what I had become. Detesting the sight, I felt sorrow rush over me. "Lord," I prayed, "if You're ready to work with me, I'm ready to work with You."

All heaven seemed to move on my behalf. Within weeks, I accepted a new position back in Iowa, where I'd grown up. I left the anything-goes West Coast lifestyle in my rearview mirror. Best of all, my quest for the Meaning of Life—for truth—was over. I had accepted Christ as Lord of my life. Finally, I had peace.

Planting my feet squarely in Des Moines, Iowa, I found a church home. In addition, I decided to attend a married couples Sunday school class—which raised a few eyebrows, since I was a bachelor. You see, I had stopped dating, suspecting I understood little about women and knowing I couldn't treat them with honor. I had heard that the pastor teaching the class would unveil the wonderful intricacies of women. He did, which only confirmed my ignorance about females, despite all the "intimate" time I had spent with them.

As the months passed, a desire grew within me to understand the lessons better. One night I simply prayed, "Lord, You've taught me so much about women. Can You show me someone who embodies these characteristics?" I wasn't asking for a girlfriend or even a date. I just wanted to see such a Christian woman in real life.

One week later, my father, now married to my stepmother, called me from Moline, Illinois, and said, "Freddie, I have a deal for you! I know a family in our church with a nice Christian daughter, and I've arranged a double date for us. My treat." I thought it was kind of cute that Dad wanted to double-date with me, but then I remembered the last time Dad had tried to play matchmaker. He sent me on a day ski trip with a date who wore tight stretch pants, had big hair, and used so much makeup she must have applied it with a trowel.

Despite the bad experience, I decided to play along again and make the three-hour drive to Moline. Dad meant well, and a church service capped with a free lunch seemed tame enough. With a little luck, I'd be home in time for the second NBA game on television.

The day began when I took my seat right next to Dad just a few minutes before the church service was to begin. He leaned over and whispered, "Freddie, here she comes."

Brenda Hulett stepped into our row, and I stood up to shake her hand. As our eyes met, my heavenly Father seemed to lean down and whisper, *This is the girl you're going to marry.* I really felt that I would become her husband! This thought, premonition—whatever you want to call it—struck me as funny, which caused me to giggle throughout the service whenever I glanced at her.

Naturally, Brenda was annoyed by my behavior, wondering who this weirdo was sitting next to her. Later that day, I naively told her why I'd been chuckling all during the church service. Now she really wanted to run! Miraculously, she resisted the urge. I was vindicated seven months later on our wedding day.

SEEKING A MOTHER'S BLESSING

So God arranged your marriage, huh? Everything must have gone perfectly for you after that. Hardly. Our courtship progressed strangely that spring and summer, beginning with a request that I made to my mother after our engagement. "When can I come to Cedar Rapids to see you?" I asked. "I want you to meet my fiancée."

An icy silence ensued. My mom and I were very close, and the thought of her only son marrying some girl she'd never met was not well received. Maybe she was thinking of her own marriage, which broke up when I was eleven years old. After my parents finalized their divorce, life became an emotional and financial horror for Mom, my two sisters, and me. The pressures of single parenting nearly leveled her, but Mom tenaciously fought through it. Working two jobs, she'd come home from her receptionist job, touch base, and grab a bite to eat with us, and then head out to sell grave plots.

Mom was easily the bravest person I knew. As she battled on, my young heart ached for her, and I vowed I'd never do anything to make Mom cry. I shouldered the mantle of manhood as best I could, and we all became closer as we passed through the trials together. That's why her silence following the news of my engagement caught me off guard. I didn't realize that my mother wanted to meet the girl *before* her son decided to marry.

Against this backdrop, Brenda naturally felt the pressure to make a good first impression upon my mother and sisters. Wearing her best sundress, Brenda fixed her hair into a wonderful cloud of curls, and she couldn't have looked nicer. Alas, at first glance my mother and siblings immediately pegged Brenda as a "sorority chick" who would never fit in with the family. No blessing was forthcoming that day, especially after Brenda accidentally stepped into a flat of fresh strawberries my mother had lovingly picked for me.

I hoped our autumn wedding would end the relational tailspin, but first impressions turned into a lasting impression. And marital adjustment turned out to be difficult for Brenda. Her father had died two months before the wedding, and although his passing was expected, his death nonetheless brought immense grief. Guilt piled on top of Brenda's grief because we were living three hours away from her childhood home in Moline, Illinois, leaving her mother alone to deal with her pain.

We settled in Des Moines, but Brenda couldn't get her bearings there. Brenda had been born and raised in Moline, had always attended the same church she'd been baptized in as a young child, and had cultivated deep friendships there. After college, she had returned to Moline to work as a registered nurse, a career that gained her respect among her peers. Now in Des Moines, Brenda had no friends for support.

To make matters worse, her new job at a local hospital was an unpleasant, vulgar work environment. Worst of all, she was living with me, a veritable stranger who had lost his temper on her wedding night and erupted far too often since. She was overwhelmed. Because of this, we often spent more time with Brenda's family than with mine when we returned to Moline for a visit. Though logical given the circumstances, the relationships with my family deteriorated further. Storms rolled in from every direction.

Trying to mediate both sides was no fun. Where I come from, the louder you were, the righter you were. So every few nights, I received another railing phone call from my family regarding this "insensitive woman" I had married. They kept asking:

"How can she be so selfish with your time?"

"Why do you let her be so self-centered?"

"Don't you still love us?"

We lived in a small apartment, and Brenda could hear it all. Enduring a few tempestuous holidays with my family as well, Brenda soon grew frightened by their volatile outbursts. She felt nauseous for three full days before any visit to their homes.

And why not? The holidays were nothing but trouble. My family, already seeing us less than they desired, demanded a full day's visit. Frightened by their explosive tempers, Brenda preferred an afternoon schedule, somewhere in the one-to-four-o'clock range. With a bit of brokering, I'd negotiate a noon-until-six schedule. Upset with nerves, Brenda dawdled till the last minute, and we often arrived late. This annoyed my family to no end. Of course, the roles reversed in the afternoon as they demanded we stay until the very last minute, while Brenda ached to return to the safety of our car at the first possible moment. Everyone watched the clock all day. It drove me nuts.

Was I frustrated with my family? Sure. They were wrong about Brenda and made impossible demands on me. But I was even more frustrated with Brenda. We were teammates, and I expected that we would pull from the same rope. I felt she should be more flexible in the negotiations to help me bring us together. I began calling her names, like "big baby" and "spoiled brat."

Did Brenda agree? Not on your life! She felt that I loved my family and relatives more than I loved her. "After all," she said, "I don't hear you calling them nasty names." She felt that I should defend her and halt their demeaning tirades. My temper became sickeningly manifest. Often, I'd stand toe to toe with Brenda and shout until she cowered. I twice broke holes in the Sheetrock walls with my bare fists. During one of my many tantrums, I threw a pot of bean soup across the floor. But I felt justified.

From my perspective, she was simply stubborn and wouldn't help.

From her perspective, she *couldn't* help.

WATCHING THE LOVE GROW COLD

The poison of in-law problems seeped into every aspect of our relationship. In the early days, my heart skipped a beat every time I saw Brenda walk across a room. Not anymore. More often than not, our evenings ended the same way: After hitting the light on the nightstand, I'd settle my head into my pillow, only to hear these sickening words in the darkness: "Fred, we have something to talk about."

On Valentine's Day, I went to buy a card. Fingering through the cards and reading the texts, I returned them one by one to the rack as "too mushy" or "too contrived" or "too romantic." Little by little, panic settled in as I faced the truth: I couldn't give any of those cards to Brenda with any measure of sincerity.

The onslaught of our in-law problems resembled what the Allied air forces inflicted upon enemy cities in World War II. Our pilots dropped their bombs and then returned to base where life was pretty normal—eating, sleeping, playing cards, and preparing for the next sortie. But for the people back in the burning rubble of the bombed cities, normal life was impossible.

So it was with us. My family dropped their bombs over the phone and then, with the click of the receiver, returned to "base" and their normal life with friends and family. But for Brenda and me, our marriage was crumbling, with rubble smoldering all around us. There was no safe haven—only desperation. And, sadly, Brenda sensed she was living with the enemy because I continued to defend my family during our arguments. Besides, I was just as volatile as they were. I'm sure my scowl reminded her of them.

All this laid the groundwork for Brenda's sorrowful statement: "I don't know how else to say this, but my feelings for you are dead."

Now it was my turn to feel nauseous! Long ago, when my parents' divorce loomed over my life, a merciless question swirled over and over within my frightened heart. *What are we going to do?* I asked myself. *What are we going to do?*

Brenda's words brought the question sweeping back, with an even more personal twist: "What am *I* going to do?"

Her declaration took me by surprise. This is the girl God Himself chose for me. This is my wife…and all my hopes and dreams are tied up in her. I'd do anything for her. So how is this happening? I still love her! Sure, the romance is gone, but she's my best friend. We can still talk to each other. I love our walks.

I asked Brenda a few questions. "Honey, what about it? Do you still love me?"

"Yes," she said. "I still love you."

"If the love is still there, then how come your feelings for me are dead?"

Brenda couldn't put it into words, which left me writhing in grinding confusion. Waves of panic washed over me for days, buckling me in unguarded moments. This isn't right. *What am I going to do?*

AVOIDING DIVORCE COURT

One day, as I stepped into the kitchen for a glass of milk, tears pooled in my eyes once again. I fought down a searing pain in my heart. Opening the refrigerator door, I listlessly grabbed the milk carton and aimed at the glass in my hand. Returning the carton to its place, I shut the door and stared for a long time at the refrigerator through tear-filled eyes. Then I pointed to heaven, declaring, "God, I don't care how much gravel I have to eat, but I am not getting a divorce."

That's how desperate I was. I'd eat rocks if that would save my marriage. I knew it was time to pay a real price, a much deeper price. God said in Ephesians 5 that I must lay down my life for my marriage, just as He laid down His life for His bride, the church. I hadn't even approached such sacrificial love.

I lifted up that desperate statement to God nearly twenty years ago. Recently, a deacon said to me, "Fred, I know only two couples who enjoy a level of intimacy that allows them to talk to each other about absolutely anything—even their sins—without fear and with total love. You and Brenda are one of them."

I smiled and thanked that deacon. How did we get from there to here? What you're about to read is our story.

Questions for Reflection and Discussion

1. As honestly and fully as you can, describe your own journey in encountering any of Fred's experiences and discoveries as presented in this chapter. How much can you identify with him?

2. Which part of Fred's story can you identify with most?

3. Have you ever come to the point of making a significant and memorable decision to save or strengthen your marriage? If so, what brought this about?

4. How would you express your personal goals or expectations for your marriage from reading *Every Man's Marriage*?

how did the feelings die?

When my marriage went south, I hadn't a clue about how to fix it. Certainly, the state of my union hadn't turned out one bit as I'd expected. All I knew was that my marriage had collapsed under my watch. If I learned anything in that Sunday school class for couples, it was that men are primarily responsible to complete God's call to marital oneness (drawn especially from Ephesians 5:23, where we're told, "For the husband is the head of the wife as Christ is the head of the church, his body, of which he is the Savior"). While women have clear responsibilities in a marriage, let's speak plainly: Who is God likely to hold most responsible?

I didn't like this call to "marital oneness." For one thing, I didn't really understand it, and it didn't seem fair at all. I especially hated bearing the primary responsibility, since I thought Brenda was immature and spoiled. Why was *I* responsible when *she* was so stubborn? She was the one who wouldn't yield to my leadership.

I knew I'd have to answer for my marriage, no matter how I tried to twist out of it. God gave me my wife and, as I understand Scripture, asked me to lead well as the head of my family. I knew marriage and my love for Brenda were my highest calling. It was time to step up and make a deeper commitment, but I was clueless and running out of time. To resurrect my marriage, I was willing to take drastic action at any cost, even if that meant bringing in a third party.

STUMBLING ON SOMETHING ESSENTIAL

Here's what I did. I asked Brenda with all sincerity if we could talk for a moment. "Look," I began. "I've been thinking about all this in-law stuff, and I just don't know what to say. I think you're totally wrong, and you think I'm totally wrong, so let's go see Pastor Ron. He knows nothing of our situation, and I have no idea what his advice will be. But whatever he tells me to do, I will do it. I don't care what he says. I love you, and I want to fix this problem we have."

Brenda's mouth dropped open. "Whatever he says? Anything?"

Brenda doubted my word, though she had nothing to lose. After all, I'd given her a blank check. But she also knew something I didn't yet know: I'd been wrong in the way I'd been treating her. She was quite certain Ron would see things her way.

Pastor Ron patiently listened to each of us lay out our side of the conflict. As usual, he addressed the situation with vast wisdom and at great length. His conclusion was this: "Fred, you've been sitting on the fence between your wife and your family, trying to bring them together. Brenda feels as though you aren't placing her first. You must climb down squarely onto Brenda's side of the fence and make a stand for her." He then detailed what he considered a reasonable action plan, pointing out several Bible passages pertinent to our situation, including one that talked of me "submitting" to Brenda.

I didn't see how Pastor Ron's advice would work, and I told him so. His naive reasoning required that I "submit" to Brenda, which didn't sound right to me. But I was desperate, and I *had* given my word that I would follow Ron's advice. In addition, giving in would buy me some time to sort things out.

Brenda would later say, "I felt absolute and immediate relief when we left that session." As for me, I followed Ron's advice to the letter, calling my family and telling them I was climbing down on Brenda's side of the fence. She overheard my phone calls and reacted in complete astonishment. This is how she recalls her response:

When you acted upon Ron's advice, I immediately felt as though we were one, and not "me against you" all the time. Before that, because you only partially supported me, I felt you were as much of an antagonist as they were. Like Jesus said, "You are either for me, or against me." It was always hard on me when you cared so deeply for people who were so hurtful to me, although they were your family.

Through this process, I had stumbled onto the most essential biblical truth on marital leadership I've found. To my amazement, my marriage did more than stabilize. It blossomed. Now I was really confused! Why? It was *my* submission that revived our marriage—not Brenda's. Men aren't supposed to submit, are they?

And thinking further, why did the resolution of a simple conflict of wills have such an impact? I mulled over Brenda's words: "When you acted upon Ron's advice, I immediately felt as though we were one, and not 'me against you' all the time." Evidently, I had been crushing our oneness, but there was far more to it than that. How did I know? Because she also said, "I felt absolute and immediate relief when we left that session"! Relief? That's a term you use when you exit a haunted house or a raging river, not when you get your way. What was scaring her?

ME: ESSENTIALLY WRONG!

I soon stumbled upon a second essential insight—all about me. You see, for months Brenda had stated over and over that my family was treating her worse than I knew. She said I was blind to it. I sarcastically responded, "Don't tell me I'm blind! I've lived with them for twenty years, while you hardly know them. Don't you think I just might know them a bit better than you do? Hmm?"

But she never wavered. "When you aren't in the room, they're like ice, but when you appear around the corner, it's sugar time."

"Brenda, that just can't be true. Your imagination is working overtime. They would never do that!"

Each time it happened again, she would flesh out the scene in great detail in an effort to convince me. "C'mon," she said, as we drove back home toward Des Moines. "You know I can't be making this up!"

I did my best to stiff-arm her. "You can imagine it a million times if you want! That won't make it true."

Then one day we traveled to Chicago to attend the wedding of a family friend. I was the best man, so Brenda and I arrived early for the Friday afternoon rehearsal. My family would arrive later for the rehearsal dinner.

Inside the large church, Brenda sat in the rear by the doors passing time with a novel, while I stood far away at the front of the sanctuary, memorizing my moves. When my family arrived, they didn't notice me standing up front. Brenda stood to greet them with a cheerful smile. When they responded by "dissing" her, I could feel the chill from that distance. She tried to engage them in conversation, but they largely ignored her and soon moved stiffly away.

Suddenly, I *knew.* Brenda had been right all along, and I'd been wrong. She wasn't a spoiled brat after all. She had gifts for discerning relationships that I simply didn't have, and by arrogantly blowing off her insights, I had really hurt us. Most of all, I knew that if our roles had been reversed, my feelings for Brenda would have died, too.

I ached at that moment to reach Brenda, to tell her I understood, but the rehearsal ran long. Late for dinner, we rushed off in a car stuffed with people, and it was hours before I could finally tell her that I had seen the light.

Our communication patterns changed that day. I had once been blind, but now I could see. Over the next days and weeks, I listened closely when I asked her, "What exactly have I done? How did I kill your feelings?"

I found that we hadn't been locked in a simple conflict of wills at all. I had been trampling her to the depths of her soul. To rectify the matter, I had to discover the role of "male submission" in marriage. But first, of course, the trampling had to stop.

Questions for Reflection and Discussion

1. How do you understand your biblical responsibility for leadership in your marriage? How would you express it in your own words?

2. How do you understand your biblical responsibility for submission in your marriage? How would you express it in your own words?

3. As you went through this chapter, what questions came to your mind about your own responsibility for both leadership and submission in your marriage? In what ways is it easy for you to agree with the conclusions Fred came to? In what ways, if any, do you find it difficult to agree with him?

4. In what ways, if any, have you discovered that your wife was right all along about something you thought you fully understood but didn't?

trampling the one you love

I had trampled Brenda, crushing the opportunity for oneness in our marriage. I had stampeded her concerns, stepped on her feelings. Such trampling is sinning against your wife.

Yes, I said *sinning*. If you're thinking I'm off the wall and you're ready to put this book down, don't move so fast. Most of us Christian men sin against our wives regularly, but we're just too blind to see it. Odds are, you're a bit blind too. So why do I say *trampling* instead of *sinning*?

The word *sin* has lost its communication value in our culture partly because it's considered too judgmental. No one likes to be called a sinner. *That's for people who are really bad.*

More important, *sin* no longer has a consistent meaning among Christian men. While we can all agree that sin is bad, we have trouble agreeing upon what qualifies as sin. Most of us smugly believe that we never sin against our wives. Our Hit Parade of Sins comes from the Ten Commandments, and since we haven't stolen from or lied (oops) to our wives or cheated on them, we're in the clear, right?

Not really. Our definition of sin is far too narrow. Many of us go through life without understanding the full height, breadth, and depth of God's definition of sin. Instead of asking, "How holy can I be?" we prefer to ask, "How far can I go and still be called a Christian?"

And how far we go depends upon the benchmarks set by our peers rather than by God. Under such a scenario, we miss standing in the center of God's holy ground, preferring instead to roam the outer edges where we step outside the lines too often. And if we find a few Christian brothers out there with us, we simply move the boundaries out a bit farther.

This is how someone describes a Christian couple he knows:

> There's something in Tim's "bag of tricks" that really kills Sally. When they're out together, his ogling of other women is a major problem. At work, Tim always seems to gravitate toward the cute, young female associates to form working relationships that are closer than necessary. It's a big problem between them. Huge!

Tim is sinning against his wife. He doesn't call it sin, and if you pressed him on the matter, he would open his palms and say, "My looking at women? It's a weakness for all guys. And my 'sensitive guy' routine at the office is just the way I interact with women. What's the big deal?"

Tim doesn't view his wandering eye and overly solicitous helping as anything close to sin. "Just because I can't order doesn't mean I can't look at the menu," he chuckles as he glances at a pair of breasts bouncing by. But listen to what God says in Scripture regarding our eyes and our heart:

> Above all else, *guard your heart,* for it is the wellspring of life. Put away perversity from your mouth; keep corrupt talk far from your lips. *Let your eyes look straight ahead, fix your gaze directly before you.* Make level paths for your feet and take only ways that are firm. (Proverbs 4:23-26)

Fix your gaze directly before you. That's something to consider, along with this sentence from a great Old Testament role model: "I made a covenant with my eyes not to look lustfully at a girl" (Job 31:1).

This is God's standard, and He made no secret of His pleasure with Job's commitment to His standards. He even bragged about Job to Satan: "Have you considered my servant Job? There is no one on earth like him; he is blameless and upright, a man who fears God and shuns evil" (Job 1:8).

God would have each of us live as blamelessly as Job before our wives. Tim agrees in principle, but his narrow definition of sin keeps him sinning against his wife. Though his ignorance reduces his guilt, it does not reduce the effects of his sins. Marital oneness with Sally is still being crushed.

A BROADER DEFINITION NEEDED

Clearly, we must broaden our definition of sin to match God's. But there's another thing we should also do: We must allow our wives to define our sin as well.

Wait a minute. I'm the husband and spiritual leader. Shouldn't I define sin for our household? To a certain extent, yes, you're responsible for defining and exposing sin in your family as a part of your leadership, but your relationship with your wife is at least as important as your position in defining sin. Maybe more so.

We find a great deal to think about this in the clear teaching the apostle Paul gave about "the weak" and "the strong." In the book of Romans, when discussing what foods were okay (or "clean") for a Christian to eat, he acknowledged that "disputable matters" would be normal in the Christian community. As you read his words, think about how they are just as true in a Christian marriage:

> Accept him whose faith is weak, without passing judgment on disputable matters. One man's faith allows him to eat everything, but another man, whose faith is weak, eats only vegetables. The man who eats everything must not look down on him who does not, and the man who does not eat everything must not condemn the man who does, for God has accepted him. (Romans 14:1-3)

The term *faith* here refers not to saving faith in Christ but to the sense of confidence in one's liberty in Christ. In this case, "strong" Christians such as Paul understood that their diet had no spiritual significance. The "weak" simply were not yet clear as to the status of the Old Testament regulations under Christ's New Covenant. The motivations behind both the weak and the strong were the same. Both wanted to avoid sin and to serve God fully. The point, Paul said, is that unity among Christians must not be based upon everyone's agreement over disputable questions. Christians won't agree on all matters pertaining to the Christian life because God didn't address every matter in Scripture. Nor do they need to agree, as long as they handle their disputes lovingly.

When it comes to disputable matters of conduct, recognizing the importance of personal conviction is critical. Paul went on to say,

> As one who is in the Lord Jesus, I am fully convinced that no food is
> unclean in itself. But if anyone regards something as unclean, then for
> him it is unclean. (Romans 14:14)

Don't generalize from this that sin is only a matter of subjective opinion or individual conscience. Paul is not discussing conduct that's clearly sinful in light of Scripture, but conduct over which Christians may legitimately differ.

We have such situations today. Paul had his meat, and we have our Halloween, for instance. Halloween is a high holiday for Satanists, and the dark history of the Druids and jack-o'-lanterns is sobering, to say the least. Hence, many Christians believe that celebrating Halloween is evil and that pumpkins are lightning rods for demon activity. Open your front door on Halloween, and you open your door to the dark realm.

Others feel that Halloween is no more than a kiddy costume party, a time to walk through the neighborhood while your wannabe ballerina and make-believe G.I. Joe knock on doors and scream, "Trick or treat!" Pumpkins are just a hollow orange fruit to carve up with the kids, not the manifestation of some occult activity.

It isn't that the truth changes; it's just that such matters should be guided by conscience. And when consciences guide, personal convictions can and will create impasses between believers, including between husbands and wives. Sometimes it will be the husband "whose faith is weak," and sometimes it will be the wife. But these differences need not break their marital unity. So how do we resolve such impasses lovingly?

The natural pattern is for the "leader" to call for a vote, as it were, and break the tie in his own favor. Isn't that what guys do all the time when impasses involve whether to play in a weekend bowling tournament or to watch a violent flick? Don't they break a one-one vote with their tiebreaker vote? That's what Paul, as an apostle, could have done. But he chose not to, and he teaches us to do the same:

> Instead, make up your mind not to put any stumbling block or
> obstacle in your brother's way. As one who is in the Lord Jesus, I am
> fully convinced that no food is unclean in itself. But...if your brother
> is distressed because of what you eat, you are no longer acting in love.
> Do not by your eating destroy your brother for whom Christ died....
> Let us therefore make every effort to do what leads to peace
> and to mutual edification. *Do not destroy the work of God* for the sake
> of food. All food is clean, but *it is wrong* for a man to eat anything
> that causes someone else to stumble. *It is better not to eat meat* or
> drink wine or to do anything else that will cause your brother to
> fall. (Romans 14:13-15,19-21)

If anyone was a leader in relationships, it was Paul. A brilliant apostle who had once been swept up into heaven to be taught directly by God, his knowledge regarding right and wrong was unassailable. He knew for a fact that all food was clean before God. As for authority to press his case regarding food, Paul could have demanded that everyone believe his way, but he didn't. Instead, Paul submitted to his brother in Christ. In other words, he yielded his right to assert his authority to make room for the beliefs of his weaker brother.

Why did he do this? First, Paul knew that we're all called to "do what leads to peace and to mutual edification." Christ so valued our weaker brother that He died for him. Surely the strong Christian leader should be willing to adjust his behavior for the sake of such brothers. Paul would not sin against his brother by eating meat.

Second, Paul submitted for the sake of God's work. This weak Christian brother, a redeemed work of God, is one in whom God continues to work. Paul understood that pressing his rights at the expense of God's purposes was wrong. Paul would not sin against God by eating meat.

Sin against God? But Paul knew that God approved this meat as clean! Eating meat was not sin per se from God's point of view, but it became a sin within the context of Paul's relationship with his brother. To trample that conviction may cause disunity and damage his brother's spirit. It wasn't important to Paul that his brother be like him. It was important that his brother become like Christ. To be concerned with such trivial matters as one's freedom from food regulations at the expense of someone else's tender, fragile faith is to miss the essence of Christian living.

A CASE IN POINT

Let's return to Tim and Sally. Suppose that God didn't disapprove of ogling other women and hadn't warranted against it in Scripture. Let's also suppose that Tim was "convinced in the Lord Jesus" that ogling other women was "clean" conduct. It's nevertheless still sin for him because of Sally. Sally hates his ogling, which makes it a huge problem between them. His wandering eye breaks oneness with her, and oneness is God's primary design for marriage.

Tim's position as the spiritual leader in the family, as he understands it from Scripture, doesn't trump God's purposes for his marriage any more than Paul's position as an apostle trumped God's purposes in Paul's relationship with the weaker Christian brother. Paul was willing to give up eating "unclean" food rather than hurt his brother in Christ. Is Tim willing to give up ogling rather than hurt Sally?

To paraphrase Paul's words in Romans, we might say, "Look, Tim, your freedom in Christ is not to be your only focus, although you're the leader of your home. No Christian lives for himself alone, but rather for Christ's purposes. God called you to lead your marriage into oneness. Why are you putting a stumbling block in Sally's way?"

Then a follow-up point: "You, Tim, believe ogling is okay. So what? When you do it, it hurts Sally, so you're no longer walking according to love. Don't tell her it's not harming anybody! Instead, decide to remove this stumbling block from her path. It's now a sinful pastime because it offends Sally. Aren't you willing to give up ogling women rather than hurt your wife and block God's work in your marriage?"

Husbands' submitting to our wives for the sake of oneness is a bedrock biblical principle. And it's here that we begin to understand the role of male submission in marriage. For us husbands, as for Paul, there are more important things than exerting any authority in our marriage—things like oneness and the growth of a tender, fragile relationship. I call this "submission to oneness."

I learned a quick but difficult lesson about the need for submission not long after Brenda and I were married. Before I met Brenda, before I became a Christian, I loved a little pastime called "parking." You know, driving to Lover's Lane or some stretch of secluded beach for some "fun." You catch my drift. When I was courting Brenda, parking was much too risky to our purity before marriage. But after the wedding, I wasted little time before trying it again. Driving along one crisp autumn evening, I turned to Brenda with a wink, wooing, "Hey, baby, what do you say we find a quiet spot to have some fun?"

Brenda looked at me as though I had just dropped down from the moon. "What are you talking about?"

So I spelled it out for her—parking.

She squirmed. "I don't know. Parking feels funny to me. What's the point? Can't we just go home where it's private?"

"What do you mean, what's the point?" I stammered. "Parking makes life worth living!"

Brenda insisted the whole notion made her feel uncomfortable. "What if somebody comes up to the car? That would be so embarrassing."

"C'mon, no one will come up to the car. What are the odds of that? It's not like we'll be there all night. Besides, it'll be secluded."

"I really don't want to do it. It just doesn't feel right. Let's go home," she pleaded, "where we can be alone."

"We'll be alone," I cajoled. "Just try it once with me. You'll love it."

I prevailed. And soon we were deep into action. Suddenly, without notice, a spotlight burst through the driver's-side window. We scrambled into our seats just as the officer tapped on the glass. "Move along, kids," he said. Firing up the engine, I shifted into gear and we slunk on down the road.

It took about two minutes, after the coast was clear, for Brenda to launch her attack on me. Talk about incoming missiles! She thoroughly scorched my ears, and I'll not reconstruct her full and passionate expression. Let's just say it was imperative that I listen closely or risk some devastating consequences.

The text for Brenda's sermon that evening was 1 Timothy 2:9, which talks about a Christian woman's need for modesty and decency and propriety. I can summarize her four points this way: "It's impossible to go parking without breaking this command. Anyone at any time could walk up to the car and find us indecent. So parking is sin to me. I refuse to sin against God in this way."

Mercifully, she eventually closed the service. I remember thinking that her application of this Scripture to parking was quite a stretch indeed, but I wasn't about to say so at the time. Parking just wasn't a sin to me, but I have never again asked Brenda to go parking, even in jest. It's sin to Brenda, and she has Scripture to back up her case. To her, parking tramples her personal convictions as a Christian. I'd be asking her to sin no less than if I'd suggested she rob a bank with me. In the context of our relationship, parking is now sin for me too, which is an example of my submitting to oneness.

A KEY QUESTION: RIGHT OR RIGHTEOUS?

How far must we take submission to oneness? Do we stop at personal convictions? Does our wife need a text of Scripture to back her up, like Brenda did?

Not really. Regardless of whether Scripture is involved, any stumbling block we place in the way of oneness with our wives is sin. It weakens God's purpose for marriage and flaunts our leadership at the expense of God's work.

I once talked with a fellow named Richard, who said, "Fred, my wife doesn't like French kissing. She says it makes her feel nauseous and totally ruins the whole sexual experience for her. She's nuts! French kissing really turns me on, and I feel cheated and downright furious when she won't do it. After all, the Bible says that we aren't to deny our bodies to each other. To me, that means I should get what I want, but I don't! She just won't give in. From time to time, we'll be in bed and things will be going along so well that I'll give it another try. But she immediately goes rigid and loses all interest. She acts as if it's a big sin, yet there isn't a single Scripture verse against it. If God has no problem with it, why should she?"

Richard has a point. There's no Scripture against French kissing. His wife doesn't even call it a sin. But for Richard, French kissing is a sin because it tramples his wife's sexuality, a precious essence of her soul. Nothing breaks oneness like trampling your wife's soul essence—that mysterious, God-created combination of her innermost qualities.

Based upon an incorrect interpretation of 1 Corinthians 7:4 ("The wife's body does not belong to her alone but also to her husband. In the same way, the husband's body does not belong to him alone but also to his wife"), Richard felt justified in demanding that his wife submit her body to him as he saw fit. He did so at the expense of God's call to oneness. His wife told me, "Richard is so selfish in this thing. It's so demeaning when he pushes his tongue into my mouth because he knows I hate it. Is that all I'm worth to him?"

Is French kissing a stumbling block to oneness between them? Absolutely! Paul taught that we must submit our rights as leaders in such circumstances.

To paraphrase Romans 14:15-21, "If your wife is distressed because of French kissing, you're no longer acting in love when you push for it. Do not destroy the work of God (oneness in your marriage) for the sake of French kissing. French kissing is 'clean,' but it's sin for you if it causes your wife to stumble in oneness with you. It's better never to French kiss again than to break oneness in your marriage."

Paul went on to say:

Do not allow what you consider good to be spoken of as evil. For the kingdom of God is not a matter of eating and drinking [or parking or French kissing], *but of righteousness, peace and joy* in the Holy Spirit, because anyone who serves Christ in this way is pleasing to God and approved by men. (Romans 14:16-18)

Paul teaches here submission for the sake of oneness. This fosters peace, joy, and righteousness.

Another way to break a tie in such a situation is for the "weak" to simply submit to the "strong," especially if the stronger person is in a position of leadership. Paul could have ordered all the Christian Gentiles on the planet to submit to his personal convictions as an apostle. After all, he was appointed by God Himself to teach them. When the "weak" submit to the "strong," this, too, seems to fosters peace (on the outside at least). But not joy or righteousness. Let's see why.

What happens, for example, if Paul uses his authority to insist that his Christian brother eat meat with him? Paul can eat freely, but his brother, who considers eating meat a sin, violates his conscience with every bite. Although the tie is broken and the impasse apparently resolved, there's no joy in the heart of the weaker brother. Nor is there any righteousness in Paul's disregard for his brother's conscience.

But what would happen if Paul submits? Paul would merely forgo sharing a barbecued steak with this brother, while his brother would maintain a clean standing in his heart before God. A worthy trade!

If Richard's wife yields to his authoritative demands for French kissing, he may think he's gaining pleasure. But his wife will only be nauseated and seethe deeply in her soul. In the future she's more likely to avoid sex at every possible turn, going to bed early to avoid what has become for her a demeaning, joyless act. But if Richard submits? He merely loses one aspect of his sex life. His wife, though, gains so much respect for his leadership that she doubles her commitment to fully give her body, mind, and spirit in the other areas of the marriage bed.

Smart husbands always ask: *Would I rather be right or righteous?* Do not destroy the work of God for the sake of parking, French kissing, or any such thing. More often than not, we must give in at impasses for the sake of God and for the sake of oneness. That's called servant leadership.

Questions for Reflection and Discussion

1. To what extent do you agree or disagree with Fred when he says that for a man to "trample" his wife is a sin?

2. This chapter says that our definition of sin tends to be too narrow. In what ways would you say that this has ever been true for you?

3. Read carefully through Romans 14. How would you summarize the most important points Paul is making in this chapter?

4. What principles or commands in Romans 14 do you think are the most helpful for you in pursuing a godly marriage?

5. What is your understanding of the phrase *submission to oneness,* as you see it discussed in this chapter?

6. This chapter asks how far husbands should take submission to oneness. How would you answer that question?

7. This chapter also asks if we as husbands would rather be right or righteous. How would you honestly answer that question?

8. In your own marriage what do you believe God wants you to do, if anything, in response to what you've read in this chapter?

PART II

starting to breathe again

from trampling to submitting

When Brenda first announced that her feelings for me were dead, I was unaware of any possible place for male submission in marriage. As I think back on those dark early days, God helped me stumble across certain passages in the Old Testament when I needed them most.

I found the story of David and Bathsheba to be particularly compelling. God sent Nathan, a prophet, to confront David about his sin of adultery. Nathan reached David's hardened heart by telling a simple story.

> The LORD sent Nathan to David. When he came to him, he said,
> "There were two men in a certain town, one rich and the other poor.
> The rich man had a very large number of sheep and cattle, but the
> poor man had nothing except one little ewe lamb he had bought.
> He raised it, and it grew up with him and his children. It shared his
> food, drank from his cup and even slept in his arms. It was like a
> daughter to him.
>
> "Now a traveler came to the rich man, but the rich man refrained
> from taking one of his own sheep or cattle to prepare a meal for the
> traveler who had come to him. Instead, he took the ewe lamb that
> belonged to the poor man and prepared it for the one who had come
> to him." (2 Samuel 12:1-4)

When David inquired who this rich man was, he heard Nathan reply, "It's you!" Everything clicked for David. He'd seen Bathsheba as someone he could virtually devour to satisfy his sexual longings, but Uriah, "the poor man" who viewed his "ewe lamb" as the joy of his life, had his cherished wife stolen from him. David also had Uriah murdered to guarantee his silence.

While most people read this story as a reminder that sin catches up with the sinner, the key focus for me was Uriah's love for Bathsheba. The Bible says the lamb "was like a daughter to him." The Bible uses the terms "daughter" and "ewe lamb" to capture a heavenly message. Just as Bathsheba was precious to Uriah, your wife is precious to you. She lives with you and lies in your arms. She's to be treated according to her value to God as a child created in His image. You've been entrusted with the priceless essence of another human soul, so precious to God that He paid dearly for her with the death of His own Son.

I came to the stunning realization that the Lord Himself created Brenda and loves her very essence. I described this thought in *Every Man's Battle:*

> He saved a precious ewe lamb for me, a pure one without spot or blemish, with sparkling eyes and a soft heart. He formed Brenda in the womb and looked on with joy when she crawled and then walked and talked. He saw her sing "Throw Out the Lifeline" as a member of the Singing Cousins. He saw her crowned Harvest Festival Queen at church as a teen. He sent His only Son to provide for her future, to protect her, and to bring her home to heaven safely.... God raised her and cherished her, and I must do the same.

Earlier in our marriage, I hadn't seen Brenda in this light. Truth be told, there were times when I viewed her as a stubborn old goat or, worse, a mule. I never saw her as a precious ewe lamb. After reading these Scriptures and watching my family ignore her at the Chicago wedding, I suspected that I'd been trampling Brenda's essence for a long time. I had allowed my family to blitz her treasured, precious soul. I had joined in the fray, shouting until she cowered. Yet the Bible says, "Husbands, love your wives and do not be harsh with them" (Colossians 3:19). This command is no less important to God than "You shall not murder." Yet I somehow seemed to gloss over that sentence of Scripture, as well as this one: "Husbands, in the same way be considerate as you live with your wives, and treat them with respect as the weaker partner and as heirs with you of the gracious gift of life, so that nothing will hinder your prayers" (1 Peter 3:7).

These were commands, and I had been ignoring them just as my family had been ignoring my wife. Then I learned that the Greek term for "weaker partner" can also be translated "fine china," which I think is a better translation within this discussion of marriage. How do you handle fine china? With respect, as you tenderly appreciate and even display its finest points. You don't slam fine china around or put it through the blast of the dishwasher.

My Brenda is a piece of God's finest china, lovely in His sight. But I treated her like an old tin plate, trampling her soul's beauty because she wasn't like me. I trampled her femininity and godly character, honed as it had been by years of obedience and generations of Christian heritage. How could oneness survive, much less thrive, in the shadow of such darkness?

FEELING NO ONENESS

Before marriage, Brenda freely ministered to God without interference, using her gifts for His pleasure. She was free to avoid sin and to live purely. I stole this freedom. I sinned by making no room in our marriage for her to exercise her Christian gifts. Worse still, I forced her to sin.

You see, Brenda has the gift of discernment. When it comes to family relationships, she knows the good from the bad (Christianity stretches back at least four generations into every branch of her family tree), and what she saw in our in-law relationships made her uncomfortable. For example, after each visit with my father, I inevitably left his home angry or depressed because he constantly cut me down in Brenda's presence. Sometimes it took two weeks for my emotions to stabilize.

My dad was taking a toll on my young family. Before long, even Brenda began riding that emotional coaster with me after our visits. She was frightened. "If I can be sucked in," she said, "it will likely happen to the kids!" Brenda's gift of discernment was meant to bless and protect our marriage and family. She had to fight the emotional abuse coming from Dad. But I had lived with it so long that I was blind to the danger. I coldly shut her gift down. "A family doesn't have to be perfect like yours to be acceptable," I declared. "If you'd been raised in a regular home, you wouldn't be so weak in facing all this."

In truth, she wasn't weak at all. She was standing up for the convictions in her heart. To Brenda, subjecting her young family to my father's unfettered criticism was a sin, which should have made it a sin for me. Instead of making room for her personal convictions, I blindly ridiculed her gift of discernment and loudly demanded that she do what I wanted her to do. In short, I was commanding her to sin. No wonder our oneness died.

There were times, however, when Brenda actually *was* weak (as is true for all of us at times). My wife became depressed when life was full of conflict and interpersonal confrontation. Did I make allowance for this, using my strengths in these areas to complement her and protect her? No. I chided her, saying things like, "Adults have conflicts, and they need to be able to deal with them. You need to grow up."

I'm commanded by Scripture to love Brenda as Christ loved the church. How did Christ love the church? In perfect kindness: "A bruised reed he will not break, and a smoldering wick he will not snuff out" (Matthew 12:20). Christ doesn't trample us in our weaknesses. But I trampled Brenda.

I'm also commanded to love Brenda as I love myself, but upon reflection, I'd have to agree that I treated my own weaknesses with far more understanding and grace than I did hers. I was merciless with her. "And you call yourself a Christian? Jesus knew how to confront men. What's wrong with you?" Demeaned and belittled, she felt no oneness with me.

BEING A "TIEBREAKER" DOESN'T HELP

When we husbands insist on being Chief Tiebreaker in our tribe and refuse our role in mutual submission, the relationship becomes so unbalanced that our wives can scarcely fulfill their role of submission. I recently read an article about Donna Collins, the first Western child born into the Moonie church decades ago. Now a grown woman, she has left the Moonies and speaks out against their horrible mind control. It was difficult to leave the cult, she said, because that was the only life she'd ever known and everyone she loved was a Moonie. She was torn in both directions. This comment especially hit home with me:

> It was becoming clear to me [at age eighteen] that I was headed toward
> leaving the church. But if I left, I knew everyone I loved would treat
> me like a leper. I had shamed my parents, and my friends told me I
> was asking not only for exile, but also for eternal damnation. I couldn't
> imagine leaving, and yet I knew I couldn't stay. I felt crushed, broken,
> and increasingly depressed.

As Chief Tiebreakers, we let our personalities so dominate that we can tear and confuse our wives in this same way. Brenda had once expressed these very same emotions regarding our home together. On one hand, Brenda knew divorce was wrong. If she divorced me, she'd feel like a leper in the midst of her strong Christian family. She loved God deeply and wanted to submit to me for Christ's sake. On the other hand, submitting to me and ignoring the dangers seemed evil. To submit would be selling out on everything she believed in. So, with emotions much like Donna's, Brenda once told me through wrenching tears, "I knew I should stay, but I knew that I couldn't. It was awful." She recently wrote these recollections for me:

> I felt there was great danger in being closely associated with your
> family. I saw generations of widespread, deeply rooted sin, and that

sin had destroyed many family relationships. I knew there were suicidal thoughts, emotional breakdowns, and a general blindness to truth throughout your immediate family. I felt its impact on me, like when your father could be so nice and then so quickly become cutting and mean. Your family felt free to unleash unrestrained anger at any time on anyone.

I was very unwilling to allow my kids to be raised in that atmosphere. Your family lived in a frequent state of anger with each other. Remember the fight your mom and sister had in our front room when Jasen was born? I thought for sure they were going to hit each other. I remember going into his room, holding him in the dark, and whispering to him, "I won't let you be a part of this. I'll never let them affect you." I could never submit to something that might mean danger to my kids spiritually. That would be a sin to me.

SUBMITTING BRINGS RELIEF

During the weeks following my friend's Chicago wedding, Brenda and I talked regularly about my marital leadership. The picture she painted was ghastly. While I'd honestly been trying to lead in the best way I knew how, I'd been entirely flubbing up all over the place. I decided to reread the essential section on marriage in Scripture:

> Wives, submit to your husbands as to the Lord. For the husband is the head of the wife as Christ is the head of the church, his body, of which he is the Savior. Now as the church submits to Christ, so also wives should submit to their husbands in everything.
>
> Husbands, love your wives, just as Christ loved the church and gave himself up for her to make her holy, cleansing her by the washing with water through the word, and to present her to himself as a radiant church, without stain or wrinkle or any other blemish,

but holy and blameless. In this same way, husbands ought to love their wives as their own bodies. He who loves his wife loves himself. (Ephesians 5:22-28)

My marriage looked much like the first portion of this passage. I was the head, sure enough. But it looked nothing like the last part, the very part for which I was solely responsible.

One time I got it right when I followed Pastor Ron's advice by coming down on Brenda's side of the fence. For the first time, my marriage paralleled this whole passage. She felt oneness with me, and we both felt great. Our marriage soared. I had submitted to her thoughts and convictions. I should have hated it, as I once hated submitting to my big sister or the seniors on the high-school football team.

I didn't hate it, though. I felt great. But I was troubled that the word *submit* didn't appear in the husband's instructions in the last half of this passage, yet my marriage bloomed as if it did. How could this be right? Wasn't submission the wife's job?

I meditated long and hard over this. As my understanding cleared, I realized that I hadn't been *forced* to submit. I had chosen to. I hadn't submitted to her authority or her will; I had submitted to *oneness*. I had yielded my rights as leader for the sake of the relationship and for the sake of God's work and purposes, just as Paul had done. I had *chosen* to sacrifice something for her.

I had stumbled onto these truths that Paul taught in Romans 14. My submission reversed the trampling. I had chosen to yield my rights that she might *fully live* in this relationship with me. My decision spawned deep relief in me and radiance in Brenda's soul. I was reminded of these words from Scripture:

Christ loved the church and gave himself up for her…to present her to himself as a radiant church. (Ephesians 5:25,27)

With my submission to oneness, my marriage momentarily paralleled Christ's relationship to the church. I looked closely at passages that described that relationship. Could I find a parallel "submission to oneness" in Christ's relationship with His church? Did Jesus submit to His bride? Yes, He did.

READY TO FOLLOW THIS KING?

Jesus submit? But He's the King of kings! That's true. He is supreme and submits to no one's authority. But He submitted His rights and glory as King out of reverence for His Father. As head, Jesus could have demanded that we submit to His authority unconditionally. But like Paul, He didn't. Jesus was about more important things than merely exerting His rightful authority in the relationship: "For I tell you that Christ has become a servant of the Jews on behalf of God's truth, to confirm the promises made to the patriarchs so that the Gentiles may glorify God for his mercy"(Romans 15:8-9). Furthermore, "Your attitude should be the same as that of Christ Jesus: Who, being in very nature God, did not consider equality with God something to be grasped, but made himself nothing, taking the very nature of a servant" (Philippians 2:5-7).

Jesus submitted, through suffering and death, to oneness with us. He came to do the will of His Father, not His own will. His Father's will was for Jesus to bring us to God.

Jesus taught us submission to oneness by example. He laid down His life in full submission for the sake of our relationship with Him, though we were yet sinners. Only then did He ask in return our full submission to His authority. His submission to oneness and our submission to His authority made oneness possible. This mutual submission makes us fellow heirs with Him to rule and to reign as His bride. Oneness always requires mutual submission. Mutual submission is God's will for Christian relationships: "Submit to one another out of reverence for Christ" (Ephesians 5:21).

Even in marriage? Look again at that essential passage on marriage,

Ephesians 5:22-28, and think about this: My friends Bill and Nancy argue that since the word "submit" doesn't appear here in the husband's instructions, God intended to suspend the command of mutual submission within marriage. Bill says, "Christian couples are no longer brothers and sisters in Christ, but husband and wife. The husband leads and the wife submits. Mutual submission does not apply to marriage relationships."

In response, I would point out that in another Scripture passage (1 Peter 3:7), the apostle Peter commands that couples treat one another as fellow heirs of eternal life in Christ. In Peter's mind, husbands and wives never cease being brothers and sisters in Christ. So I don't think verses 22-28 in Ephesians 5 were intended by Paul to suspend the command of mutual submission given in verse 21, but rather to deepen the scope of the command in marriage beyond that expected in other Christian relationships. Our mutual submission in marriage must deepen until it parallels the mutual submission found between Christ and His bride. The wife must submit fully to her husband's *authority,* as the church submits to Christ's authority, out of reverence for God. The husband must submit fully to *oneness,* as Christ sacrificially submitted to oneness with His bride. Thus both husband and wife submit, but differently.

While the word *submit* itself may not appear in this passage's instructions to husbands, Paul clearly teaches in verse 25 that this is not a one-sided submission at all. The phrase "gave himself up for her" is not only an expression of love, but also an example of how the husband should give himself for his wife's good. To give oneself up to death for the beloved is a more extreme expression of love and submission than the one God calls upon the wife to make, just as Christ's submission unto death was a more extreme expression of love than we, His bride, are called upon to make (except for those called to be martyrs in His service). A husband must "die" for the sake of oneness with his bride, just as Christ Himself did.

Of course, you may not like the term "male submission." Bill and Nancy refuse to use the word "submission" in relation to Bill's role in marriage, but this is purely semantics. There's no oneness in marriage without male submission, whatever we call it.

Early in their marriage, Bill regularly trampled Nancy. For example, he reluctantly let her spend an evening with a girlfriend now and then, but the cold-shoulder treatment and the heartless peck on the cheek he gave Nancy as she left home let her know that he wasn't fond of the idea. Then he'd scold her when she came home a little later than promised.

Their marital oneness clearly suffered. "I felt he was being selfish," explained Nancy, "and it destroyed some oneness. I was then less inclined to respond positively to him because there was no reciprocal love in motion. It's hard to pedal a bike up a hill with one foot." What a great word picture. Besides trampling her freedom, Bill also trampled Nancy's weaknesses, often criticizing things she had said and making her feel really small. When he realized how sensitive Nancy was and how his reproaches hurt her, he softened his speech. He submitted by watching what he said.

Though Bill hates the phrase, he began living out his role of male submission as well as anyone I know. He doesn't trample on Nancy anymore because he has submitted to oneness and to the well-being of her very essence. Nancy recently related, "God has blessed Bill and me with great oneness in our marriage. He has given us the grace to shift our behavior when one of us becomes aware of the other's need."

Of course, Bill is still the head. He still expects Nancy to submit to his authority, and she does. But like Christ, Bill first leads by example. Because of this, Nancy finds submission easy. "If Bill is fulfilling his role to love me as Christ loved the church, he'll be unselfishly seeking my best. His expectations will be reasonable, and he'll make decisions with the highest good of our family in mind. For me, submission to Bill is almost a reflex because I trust him so."

Submission in marriage is not just for women. As men, we must learn submission to our Father in relation to our wives. We'll have no oneness in our marriages without mutual submission, anymore than Christ can have oneness with His bride without it.

What is every woman's desire in marriage?

Oneness.

In other words, a man who lives with her in mutual submission. This is what God intended for her. So why is male submission in marriage necessary for oneness? What exactly is oneness? We'll explore some answers in the next chapter.

Questions for Reflection and Discussion

1. Look carefully at the Bible's commands for husbands in Ephesians 5:22-28, Colossians 3:19, and 1 Peter 3:7. How do these passages relate to any struggles you may be having in your marriage? In what ways, if any, do you view these passages differently than before?

2. How do you respond to the guidelines and observations presented in this chapter? Do you find yourself mostly agreeing or disagreeing with them?

3. What are your own convictions about the issue of whether "mutual submission" (as taught in Ephesians 5:21) applies to the marriage relationship?

4. From your perspective and understanding, do you agree that every woman's desire in marriage is essentially oneness? Why or why not?

5. According to your current understanding, how would you define *oneness* as it relates to marriage?

6. What for you has been the most meaningful concept or teaching presented in this chapter?

pursuing your woman's desire: oneness

The man said, "This is now bone of my bones and flesh of my flesh; she shall be called 'woman,' for she was taken out of man." For this reason a man will leave his father and mother and be united to his wife, and they will become one flesh.

Genesis 2:23-24

When I turned to Christ at age twenty-three, terms such as "one flesh" sounded quite strange to me. *What in the world is that?* I wondered. Yet the phrase was uttered so often from the pulpit and in my Sunday school marriage class that I figured everyone knew what it meant. When I asked around, however, I saw many vacant expressions. Furthermore, I noticed that many married couples didn't seem to be emotionally close, so they surely weren't of "one flesh." Oneness was clearly not automatic, nor even semiautomatic, after the marriage vows were made.

I remember once talking with Al, a bachelor who hoped to marry one day. "I want a guarantee that marriage and sex will only be successful and never fail," Al mused. "I come from a healthy family, and I want only the best."

Oh, really?

I replied by reminding Al that he, as head of the home, was the guarantor of a successful marriage. "If you want success, it's yours. You must merely submit to oneness, in reverence to Christ. While no small task, at least it's your choice."

I don't know if Al ever made it to the altar, but I do know this: Too few couples achieve oneness because of the many obstacles they encounter. Achieving emotional closeness has little to do with emotions; it has everything to do with actions. Oneness has terms. Comply with the terms and emotional closeness follows. If you don't comply, the emotions will die. We need to act right or, more precisely, act righteously. If we do, the feelings follow.

Brenda's "feelings" for me had died. The feelings she spoke about were not of oneness, but of the intimate feelings that flow from oneness. When it came time to revive those feelings, I had to do more than buy flowers and take her out for a candlelight dinner, although those things had their place. I had to act as if we were one. When I did, the feelings of intimacy returned.

This is an awesome thing I'm talking about—the powerful experience of oneness with your spouse. But to achieve it, you'll need to recognize at least two things about oneness: (1) it's an action word and (2) it requires sacrifice.

ONENESS IN ACTION

Let me quote from one of my love letters to Brenda dated March 4, 1981:

> I bring promises. I promise a love for you that you have only hoped
> for. You asked God for a Christian to love you, and He's provided one
> aching to pour love over you, to exalt you above every pedestal, to
> cherish and hold you and gently whisper your name forever, come fire
> or rain, poverty or riches. A man bursting with floods of love to sweep
> over the girl with the key to his floodgates—you, the kindest, most
> loving, trusting rarity I've found.

Okay, so I'm no Shakespeare! Yet allow me to point out that love and oneness aren't the same. In fact, they're only loosely related. Love can live on despite the trampling. Brenda and I still loved each other during the darkest days of our marriage, though our oneness had died completely.

Let's compare love and oneness in our relationship with God. God's love for you is unconditional; it never changes. Before you were formed in the womb, He loved you. He's watched over you lovingly from your earliest days, longing for your heart to call His name. When I rampaged through pornographic magazines, He still loved me. When I lay in the arms of too many women, He still loved me. He chased me desperately, aching to reach me before it was too late. Cornering me in my California office, He captured my heart in a moment. Although I knew better, I splurged in sexual sin a while longer, yet His love never waned.

You, too, are the apple of His eye. His love for you has no limits. Your service can't make God love you any more, and your sins can't make Him love you any less.

Not so for oneness. Oneness has terms, it isn't unconditional, and it calls for action. While God loves everyone equally and is unwilling that any should perish, He is more intimate with some than others. He spoke with Moses face to face. He walked with Enoch. When angels dropped by to see Daniel, they addressed him as "highly esteemed" by the Lord. And God called David a man after His own heart. Think of your children. You love them all the same, of course, but with some you are more intimate. Which child do you feel "one" with? Probably the son or daughter who walks with you and talks with you. The one who obeys.

Man once had perfect oneness with God in Eden. God walked with Adam and Eve in the cool of each day. What happened? They sinned. Not satisfied to be one with God, Eve desired to be God. She disobeyed, and then she got Adam to eat from the apple as well. Oneness with God died.

Oneness has terms. Can oneness with God return? Yes, but on His terms, through salvation. Salvation happens on two levels. In the truest sense, oneness with God happens at salvation, in a single moment in time. When you commit to Christ, you become one with God.

But in another sense, oneness doesn't happen in a moment at all. Oneness with Christ happens over time, as we "work out our salvation" through sanctification (see Philippians 2:12). We *become* like Him. In this sense, salvation merely gives us the opportunity to be one with Christ. We know from experience that oneness is no more automatic with Christ than it is with our wives. Our salvation is expressed in an ongoing process of spiritual growth in which we're strenuously involved.

Take sexual purity, for example. At a single moment, salvation freed us to be sexually pure. But in another sense, salvation gave us only the *opportunity* to be sexually pure. We still must choose oneness with Christ.

"It is God's will that you be sanctified: that you should avoid sexual immorality" (1 Thessalonians 4:3). Oneness, then, is an act. While feelings of intimacy flow from oneness, oneness itself is not a feeling. It's a state of being. Feeling regret over my sexual sins did not make me one with Christ. Preaching against sexual sins did not make me one with Christ. Walking purely makes me one with Christ. If I'm sexually pure, Jesus and I are one in this regard. If I'm not, we aren't.

Many men whitewash their lives with the language and customs of the Christian culture. Satisfied with salvation alone, they avoid the strenuous work of submission necessary for oneness with Christ. So singing in the choir by day, they hit their wives by night. Nodding their heads about the sanctity of marriage by day, they wallow in cyber sex by night. Ravaging their homes with verbal abuse by day, they serve at deacon meetings by night. On the outside they seem Christian enough, but they refuse to meet the terms of oneness.

Who sets the terms? Christ. More accurately, Christ's essence. What is Christ's essence? Holiness. The original Hebrew word for holiness conveys far more than sinlessness. The term encompasses Christ's full essence, the matchless beauty and wonder of God, a beauty so awesome that the four living creatures in heaven cry out continually, day and night, "Holy, holy, holy is the Lord God Almighty!"

Holiness—it's making Christ's essence ours in practice. To submit to holiness is to submit to oneness. When we turn on the computer and masturbate to naked, nameless lovers lying across our screen, we trample His essence. We sin against Him, and distance grows. When we choose sexual purity and walk in the light, we're one with that part of His essence. Action is everything to our Lord:

> Whoever has my commands and obeys them, he is the one who loves me. He who loves me will be loved by my Father, and I too will love him and show myself to him. (John 14:21)

When we call ourselves Christians but don't act like it, Jesus indignantly objects: "Why do you call me, 'Lord, Lord,' and do not do what I say?" (Luke 6:46). With a deep singleness of purpose, we must set ourselves apart unto Him, yielding our right to choose our own way. After all, God is aching for us to be one with Him. The whole plan of salvation was designed that He might have a relationship with us. Have you met the terms?

Oneness in marriage is very similar to this. Like salvation, oneness in marriage happens in a single moment. During your wedding, God declared you one with your wife. Yet for me, that oneness was certainly not evident at our hotel room on my wedding night. My flaring temper and a flying brush (I'll tell you the story later) revealed that our oneness was a bit of a sham. The wedding merely gave us the opportunity for oneness.

I know five couples who once led important marriage ministries. They're now divorced. All five husbands, who could articulate the language and customs of a Christian marriage, seemed to have marriages made in heaven. One proclaimed openly, "God hates divorce." But later his actions said, "God told me to marry my mistress so I can have a happy life."

One sent a newsletter proclaiming the sanctity of marriage, but later his actions inexplicably declared, "God told me it's okay to divorce my wife, since He never wanted me to marry her in the first place." Another proclaimed, "The marriage bed must be kept pure," but he later hit the sack with his mistress, protesting, "My wife hates oral sex. If I can't get it at home, I'm getting it somewhere else!"

Who sets the terms for oneness in marriage? Your wife. More accurately, your wife's essence. And that means there will be some sacrifice on your part.

SACRIFICIAL IN APPROACH

A simple word picture involving candy canes, along with the following Scripture passage, can help illuminate the picture:

> In this same way [as Christ loved the church], husbands ought to love
> their wives as their own bodies. He who loves his wife loves himself.
> After all, no one ever hated his own body, but he feeds and cares for it,
> just as Christ does the church—for we are members of his body. "For
> this reason a man will leave his father and mother and be united to his
> wife, and the two will become one flesh." (Ephesians 5:28-31)

Oneness lies not in the *sentiment* of loving our wife as ourselves, but in the *act* of loving her as ourselves. We must treat the convictions and gifts of her essence exactly as our own.

Let me use the common candy cane to help us visualize oneness. God says the husband and wife shall be "one flesh." Envision the groom as a solid red candy cane, and the bride as a solid white candy cane. Through marriage, these two canes become woven into a single candy cane. The colors of both the husband and wife, though distinct, now intertwine and are expressed together. In this striped piece of candy we clearly visualize the role of male submission and the consequent oneness in marriage.

The husband is the "head of the wife," as Ephesians 5:23 expresses it. His red is the dominant color, but he must make room for her white essence to play its part in the beauty of their marriage. The role of male submission is to yield his rights as the dominant color so that her gifts and essence might be expressed in their own distinctive beauty. The role of female submission is to allow the husband the discretion to place the red and white stripes on the cane, but he must allow the white to take its place side by side with equal honor. This is where loving her as he loves himself comes in. He must love the white and make room for the white, as much as he loves the red and makes room for the red.

Guess what that means? Sacrifice, especially in the sense Paul spoke of where we yield our rights to honor her personal convictions and her soul essence. Of course, sacrifice is always easier on paper! I found making room for Brenda's white essence on the cane to be very difficult. It was one thing to admit, for instance, that Brenda's gift of discernment in relationships was stronger than mine. It was quite another to give this gift real sway in my day-to-day decisions. I had to make room for this white on our cane, but it meant real sacrifice, costing deeply in my relationships with the family in which I was raised.

But there are more important things than exerting our authority in the marriage relationship. One, for instance, is encouraging God's work of oneness in our marriage. To be concerned with relatively trivial matters, even painful ones, is to miss the essence of a good marriage.

You see, loving our wives as ourselves has nothing to do with emotions. You either sacrifice for her essence as you do your own, or you don't. You either place her essence on the cane, or you don't. If you have a striped cane, you are one. If the cane is totally red, then you haven't done a thing.

Let's use a goal-setting exercise from the premarriage classes I teach. In the class, we ask each student to work separately and list his or her top ten goals for marriage. We then ask the students to pick their top three goals and compare them with what their fiancés wrote. Rick and Kelley's are typical responses:

Rick:

1. To make God the center of our home.
2. To establish a strong career.
3. To save money for a down payment for a house.

Kelley:

1. To let God rule our marriage.
2. To make family our priority.
3. To build communication together.

What does it mean for Rick to love Kelley as himself? It means that Kelley's second goal has to be as important to him as his own second goal.

And Rick must ensure that Kelley's third goal receives as much time and attention as his third goal. That's how oneness looks in practice.

I checked up on Rick a few years later. By this time, the young couple had a two-year-old daughter named Clare, and the number-two child was on the way. Rick's second goal had been to establish a strong career path, and he was well on his way. He had been so successful that a headhunter had hired him away to a large company in another state. In his previous job, Rick was coming home between 5:30 and 6 P.M. Now he stretched it to 6:30 or 7 P.M. Rick saw nothing wrong with this because it still aligned with his second most important goal in his marriage. Kelley, however, began complaining that he wasn't making the family a priority.

From his point of view, Rick offered a reasonable explanation: "Since I started working at this new company," he said, "I noticed an unstated expectation that everyone must stay late like this. It's strange, though. Practically no one gets anything done during the last hour, and it seems like a waste. Still, Kelley, you and I are in this together. I'm doing it for you and the kids, sweetheart. It's only an extra hour per night. You're just going to have to adjust."

Kelley didn't think so. "I agree that we're both in this together, Rick. But if you're so concerned about doing something for the kids and me, you'll start coming home earlier. We put Clare to bed at eight. You used to get home by six and have two hours to play with her at night. While working one extra hour seems small to you, it cuts Clare's time with you in half. From her perspective, that's huge. If you were actually getting work done during that hour, I might consider it worthwhile, but our family is just as important as your career, is it not? Rick, you shouldn't sacrifice your family time for an hour of nothing!"

What was Kelley asking? That Rick would value her second goal equally with his own. A few more years passed, and I asked Kelley what happened. "I fought it hard for about eighteen months," she snapped. "Finally, I just gave up." The dark flash of anger in her eyes said far more than the words. She was forced to a painful resignation. He would never respond, and her resentment burned.

Kelley was no weak woman, and she could handle home life without Rick. She'd been successful in the corporate world before quitting to stay home with Clare. Though she loved working outside the home, she'd made the painful sacrifices necessary to give her second goal in marriage its proper priority. Showing her love for Rick, she'd also made an equal sacrifice for Rick's goal by moving a long distance for the sake of his career—even though that meant leaving her friends and family behind.

Had Rick made an equal sacrifice for her? No. He refused to even make the far lighter sacrifice of coming home an hour earlier. He even had the gall to suggest that Kelley didn't understand that they were both in this marriage together. Excuse me! Her sacrifice clearly displayed that she understood this quite well. It was Rick who didn't understand. This situation stabbed Kelley deeply. She'd been trampled.

There's nothing emotional or mystical about the command to love our wives as ourselves. If Rick came home an hour earlier, he'd be loving her as himself and making room for her essence on the candy cane.

It's all about action; it's all about loving sacrifice.

ARE YOU CLUELESS?

Let's talk a little more about the wife's goals, about which many husbands are clueless. Bernice told me, "My husband doesn't get the concept that a woman's house is a reflection of her, even though I've tried to explain it to him a million times. I really believe he wouldn't care—or even notice—if he lived in a barn."

When Bernice and Stan bought their new house, she wanted to remodel the two bathrooms, which she found extremely ugly. She picked out new flooring and wallpaper and asked Stan to find some time to spruce up the rooms.

That was six years ago.

"I waited and waited," said Bernice. "In six years, he couldn't find a single weekend to make me happy. I wasn't a priority to him. Every time I stepped into those bathrooms, I was reminded that he didn't care about me. I was hurt, and then I became angry. I resented all the things he made sure he did for himself and especially those things he expected me to do for him."

The beauty of her home was a deep part of Bernice's soul essence. Her husband needn't *enjoy* hanging wallpaper. He just had to *do* it. And if he couldn't do it, then he needed to hire someone who could. He needn't develop the same emotional attachment to their home as Bernice experienced, but he did need to exert himself in the same manner that he did for his own projects.

This is male submission to oneness. This is honoring her essence equally with his own essence. Like a double-stuffed Oreo in marriage, there's now double the essence, and you must love all of the "stuff" with the same love. Your wife is aching to be one with you. The whole plan of marriage was designed that you might be one with her. And because women were created for relationship, her highest priority is that you would honor her essence as you do your own, living in mutual submission with her. This is every woman's desire.

On the first night of premarriage class, I always ask, "What do you hope to get out of your marriage that you wouldn't get if you were to remain single?" Here are some of the women's responses:

Anna: "I want companionship and a sharing of intimate moments together. I want to have a relationship with the Lord together. What I long for is bonding together."

Vickie: "I can't explain it real well, but I want a partnership, emotionally and physically. I haven't got a best friend and haven't had one for a long time. I want that in Craig."

Kathryn: "I would like a bond that no one and nothing can touch, through good times or bad."

Jennifer: "I want companionship and someone who will be there when I need him. I want to be happy."

Stacy: "I want companionship and love and my very own cheering section. I want someone to be there to accept me as a whole person, good and bad, someone that I can count on."

Early in my marriage, it would have hurt me to read this list. Had I been Brenda's cheering section? No, I had been more like the drunken, babbling sports fan throwing batteries at her head. Had I accepted her as a whole person, loving her weaknesses as well as the good? No, not at all.

Most of us husbands aren't thinking about what our wives truly desire. Our wives want rich communication and a bond that no one can touch. They long to blossom in marriage. They long for our eyes to meet in meaningful dialogue.

Go into any restaurant and watch the older couples. Most take a small corner table, order off the menu, and barely speak a word to each other during the entire meal. Their eyes rarely meet. As they shuffle past on their way out the door, look at the woman's eyes. It's truly harrowing. She's just playing out the string. Was this God's dream for her in marriage? For us? In premarriage class, every female eye is bright with hope and anticipation. The trampling of marriage brings death to those eyes.

Your wife didn't expect you to trample her. You seemed kind and godly before marriage. She never dreamed you would treat her like this. In premarriage class, we ask women, "What impresses you most about your fiancé?" Their answers are beautiful:

Denise: "What impresses me the most is his kindness and honesty."

Karen: "He's so attentive and respectful."

Penny: "I'm most impressed with his patience."

Marsha: "He's a very compassionate guy."

Amy: "He's so caring and sensitive toward me."

Jodie: "He's just such an encourager."

Ruth: "I've never met such a kind man."

Deb: "He shows such patience in our impasses."

Diane: "He wants to do anything and everything to be a better husband."

Ten years from now, will these same women say that they'd been snowed by their husbands?

What impressed your wife the most about you before you got married? Do you still impress her in this way? Are you still an encourager? Do you still have patience in the impasses? Are you attentive and respectful enough to submit to oneness?

Kindness, patience, respect, honesty, and compassion are necessary for male submission. Perhaps your wife once saw these things in you. Were they a mirage? Your soul once seemed a cool pool in her dry and thirsty land, and she dived headlong into marriage in total trust. Did she find a companionship or a mouthful of sand? Consider this letter I received from a female reader of *Every Man's Battle:*

Things aren't so good here in my marriage. I'm so angry with my husband for so many things that I don't know what to do with it all. It seems like it's finally all come to a head, and the floodgates are open. I feel like the life has been sucked out of me, and I don't know what to do. I can look at him and not feel anything! Or I feel such an irritation that I want to scream. He will not face anything or work on anything that is difficult. He avoids the hard stuff no matter what it is until it is so insurmountable that it is torture to fix or ruined completely. No disagreement ever seems to come to resolution. We separate into our corners and come out ignoring each other. He is so impossible to reason with and won't stay on the subject in a discussion, dancing around it and throwing smoke. He will always find a way to twist it and make it my fault. In his mind, he is never responsible for anything.

Now that the kids are older, he is making them crazy, too. I never thought I'd get to this point, but I'm so tired that I don't care about holding it together. And I can't defend him to the kids anymore because they're too smart and they know better. Besides, how do you defend his stuff? I hate it here. I love my kids, but they will be gone too soon. Then what? I probably need to see a counselor to work through some feelings, but it would have to be at divorce's door before he would be threatened enough to come along. My marriage stinks, and I'm too tired to care.

Sadly, most men are a mirage. According to one recent study, our report card is shameful:

- Eighty-four percent of women feel they don't have intimacy (oneness) in their marriages.
- Eighty-three percent of women feel their husbands don't even know the basic needs of a woman for intimacy (oneness) or how to provide intimacy for them.
- A large majority of female divorcées say that their married years were the loneliest years of their lives.

How can this be? Our wives had such dreams of oneness and intimacy. God has called us to love our wives as ourselves and to lay down our lives that we might be one with them.

My friend, you must submit to oneness. You owe it to her, in honor of her trust in you. Furthermore, the Lord bought you at a price, and He even gave you one of His precious daughters as a mate. What in the world has happened? How can 84 percent of today's married women feel that they don't have intimacy with their husband? What obstacles have blocked us from answering God's call to oneness with our wives?

We'll explore some answers in our next chapter.

Questions for Reflection and Discussion

1. How would you define *oneness* as this concept is taught in this chapter? And how would you define *essence* as the word is used here?

2. This chapter states that it is your wife's essence that sets the standard for oneness in your marriage. How do you respond to that statement?

3. What do you think it takes for a husband to be totally convinced that his wife's essence sets the standard for oneness in his marriage? And how important is it to have this conviction?

4. In practical, everyday terms, what would it mean for you to let your wife's essence set the standard for oneness in your marriage?

5. What are your top ten goals for your marriage? And from that list of ten, which goals are the top three? How do you think these would compare with your wife's top goals for your marriage?

6. In what significant ways have you recognized the importance of making loving sacrifices in your marriage?

7. What impressed your wife the most about you before you got married? Do you still impress her in this way?

facing the top ten
love-chillers

My bachelor friend was puzzled. "Most Christian couples pray their hearts out before marriage, and they feel that God has brought them together," he said to me. "Then they marry and find more differences than common ground. They assume that God didn't bring them together after all. What's going on here?"

Nothing. Marriage is just a ridiculous concept, that's all. First, we take a male and female and tell them to become one. This alone is preposterous, considering the vast differences between men who are from Mars and women who are from Venus. Then throw in a host of other differences, such as temperaments, family environments, and religious backgrounds. After that, place them in a melting-pot culture inundated with sexual images and warped by no-fault divorce with little social stigma. Grant the blushing couple a kiss for luck, pronounce them man and wife, and boot them into the great unknown through a hail of rice and a mountain of gifts. As they disappear around the corner in blissful ignorance, snort with a wink and a hearty chuckle, "The fun's just beginning! They don't even see it coming!"

I certainly didn't see the train coming my direction. Brenda and I never fought before the wedding, and we even liked the same pizza—Canadian bacon and pineapple. Surely our marriage was a match made in heaven. Yet on one lovely September evening the chiming of wedding bells faded quickly in the din of a terrible row between us.

We had stopped by her mother's house after the wedding reception to pick up a few things. Suddenly, the reality hit Brenda that she was really leaving home—for good. She couldn't tear herself away. As for me, I had been celibate for a year, and I was anxious to, well, you know, get moving to the honeymoon suite reserved for us at a nearby hotel. I certainly didn't want to hang around my mother-in-law's house sharing soup and crackers.

Two hours later, moments after I had finally carried Brenda over the threshold, I was steaming. Brenda had announced that she'd forgotten a bag. "We have to run home and get it," she said.

I flipped out. "Then you'll go without me!" I violently rifled a hairbrush across the hotel room.

After that inauspicious beginning, we got up the next morning and drove westbound toward Des Moines to begin our honeymoon. Destination: the Rocky Mountains. I insisted that we stop for a day in Des Moines, however, so I could catch up on some work before leaving for Colorado.

Brenda was appalled. "Our honeymoon should take precedence over work!" she protested.

"What good is a nice first week together if I can't support us when we return?" I sneered.

On day three, I checked us into a hotel that, in Brenda's words, was "a fleabag."

"Be thankful for what you have!" I snapped. "We'll only be sleeping here anyway."

She began crying. "This is so unromantic," she whimpered. "I can't even put my feet on the floor without socks and shoes. Feel the carpet. It's gross!"

By the fourth night we clearly needed intervention. Brenda innocently asked, "Shouldn't we have devotions tonight? We haven't prayed together since our wedding day."

I don't remember why, but I exploded. Maybe I was insecure. I didn't really know how to lead devotions with a wife. Or maybe I was tired. But if I had to, I'd bet on something much less noble. I likely suspected that devotions would rob us of sex that night, that praying together would somehow take her out of the mood. Whatever the case, I stormed out of the room, blasting, "You're so holier than thou!"

During our first week back home, I discovered that Brenda didn't know how to cook. A few days later, she returned fearfully from the laundry room down the hall. "I think you'd better come take a look," she said. Inside a clothes hamper, all my white dress shirts had turned a pale pink.

"You didn't know you can't wash whites with colors?" I demanded. She meekly shook her head. I exploded, tearing the shirts into shreds.

HOW DID THE PROBLEM BEGIN?

You probably have a few stories of your own to tell from your early days of marriage. In case you're wondering how this guy-girl thing started, here's how it all began:

It seems that Adam was walking around the Garden of Eden one day, feeling very lonely. The Lord took notice and felt sorry for Adam. "Is there anything wrong with you?" God asked. "Is there anything I can do for you?"

"Well, it would be nice to have someone to talk to," said Adam. "You seem awfully busy these days."

"Okay, tell you what. I'll create a companion for you. She'll be a woman. She'll gather food for you, cook for you, and when you discover clothing, she'll wash it for you. She'll agree with every decision you make. She'll bear your children and never ask you to get up in the middle of the night to care for them. She won't nag you, and she will always be the first to admit she was wrong when you've had a disagreement. She'll give you love and passion any time you want it, and she'll never go to bed with a headache."

"Wow, that sounds great!" said Adam, his interest rising. "What will a woman like this cost me?"

"An arm and a leg."

This seemed like a lot to Adam. Then he had a brainstorm. "What can I get for a rib?" he asked.

The rest is history…

We laugh, but it does seem like our expectations in marriage keep getting shortchanged. Like right after the wedding. Did you ever wonder if you married the right person? Did you ever think that you might have missed God's will in whom you should marry? If so, welcome to the club.

We're so different! So what? Aren't we all? Once this truth settles in, the climb to marital oneness seems impossible. We panic, sensing fraud; we may look for a way out of the deal. Yet Paul said in Romans 14 that compatibility isn't at all necessary for unity. Disputes and incompatibility are always going to exist in a marriage.

This is why it's necessary for you to be a leader with a soft heart, a man who can submit his rights for the sake of oneness. Hardheadedness, however, keeps getting in the way. Consider this passage from Scripture:

Some Pharisees came to him to test him. They asked, "Is it lawful for a man to divorce his wife for any and every reason?"

"Haven't you read," he replied, "that at the beginning the Creator 'made them male and female,' and said, 'For this reason a man will leave his father and mother and be united to his wife, and the two will become one flesh'? So they are no longer two, but one. Therefore what God has joined together, let man not separate."

"Why then," they asked, "did Moses command that a man give his wife a certificate of divorce and send her away?"

Jesus replied, "Moses permitted you to divorce your wives because your hearts were hard. But it was not this way from the beginning." (Matthew 19:3-8)

Notice that it was not our irreconcilable differences that couldn't allow us to love our wives as ourselves. It was because we *wouldn't* love our wives.

WHAT IS IT ABOUT MEN?

Why won't we love our wives? Why do we have such hard hearts?

For starters, we're males. We men are just different from women—and there are some qualities about us and how we relate to women and marriage that we definitely need to understand and confront. We might call these characteristics potential "love chillers" in a marriage because they tend to induce a cooling effect on the flow of warmth and affection in the relationship.

We aren't by nature worse than women. But as you read the following list of ten traits that males typically bring into a marriage, you'll see how they can render us eminently unqualified to love like Christ:

1. Men Are Rebellious By Nature

Sure, Eve was the first to be deceived in the Garden of Eden, but Adam, on the other hand, knew that eating the fruit was wrong and did so anyway. Through the millenniums since, Adam's sons (that's us) have been just as rebellious, choosing our own way with an intensity far beyond that shown by most women (as evidenced by, among other things, the far greater crime rates among males than females).

We get bored fast with the straight life. By nature, we quickly tire of submitting to the needs and essence of our mates. We'd rather have things our own interesting way.

2. The Male Ego Is Bigger but More Fragile Than the Female Ego

The fragility of our egos easily prevents oneness and intimacy. Tracy said, "Most things in our marriage are Gil's plans and desires. Gil never shows me any of his deep feelings, and I can't say that I've ever felt one with him. He once said, 'If I let you in and show you my feelings, I'd be vulnerable to becoming hurt.'"

And while as husbands we must make room for our wife's gifts to blossom, our big but fragile egos can easily see the expression of our wives' superior gifts as a threat. Monica told me:

After a while, I felt that I could manage raising our kids if my husband weren't around to frustrate us. It always caused confusion when my husband came home and wanted to be in charge. Most of the time, his choices about what to do for family fun didn't fit with what the kids wanted to do. If I tried to make another suggestion, he would be crushed. This led me to take even more control by trying to have things already planned. I was only trying to help him become a better father. Besides, it only seemed natural for me to choose the family activities, since I knew everyone's schedules. But he couldn't see it that way, saying I was hooked on controlling things. It made me very angry, and it was hard to feel as though we were a real team.

3. Men Are Relatively Less Sensitive to the Needs of Others

In a perfect world, the head of the home would be the most sensitive one in the house. We don't live in a perfect world! Mary said:

Early in our marriage, my husband wanted to be intimate at the most inconvenient times. It seemed that if company was coming over, he just had to have sex. But my mind was spinning, trying to keep every-thing going. I was exhausted with cooking, doing the laundry, and just trying to keep a clean path through the house as I prepared for the guests. Suddenly, I'd find him lying in the bedroom like a spider just waiting for me to come and meet his need.

He never noticed that I needed his help or that it might be better to wait until our company had gone home that night. It was very hard to feel one with him at the time. He didn't care how I was doing, but he did care enough to have his sexual needs met.

Since then we've really talked about my needs and expectations, especially when we have company. He has not only given in on having sex before friends come over, but now he helps me prepare for com-pany. He's very understanding. This has brought a oneness and closeness that we didn't experience in the early years. And our sexual relationship is better than it has ever been.

For most men, sensitivity takes work at first. We aren't born with the sensitivity necessary for mutual submission.

4. Men Are Less Able to Express Emotions and Feelings Verbally Than Women Are

In one study, Stanford University researcher Diane McGinness gave young children twelve tasks and recorded any vocalization. What happened? The boys had the same amount of vocalization as the girls, but it was vastly different. The girls spoke with each other, and 100 percent of the vocalization was in language and sentences. The boys weren't verbally oriented at all. Only 60 percent of their vocalization was language, and the remaining 40 percent was nonverbal, one-syllable exclamations like "Wow!" or "Boy!" or motor noises. (Ever notice that men tend to swear and curse more than women do?) For obvious reasons, our natural verbal deficiency doesn't aid the cause of oneness.

5. The Male Brain Is More Oriented to Facts and Logic Than to Emotions and Intuitions

Because of brain differentiation during fetal development, the female brain has more lateral transmission points between the two hemispheres of the brain. She more easily consults all of her past experiences and is often quicker to make the accurate character judgments that manifest "intuition."

Women can also recall details of any fight you've had over the past twenty years—including the color of the shoes you wore as you stormed out the door. We men are often totally outmatched in conflict and often try to do everything we can to avoid it. This avoidance doesn't help communication.

Furthermore, a recent study at the Indiana University School of Medicine revealed that women use both hemispheres of the brain when they're listening while we men use only one. We're communicating with half our brains tied behind our backs!

As leaders, we should allow our wives' superior gifts of discernment to bless our marriages and to promote oneness. She's more than happy to help with her intuition. But too often we'd rather sniff at anything that smacks of intuitive thought, as Gina revealed:

> If I disagreed with Clay's opinion, he had to make me see things his way. It seemed to threaten his leadership if I expressed a contrary opinion— especially if it had to do with other people. He called me judgmental if I sensed a character flaw in someone or if I sensed that they were phonies.
>
> I could have helped him deal better with other people if he would have valued my opinion. I suspect he often knew that I was right about someone, but as a leader, he felt he needed to be the one to sense these flaws. My judgment could not be the sole deciding factor. Only his could be.
>
> In the end, if I differed with him, he acted like a wet puppy, so I usually kept silent. This silence brought him some peace, but he often made mistakes in dealing with people that he could have avoided. I resented that, which put a distance between us.

Our maleness can blind us to the finer aspects of our wives' essence, so we trample them regularly.

6. Men Are Sexually Stimulated Visually

We're more prone to straying sexually than women because our eyes chase any short skirt that moseys by. When coupled with our rebellious natures, this becomes a huge obstacle to oneness. In an effort to describe male sexuality, Debbie simply states, "Men are pigs." It's an apt indictment. Rather than purify our eyes and submit our behavior to God, we often choose our own way. Consider this letter we received from a reader of *Every Man's Battle:*

My husband has bought into the lie that "all men look" because they are so visual. He read your book *Every Man's Battle,* but he still says it is impossible for any real man to avoiding looking at a babe in a string bikini. This bothers me, but he has threatened me with divorce if I don't stop "nagging" him about this. He says that if I'm looking for a man who doesn't notice other women, I'll be waiting for a long time.

I am sick to my stomach to think that for the rest of my life, I will be robbed of fullness in my marriage. Because this bothers me so much, and because my husband is so sick of being reminded of it, he does it even more now! Can you imagine? Everywhere I go with my husband I know I can't keep his attention. NOWHERE!

Take note of her pain as she contemplates the lonely decades yawning cavernously before her. Maybe we are pigs. The lust of our eyes naturally hardens our hearts to our wives' sexual essence. We think she must meet our terms or we'll detour to the ever-ready harems of cyberspace.

7. Before Marriage, Males Take Responsibility for Nurturing the Love Relationship

After marriage, he sees the bride as someone to look after him. Having conquered this frontier called love, we turn the reins of the relationship over to our wives and climb back into our Conestoga wagon for a nap.

Our justification? Laziness, most likely. But some guys like to take 1 Corinthians 11:9—"Neither was man created for woman, but woman for man"—and stretch it entirely out of shape.

Brenda has recently been rereading all the letters I sent her during our courtship. "It's disappointing that I don't have any letters from you talking about my dad's death," she remarked. Knowing he died a couple of months before our wedding, I figured she must have misplaced them. "There must have been some, right?" I asked.

"No," she replied. "You had stopped writing by then. Your ardor had already cooled."

I guess I turned the reins over a bit early, but that's our nature, men. The sacrifice of male submission doesn't spring easily from such hearts.

8. Men Need Less Romance Than Women

We tend to forget to stoke the fires of the relationship. We say to ourselves, "Okay, now I've got a wife. What's next on the agenda?" But romance lies at the heart of the female essence. Every wife is an incurable romantic, since romantic love is the fuel that runs the female engine.

When I brought flowers home for our anniversary a few days ago, Brenda didn't know whether to gasp, jump, shake, or squeal. So she did them all at once! She loves to eat at our old haunts, drive by our old homes and apartments, and walk together at dusk holding hands. She loves my gifts of time, and she especially loves my nonsense gifts. Happy surprises are fun.

By nature, romance draws less of our focus after the wedding. To make matters worse, our souped-up, sexually charged male engines cause us to get everything mixed up. Jean said this:

> I love the romantic intimacy of a hug and extra attention, but any little hug and kiss I give John seems to suggest that I want to make love. How exasperating! I just want him to know that I love him, and I just want the same response back without feeling that I have to jump into bed. I just want him to hold me and talk to me; I just want to be near him.

Often low on romantic fuel, our wives run on the fumes of memories from days gone by when we nurtured the love relationship. We'll rarely honor this crucial area of the female essence when left to our natural male devices.

9. The Male Shield from Inferiority Is His Work

The wife's shield from inferiority is generally her husband, so she naturally places a higher value on the marital relationship than her husband does. Oneness isn't on his radar screen.

I was visiting Jeff's office one day when the conversation lulled. Suddenly, his face brightened as he asked, "Would you like to take a look at my business goals?" Jeff proudly hauled out a huge three-ring binder. Flipping it open, I found the summary of his seven-year business plan. He had detailed his sales quotas and responsibilities, the toys he hoped to acquire, and his plans to build an office building. Page after page listed the required yearly, monthly, and weekly steps to accomplish all those worthy goals.

As I left his office, I wondered why he didn't have such a binder for his marital goals. Then again, why didn't I? His wife, Janet, meanwhile, was starving emotionally. His "seven-year plan" didn't include improving his marriage. "I feel more like his business partner than his wife," Janet said, adding that she'd recently applied for a job to "get my sense of self back."

"What are your feelings for Jeff right now?" I asked.

"They're dead."

I shuddered. I'd heard that somewhere before.

10. *Men Desire Peace from Marriage, While Women Desire Oneness*

We can easily be satisfied with a "business partner" relationship in marriage as long as there's peace and enough sex. The candy cane of that kind of marriage is all red, however. Here's what Jane Fonda said (in *Good Housekeeping*, the November 2000 issue) when she was asked, "What have you learned about yourself and men?"

> My generation, for our "survival," bought into this notion that we
> have to stifle our own needs in order to stay in a relationship with a
> man. And I'm a good person to talk to about this; I've been married
> three times. And it's not that the men are bad, or mean. It's that
> that's the way I was brought up. You can be very forceful politically, or
> you can have a voice professionally, as I do. But where losing your voice
> shows up is behind the closed door of your home—in your primary
> relationship. No one ever told me to act like I did with men. It was

ingrained in our hearts and our minds that we are being selfish if we say, "That doesn't make me feel good" or "I don't want to do that" or "I really need to be alone now."

While all her husbands felt good about themselves, Jane was lonely and alone. Jane faults her generation, but females of every generation say this same thing, to our shame as men.

Rather than rise above our natural male preference for peace over oneness, we selfishly settle for what's comfortable to us. Again, it's not that we *can't* love our wives, but that we *won't*.

WILL YOU SOFTEN YOUR HEART?

Those ten male traits didn't form the most encouraging list, did they? By nature, men are insensitive, poorly focused, and have little interest in male submission. No wonder oneness in marriage is so rare. In the face of the countless incompatibilities of marriage, we need soft hearts if we're to submit our rights for the sake of oneness. We're just not naturally suited to this call.

I can relate to all ten of these traits because I was overwhelmed by every one early in our marriage. I recall attending a marriage seminar weekend with Brenda. As we left the retreat center that Sunday, I felt good—about myself, about my marriage. Then a deep sense of foreboding hit my gut. As we drove off, I told Brenda, "It feels like I'm driving toward the Promised Land, but I can see the top of a dragon's head over the horizon, waiting to crush me."

What was this dragon? That huge monster of male traits that I knew I must soon slay. So much change was necessary in me!

Do you recognize yourself in the love-chillers list? How many of those male traits have you submitted to your wife in reverence to Christ? Too many of us just shrug our shoulders and figure that's the way it goes. My father always said, "I like me just the way I am. If you don't feel that way, then you'll have to find a way to deal with it."

Then there are those of us who think we have the world figured out, including our marriage. Consider this story from Pam:

> My husband and I have been married for thirty-two years. Do you
> know what happened Tuesday night? Peter said to me, "Pam, I love you
> more than I ever have. I don't think we've ever been closer during our
> whole lives together."
>
> He really meant it too! Do you know what I thought when he said
> it? "You're crazy! You don't even *know* me!"

Peter had the peace he desired from marriage, but no oneness. How, then, could he feel closer to her than ever before? Perhaps it was because they were debt free with the house nearly paid off. Perhaps it was because he had a fulfilling job that would carry him through to retirement. Perhaps it was because the stress of raising and supporting children had passed. His grandchildren bounce on his right knee, and he has time to explore hobbies for the first time in years. Peter has peace in every corner of his life. No wonder he feels his marriage is perfect.

But not Pam. She says:

> Peter seems to be threatened or feels inferior when I'm able to manage
> things, figure people out, or be organized. This has been hard for our
> relationship. I've had to pull back from teaching or taking any leader-
> ship roles until he can figure out what his leadership role is. So much
> of me has been kept under wraps. I could have been a great help to
> him through the years, and we could have been so much closer.

Sadly, Peter is blind to the fact that he desires peace over oneness. And our blindness creates hard hearts. It's not that we're intentionally mean; it's just that we can't see very well because of these natural traits we've listed. This blindness is compounded by our overall track record. We've had few role models of men rising up to live in mutual submission with their wives. Eighty-four percent of us don't even have the first clue about developing oneness and intimacy in marriage—how could there be many role models?

Role models aside, what about you? Do you have blind spots as a result of these ten traits? How would you know? Someone has to tell you. A few years ago, God moved heavily in my life and caused some deep Christian growth. It began when I sensed that I would soon take on a more visible leadership role at church. I wanted to know if I had any blind spots in my character that would undermine my leadership in any way. So I asked four men this question: "What traits or characteristics do you see in me that would keep me from becoming an effective leader in this church?" I decided to ask a pastor and a deacon who knew me very well, plus a pastor and a deacon who knew me only in passing. I figured this would paint a broad picture of my strengths and weaknesses.

The results encouraged and devastated me. All four men named the exact same flaw in me! They found me aloof and unapproachable. This news devastated me because I knew that if all four saw it, then 98 percent of the rest of the human race probably saw the same thing. All this time these character flaws had been obvious to everyone but me. How humiliating!

But it was very encouraging to know the truth, for now I could deal with it, by God's grace. Brenda exclaimed, "That was so risky and brave! I could never do that." But it didn't seem so brave to me. If I wanted to lead, I *had* to know the truth. They were *blind* spots, after all. How else would I see the truth if I didn't ask?

Knowing the truth is half the battle. Rather than smugly step into marital leadership thinking we're God's gift to our wives, we must adjust our thinking to align more closely with the truth, that marriage will likely require much change in us.

How will you check your blind spots? Are you one of the 84 percent who aren't providing oneness to their wives? Asking others isn't the *only* way to discover blind spots, of course.

You can ask yourself. When you hear one of those oldie passionate love songs and think about the lyrics, do you always picture your wife, or do you think of some old girlfriend or some babe at work? When you sing as you cruise down the road, are you singing to your wife, and to her alone?

Perhaps your best path to the truth is to simply ask your wife, as I did these men. We've developed a set of questions that you can copy and hand to your wife. But strap on your helmet. When women read this list, they sometimes become angry. Other times, they cry as they consider what they've missed in their relationships with their husbands. Believe us, we know.

Are you courageous enough to ask her these questions? Are you brave? We think you are.

A HUSBAND'S LEADERSHIP EVALUATION

Your Evaluation of Our Oneness

1. In your opinion, what creates the most impasses between us? How do I handle these impasses? In these impasses, do I break the ties in my favor most of the time? Do my methods affect our oneness?

2. What do I do that tramples who you are, your soul essence? In my decisions, do I respect and honor your soul essence as I do my own? Do I seem more like a father trying to get you to comply with my views, or more like a fellow heir who is longing to understand you?

3. What do I do that strips you of "feeling one with me?" How does that affect your relationship with me?

4. Do you feel that we have complete oneness? Where does our oneness break down? Do I understand my role in the breakdown, and am I working actively on it?

Your Evaluation of My Spiritual Leadership

5. Who has the greater knowledge of the Word of God, you or me? How does this make you feel? How does this affect your oneness with me?

6. When character flaws are revealed, which of us is quicker to submit to Scripture and change? Are there character flaws in me that I've been slow to address? Are there some I've refused to address? What does this reveal to you about my love for you?

7. Who is the quickest to forgive, you or me? Who is the quickest to ask forgiveness? How does this affect your feelings of oneness with me?

8. Which of us is more consistent with prayer and devotions? Which of us is more comfortable in devotions as a couple? As a family? Does this affect our oneness?

9. Has the spiritual temperature of our relationship been rising or falling through the years? Has my leadership brought you to a higher level than ever before? Do I resist you when you try to raise our behavioral standards?

Your Evaluation of My Heart's Softness

10. Who gives in at impasses more often, you or me?

11. Who enjoys sacrificing and serving more, you or me? Do I have a good attitude when serving?

12. Who is inconvenienced more often in our relationship, your or me?

13. Who is the "chief servant" in our family, the best example of servanthood?

14. Let's say our pastor said to you, "I want to nominate your husband as deacon (or elder). What would be your reservations regarding his character?" What would you tell him?

15. God calls you to submit to my authority. My leadership style should make this submission easier. Does it?

Your Evaluation of Me As a Servant

16. To what extent do I understand that my time is not my own? Do I often unilaterally make decisions regarding my time?

17. To what extent do I understand that I don't have a right to make unilateral decisions regarding hunting, golf, work, my friends, etc.?

18. Do you feel I've really studied you through the years and changed my behavior and decisions in order to honor what I've learned about you?

19. Do I draw more prestige and self-esteem from my success as a leader and husband at home, or more from my work and other accomplishments?

20. Have I been quick to learn new skills in our relationship and home to serve you better and give you more freedom?

21. Do I throw my full heart into helping you to fully live and blossom in marriage? Or do you feel that you're carrying the heaviest load of responsibility regarding our marriage and family?

22. Do I make room to allow your personal gifts and your ministries to blossom? Do you sense that your gifts and talents threaten me as a leader?

23. When you have a strong gift in a certain area, do I honor you by allowing your opinions to dominate my decision making in that area?

24. Do I allow for your weaknesses, as I do my own, and lovingly make up for them with my strengths, or do I generally judge you for them?

25. Do you feel free to confront sin in my life, or am I so offended when you do that you'd rather not bother?

Questions for Reflection and Discussion

1. In what ways have you seen your own tendency toward any of the typical male traits (in terms of your relationships with women) listed below?
   —a rebellious nature
   —a bigger ego than your wife's but more fragile
   —less sensitivity to others' needs
   —less able to express emotions and feelings verbally
   —more oriented to facts and logic than to emotions and intuitions
   —sexually stimulated visually
   —less inclined to continue being romantic after marriage
   —needing less romance
   —using work as a shield from inferiority
   —desiring peace (more than oneness) in marriage

2. Take the time necessary to work through (with your wife) the Husband's Leadership Evaluation.

leading as a bondservant

If you have young children, you're probably familiar with Playmobil action figures from Germany. These round-headed plastic characters—knights, cowboys, construction workers, and farm moms—come with "curled" hands that enable them to hold a wide range of interchangeable accessories, from horsewhips and pails to dolls and carriages. My daughter Rebecca, when she was a toddler, looked at this motley bunch with their weird hands and dubbed them "pinch people," since their hands looked as though they were about to pinch someone.

One early evening, Rebecca and her friend Tracy were plunked down on the kitchen floor playing "pinch people" when I slumped into a breakfast nook chair following a hectic day. Absently gazing their way, I became mesmerized by the imaginary interplay between Rebecca and her round-headed family. Mama-doll bantered lightly with Baby-doll as she stood at the stove stirring up supper. Meanwhile, Tracy drove Papa-doll home from work. Walking him past his sweet round-headed wife, she paused so Papa-doll could give Mama-doll a peck on the cheek. Suddenly, a dark scowl rolled across Tracy's face as she marched Papa-doll into the living room and slammed him onto the couch. "Daddy's going to lay down," she announced to all with disgust. "Daddy never does anything to help."

I shivered in my chair. Tracy's dad was like the many husbands in our culture who have no idea what a good marriage should look like. Since many husbands have no idea how they're supposed to act or lead, they fall back on what comes naturally. Given the list of our natural character traits shared in the previous chapter, that's not good! Sure, we can say we want to "be a better husband" or "spend more time at home and less at the office," but these platitudes quickly fade in the face of life's temptations and pressures. Without a new blueprint to transform our minds regarding marital leadership, we revert to our natural ways and, as a result, lead mediocre lives.

To make headway, we must begin by incorporating sacrificial acts of leadership, letting Jesus be our ultimate role model. Just before His death, Jesus used a routine practice of His day—foot washing upon entering a home—to show us the way:

> When he had finished washing their feet, he put on his clothes and returned to his place. "Do you understand what I have done for you?" he asked them. "You call me 'Teacher' and 'Lord,' and rightly so, for that is what I am. Now that I, your Lord and Teacher, have washed your feet, you also should wash one another's feet. I have set you an example that you should do as I have done for you." (John 13:12-15)

But we mustn't sacrifice merely for the sake of example, or our attitudes will easily be warped. Recently, we (the Stoeker family) were at an Italian restaurant when my youngest son Michael spent five dollars of his own money to buy a cheese stick appetizer for everyone to share. We'd been teaching about sacrifice in our family prayer time, and we were pleased that Michael desired to set an example. Trouble is, for the rest of the night he bragged about his appetizer as if he'd just won the NBA slam dunk contest!

THE MEANING OF SACRIFICE

All too often, any "sacrifice" we make for our wives is more about burnishing our own images than actually doing something for our wives. Let me offer an example: When Brenda was a surgical nurse, she was often called out on medical emergencies in the middle of the night. She never rose alone on those wintry nights at 3 A.M., however. I awoke with her, venturing out to warm up her car and scrape her icy windows while she dressed to leave. I returned to my warm bed only when she was safely off.

On the mornings when she had a regular work schedule, I made up her lunch while she showered, dropping special treats like Ding Dongs into her brown paper sack. Sometimes when I passed her car in the hospital parking lot, I tucked a love note under her windshield wiper. I bought appetizers for her on our dates, splurging simply because she loved them so. Invariably, news of how "special" I treated Brenda reached her coworkers during break time. They acted jealously, saying, "You're so lucky to have such nice husband!"

Brenda smiled and replied, "Thanks. I know." But inside, because of my trampling, she didn't know what to feel. Sure, the ice scraping and Ding Dongs and love notes were nice, but they probably did more for me than they did for Brenda. I rather enjoyed my "sensitive guy" reputation. Better yet, I liked what her friends and coworkers said about me: *What a sensitive, wonderful husband you have!*

I may have done everything suggested in *Fifty Ways to Please Your Wife*, but I was still guilty of trampling Brenda during the other twenty-three hours of the day. If you as Chief Tiebreaker are crushing oneness in your marriage, it's not enough to polish your image by making "sacrifices." You need an entirely new mind-set and a wholesale change in motive.

When Jesus washed His disciples' feet, this act of submission wasn't about showing off His superior humility or sensitivity. Setting an example wasn't even His primary motive, as you can see from this passage of Scripture:

> It was just before the Passover Feast. Jesus knew that the time had come for him to leave this world and go to the Father. Having loved his own who were in the world, he *now showed them the full extent of his love....*
>
> So he got up from the meal, took off his outer clothing, and wrapped a towel around his waist. After that, he poured water into a basin and began to wash his disciples' feet. (John 13:1,4-5)

Jesus knew that His time on earth was ending, and His heart was broken at the thought of leaving His friends. He wanted to love them one more time before He left. Christ did the same for the rest of humankind, enduring the horrors of crucifixion as the ultimate manifestation of submission and as history's most wondrous act of sacrificial love.

Each one of us should do no less for our wife. The sacrifice of male submission will set an example, but its primary purpose is to release our wives to live life fully and blossom to their full potential. Recalling Paul's words again, we see that submission must be rooted in love and unity:

> If your brother is distressed because of what you eat, *you are no longer acting in love.* Do not by your eating destroy your brother for whom Christ died. Do not allow what you consider good to be spoken of as evil. For the kingdom of God is not a matter of eating and drinking, but of righteousness, peace and joy in the Holy Spirit, *because anyone who serves Christ in this way is pleasing to God and approved by men.* (Romans 14:15-18)

Servant leadership is more than washing your wife's feet once in a while or vacuuming before she returns home from a trip to the mall. It's more than washing dishes, running a load of laundry, or filling her car with gas. We have neighbors who would do these things for us in a pinch.

IT'S WHAT YOU ARE

Serving isn't something we *do*—it's something we *are.* We can't just act like a servant from time to time, whenever it happens to suit our purposes. Rather, we need to become a servant—our minds transformed to think like one, and our hearts transformed to submit like one—all of the time. Jesus *became* a servant. We, too, must *become* servants and reject our Chief Tiebreaker mindset. How do we do that?

By choice. While Jesus' beautiful example of servanthood can take us only so far in marriage (after all, He never married), the Father provides the transforming model we need when He describes the bondservant of Old Testament times:

> If you buy a Hebrew servant, he is to serve you for six years. But in the seventh year, he shall go free, without paying anything.…
>
> But if the servant declares, "I love my master and my wife and children and do not want to go free," then his master must take him before the judges. He shall take him to the door or the doorpost and pierce his ear with an awl. Then he will be his servant for life. (Exodus 21:2,5-6)

Imagine the scene. A broken Jew awakes one morning with no options. Mired hopelessly in poverty, owning nothing but an empty stomach, he stands starkly upon the auction block of slavery. Shoulders slumped, his pride long since stripped away, his ashen face conveys only a searing shame, gaunt eyes staring aimlessly into the distance.

Suddenly, a man with gentle eyes appears before him, a man he's never known. Somehow this man sees a shred of value in him. *Did I see a trace of love in this man's eyes?* the slave wonders. It couldn't be, but his hope rises as his master pays the price to bring him home. His master does love him. Clothing the man well and feeding him richly, the master speaks gently to him and calls him "brother." Six years quickly tick by, and within the slave's heart grows a deep love for his master. He longs to repay his master for his mercy and grace.

When the day of the slave's leave-taking finally arrives, his master, with moist eyes, offers gifts for the freed man to take on his way. The man declines but offers his own gift in return: his once broken life now restored by the master. Setting his lobe to the post, he joyously receives the mark, submitting his rights and future for the honor of serving and pleasing his master for as long as he lives.

We recognize this picture. It's our life in Christ. Once we were slaves on the auction block of sin. We stood broken by every evil and foolish thing we'd ever done. Yet our pure Master inexplicably saw value in us, paying for our freedom with His blood that we might serve Him. Experiencing His great love, we returned His love by working in His kingdom, happily marked by the Holy Spirit (see Ephesians 1:13).

This Old Testament scene suggests another picture that I'll paint for you. One day my eyes opened to see Brenda before me, a woman I'd never known. Seeing value in me, she paid a dear price to have me as her own. I returned this love, happily receiving the mark of a golden ring that told everyone I was now hers. She was my "master," to whom I was forever pledged to serve.

Of course, I wasn't technically a bondservant to Brenda. First of all, I was to love her as Christ loved the church, and He is not a bondservant to His bride. And unlike the bondservant of the Old Testament who had no rights, we husbands certainly have rights of our own separate from our wives. Furthermore, as I understand Scripture, we clearly carry the position of authority in our homes.

That said, our position as leader cannot be separated from God's call to submission, and this bondservant model of love can and must serve as our paradigm of leadership. A bondservant loves his master as he loves himself, and he's committed to helping his master fully live and fully blossom as a person. Sound familiar?

But Fred and Steve, my wife is not my master! True, but becoming-one-with-her-essence is your master. You submit your rights in whatever way necessary as leader to attain this, not because she has authority over you, but because you love her. You've been commanded to love her in precisely this way by someone who *does* have authority over you—Jesus Christ.

A man once asked us, "You speak so much about serving and giving in. Do you ever feel as if you aren't head of your home?"

The answer is no. We know that seems paradoxical, but obedience to Christ leads to paradoxical blessings. This servant approach has actually given us stronger leadership in our marriages, not less.

Listen to what my wife, Brenda, has to say:

Submission never came naturally to me. It was even harder to submit when my respect for Fred's spirituality was at its all-time low.
During our days of severe fighting and in-law problems, I would ask
myself, *Why should I submit to someone who is worse off spiritually
than I am?*

I knew I could always submit for the sake of the Lord. I knew His
ways were for the best. I knew Jesus had sacrificed for me and that He
wanted me to submit to Fred for His sake. But then Fred changed, and
it became easier to submit when he was leading by example.

Fred's commitment to servanthood all these years has been a wonderful teacher to me. I have been inspired to do better by watching him.
As he gave himself and his desires away, I wanted to do the same.

Did you get that? When I'm leading as a bondservant, my wife's submission becomes easier for her, which strengthens my leadership.

Another marital benefit of submission to oneness is "affair-proofing" your
marriage. Brenda explains: "I'm not a likely candidate for an affair because I
have a deep understanding that it's sin. Still, I've frequently thought, 'How
could I ever have an affair? He treats me so well and gives up so much for my
sake. How could I be so disloyal as to turn my back on that?'"

Yes, we know what you may be thinking. You may have heard it from
your father often enough: "Real men take control of their homes." But real
men aren't necessarily dictatorial leaders at home, as evidenced by Greg, one
of the toughest guys you'll ever meet. On the football field, if you ran a cross-
ing pattern at him, he'd split you in two and eat your liver as a party snack.
A bright, tough farmer, Greg is part man and part beast, but he understands
mutual submission and acts as a tender leader over his wife, Candy. Here's
how she calls it:

I am so fortunate to be Greg's wife. Each night when he comes home
from work ready for a shower, he wants me to come into the bathroom

to chat with him. That is so sweet, and I never thought God would grant me such a terrific marriage and husband, especially after all the creeps I dated in college.

Greg has four guys he meets with every Sunday night. A few don't have terrific marriages, but they know ours is something special. One of those men, speaking to Greg recently, said, "You must be doing something right because your wife obviously adores you." This made Greg feel great!

Many women have domineering husbands, but Greg considers my feelings every step of the way. Most of the time I find submission to Greg to be freeing because I know he seeks God first.

Hmm. Greg sounds manly to us. Anyone want to question the strength of his leadership?

IT's a MATTER OF STYLE

We're not talking about abdicating the crown when you choose to mutually submit. We're talking about abdicating your *style*. Playing Chief Tiebreaker will trample your wife's convictions and eat away at her soul essence. She'll never blossom under that scenario, and there'll be no oneness. You won't experience intimacy.

There's simply a better way to lead. After all, the surest sign of insanity is doing the same thing over and over—tiebreaking—and expecting a different result. Tiebreaking will always leave too many of our wives dying on the vine, with their married years being the loneliest years of their lives. It's time for a different way.

Of course, we must be wise as we become Chief Servant, because there are two sides to the coin of mutual submission. On one side are those men who think they're kings of the realm, and they lord that role over their wives. This attitude creates resentment and imbalance in the relationship. On the flip side are those men who have abdicated their godly role of male leadership because of feminism. In other words, they make *their wife* king of the realm, deferring to their wives and failing to take leadership. Both extremes are damaging to the family because the relationship goes against God's principles—that is, the marriage no longer parallels Christ's relationship to the church.

As a bondservant, you will not find yourself at either of these extremes. Rather, you are and will still be the leader. As great as Greg is at male submission, both he and Candy understand male leadership, as Candy relates:

> Employment once loomed as a big issue in our marriage. We both found ourselves working jobs that we hated, so Greg quit his to return to the University of Iowa. After graduating with a teaching degree, Greg realized he hated teaching and wanted to farm. This decision turned out to be quite stressful for me since I grew up in a stable home where my father brought home a steady paycheck. Besides, I couldn't stand the thought of being a farm wife. So I did the mature thing and locked myself in our apartment bathroom! Eventually, I came around to Greg's way of thinking and submitted to his decision. Now I am very happy on the farm.

We need to lead and to lead strongly, but we need a bondservant style of leadership that creates oneness and radiance in our wives. What does this leadership style look like in practice? Let's take a look at a snapshot of the bondservant's life in order to draw out the more important characteristics of his love for his master.

Once that awl was driven through the bondservant's lobe, *his time was no longer his own.* He couldn't get up in the morning and simply decide to go fishing. He must check with his master to see what pressing thing needed to be done. *The bondservant had few rights.* If the master were godly, the servant was granted the rights provided by the Bible, but those rights could be counted on one hand. Any other rights were granted after discussion with his master.

There was always much to do. Because of his love for his master, *he constantly studied to find new ways to better serve him.* He thought of ways to thrill his master's heart or take a load off his mind or body.

He developed new skills to better serve his master. For instance, if he knew his master loved fresh venison, he would learn to hunt in order to please his master with savory meals.

The servant did all he could to build the esteem and prestige of the master in the community, and he drew much prestige from this himself. He took great pride and honor in his role as bondservant to his master. The bondservant, though quite wise in his own right, *treated his master's thoughts and opinions as being as valuable as his own.*

As for his master's spiritual gifts, the bondservant was happy to do the most menial, thankless jobs *to make room for the master to exercise those gifts.* If his master had weaknesses that hurt his ministry and relationships, the bondservant *made allowances for the weaknesses* as if they were his own until his master was strengthened through God's grace, mercy, and the experience of time. The bondservant also actively *protected his master's faith.*

If the bondservant's own sin hurt his master, *he didn't dawdle in seeking freedom from this sin.* He loved his master, and he *completely enjoyed serving* his master in every way.

Not a bad life, actually. Of course, to Americans, this scenario seems preposterous. Who would ever give up his freedoms to enter such a relationship?

However…you should have done that on your wedding day.

IT'S A NEW WAY TO LEAD

Marital adjustment is a simple matter. Before marriage, you commanded your ship of life based upon the personal convictions and soul essence of one person—you.

You're now the skipper of the USS *Matrimony.* As captain, you must now command based upon the personal convictions and soul essence of *two* people. If this concept is new to you, you must learn quickly.

The convictions of these two people will sometimes conflict. But, according to Paul, male submission will be required to maintain unity on board. Male submission requires a humble mind-set that honors the essence of your wife.

Where do I find such a mind-set? We suggest you look at and choose that of the bondservant because, first of all, he loves his master as he loves himself, and he's committed to helping his master fully live and blossom as a person. That's the very same calling we have in our marriage—we need a servant's heart for our wives. Also, a servant's mind-set provides the humility necessary to give in for the sake of marital unity.

We've used the first two sections of this book to describe the common phenomenon of "deadness" in a wife's feelings and the male role in mutual submission as a way of reviving those feelings. Now, in the next two sections, we'll teach you to think like a servant. What's riding on it? Every woman's desire, which is oneness and intimacy with her husband.

What if I don't learn to submit? Your marital cruise could turn into an ugly shipwreck. Or, to stick with our analogy of "dead" feelings, your marriage could remain in the cemetery! Sure, you may have a compliant wife who will let you get away with a lack of submission, but odds are you'll sit together in a restaurant and she'll have dead eyes for all to see. Or you may have a strong-willed wife who chafes under your command and coexists with you as a "married single," but she may jump ship one day. In the best-case scenario, you'll get a godly wife who, while unable to submit out of respect for you, will find the strength in Christ to submit to you for Jesus' sake.

In all cases, you will not have oneness. You may have peace, you may have marital longevity, and you may even appear to have a marriage made in heaven. But you won't have a relationship based on intimacy. As a result, there'll be casualties on all sides, including one of particular interest to men—sex.

IT'S GOOD FOR YOUR SEX LIFE TOO!

For women, sexual attraction is based on relationship. If you've refused to take on a servant's mind-set, you'll have a wife with weak, little, or no sexual attraction to you. Take your pick. That's just the way it is.

A church pastor once said to someone, "See that chair over there? That's my counseling chair. Do you know what complaint I hear most often from married men?"

"No, what is it?" he was asked.

"'I'm just not getting any sex.'"

Readers of *Every Man's Battle* bombed us with e-mails asking a variation of this question: "How can I get my wife to desire sex with me?"

That's a great question. We've had men approach us with comments like Jim's:

> I'll admit I'm not perfect in my sexual purity, but can I talk to you about something else? My wife came up to me last Tuesday and said, "Jim, I have something to tell you, but I don't really know how to bring it up. I'll just say it straight out. I just don't like sex, and I really wish I didn't have to do it anymore."
>
> I was stunned. I didn't quite know what to say, but I said, "Honey, is it something I'm doing wrong, or is there something I can do better?" She said, "No, it's not what you're doing. All my friends feel this way. Every one of them."

Why don't women want sex with their husbands? The answer is that they have no real relationship with them. They don't feel intimate at all. Their husbands haven't allowed their wives' soul essences to be honored, loved, and expressed with their own.

But here's some news that should inspire you: Every male we know who is practicing mutual submission has a very satisfying sex life.

Want to learn more about mutual submission and the servant mind-set? If so, good. We'll spend the next several chapters discussing the characteristics of the bondservant model in relation to marriage. Toward the end of the book, we'll show you how to bring this new heart and new mind-set into your sex life.

Questions for Reflection and Discussion

1. What does the phrase *leading as a bondservant* mean to you after reading this chapter?

2. What tendency have you seen in yourself to make "sacrifices" more for the sake of enhancing your own image than for actually serving your wife?

3. In what significant ways have you recognized that serving isn't something we *do*—it's something we *are?*

4. This chapter says that the husband's position as leader cannot be separated from submission, and that the bondservant of love must serve as his paradigm of leadership. How do you respond to this idea? How fully do you accept and believe it? Does it raise any doubts or questions in your mind?

5. How would you describe your leadership style in your marriage? How does it compare to the bondservant style?

6. In your own marriage, what do you believe God wants you to do in response to what·you've learned so far in *Every Woman's Desire?*

PART III

manifesting your bondservant heart

the "master" defines your rights

You are not your own; you were bought at a price.

1 Corinthians 6:19-20

I purchased my first shotgun ten years ago at the urging of my buddies Brad and Dave. They helped me shop for a beautiful Browning semiautomatic twelve-gauge cannon. We celebrated by driving to an open stretch of public land for a session of skeet shooting. I was a natural at "pull and shoot," turning clay pigeons into black powder in no time. Shooting skeet by the boxful turned out to be the most relaxing hobby I'd ever found.

Brad and Dave suggested I might be interested in shooting something live, so one glorious Saturday morning before dawn I joined them on a pheasant hunt. Having grown up in a home where my father detested the practice, I'd never hunted in my life. Personally, I expected to be bored. I figured we'd walk around the Iowa brush in Day-Glo orange vests and get off a shot or two at birds darting away in the distance.

As we approached the first large clump of bushes, a cock jumped, and Brad aimed. When he fired, dozens more birds rushed skyward, and the three of us began blasting away as if we were in a firefight for our lives. My heart was pounding! I instantly knew why grown men spent every weekend for two and a half months tromping through frosty fields during pheasant season. I couldn't wait to return. I was captured.

Lurching through our door at five o'clock that afternoon, I gushed every detail to Brenda. "Honey, you won't believe this," I exclaimed. "I've finally found a hobby I love! Wow! The guys and I are going out again next Saturday, and I can hardly wait."

Brenda failed to return my enthusiasm. She couldn't imagine how climbing hill and dale and stumbling through cornstalks and switch grass could be relaxing. But there was more. Saturdays were family days, and she looked forward to them all week long.

"Sweetheart, you can't imagine how good it makes me feel to know you've found a hobby you love," she began. "You've needed one for a long time, but you need to understand what this means to my life. Hunting means I'll have to handle the kids six days a week all by myself. Besides, what good are Saturdays without the fun you bring to the mix?"

I glossed over her concerns since I *really* had fun pheasant hunting. "I know it's a sacrifice for you," I admitted. "But it's a short season—only two-and-a-half-months long. I have to make the most of it now."

Brenda wasn't tracking. "I really do wish you could do it every weekend," she said. "But hunting would steal too much time from me and the kids. With Sunday school and church, they really only see you on Saturdays as it is."

My position in this conversation was slipping.

She continued, "Since you like hunting this much, we should agree now how many times per year you can go. This way, you won't be tempted to stretch it when your buddies call."

This suggestion—a good one—caught me flatfooted. Advantage Brenda. Thinking rapidly, I knew I should be as "sacrificial" as possible. "How about three times?" I offered. That didn't seem like much to ask for when pheasant season lasted fifteen weeks.

"How about two?"

"Two? Come on, sweetheart, be reasonable! Three is already a huge sacrifice for me, and you know it. I have every right to go hunting at least three times a year!"

Let's stop the conversation right here. Make a freeze-frame. Why couldn't I do as I pleased? Hadn't I earned the right to some relaxation? Wasn't I the fellow who brought home the bacon twice a month, the leader who could unilaterally end a discussion on my terms and let the chips fall where they may? Besides, wasn't the pursuit of happiness the right of every American?

MY RIGHT, RIGHT?

Yeah, that was it, my right to the pursuit of happiness. Isn't that enshrined in our Declaration of Independence?

Actually, Brenda would have been better served had the Founders written "life, liberty, and the pursuit of righteousness" because marriage isn't about the pursuit of happiness. I should have been pursuing righteousness, and there's nothing righteous in trampling Brenda by thinking of hunting first and her and the kids second.

It's best to consider our rights with the heart of a bondservant: We have no rights except those agreed upon by our wives. James says that clambering after perceived rights is the chief reason for fighting and quarreling: "What causes fights and quarrels among you? Don't they come from your desires that battle within you? You want something but don't get it" (James 4:1-2).

Did I have the unilateral right to choose my hunting schedule, or did I simply perceive it that way? I had an easier time answering that question when I put the hunting boot on the other foot. I imagined it was Thanksgiving Day, and I was stuffed to the gills with turkey and gravy and football. As I stumbled heavily into the kitchen, Brenda squealed, "Honey, I'm so excited. Tomorrow is the start of the shopping season! The mall opens at 7 A.M., and I've got to be there early so I don't miss out on any of those 'doorbuster' sales. I'm going to meet Amy and Martha at Starbucks at 6:30 so we can get an early start. There are some incredible deals out there!"

"Okay, I'll watch the kids," I said. I figured they could play Game Boy while I watched some college football games.

"Thanks for doing that for me, honey, but I have another favor to ask you."

"And what would that be, darling?"

"I read in the newspaper that the stores will be having sales right up until early January. I'm not saying I'm going to buy something every time I go shopping, but every weekend between now and mid-January the girls and I will be hitting every sale between here and Indianapolis."

"Wha..."

"You should plan on being home with the kids when they get up until I come home late in the afternoon."

"And when might that be, my sweet little sugarplum?"

"Oh, I don't know. Around suppertime. Oh, you look sad."

"Well, all day does seem like a long time."

"Don't worry, pumpkin. It's a short season—only eight weeks. Isn't that great? Since the holiday shopping season is so short, I'm sure you'll understand!"

Everywhere across the fruited plain, I can hear the sound of roaring laughter—from women reading this book. "Oh sure, that'll be the day!"

LET'S BE REASONABLE

So how did my hunting story end?

"C'mon, Brenda," I pleaded. "Be reasonable! I don't think three Saturdays of pheasant hunting is too much to ask for."

"Okay," Brenda announced, breaking the stalemate. "I'll be reasonable and give you the three days. I'm sure you'll find it just as reasonable to provide me three full days of baby-sitting in return so I can shop with Pam."

Brenda didn't care a fig about fairness, but she cared dearly that I see the price I was asking them to pay. "Brenda, I really did think I was already sacrificing a ton to ask for only three Saturdays. Now you're making me look like some weakling who has to ask his wife how often he can hunt."

"I know that, honey, and I'm not trying to take your authority away. But we have the kids for such a short time, and then they'll be gone. You're so valuable to them that it seems crazy to spend so much time hunting, no matter how much fun it is."

It wasn't long before I said, "Okay, my dear, two it is." She gave me a big hug.

I can hear you now. *But that just didn't seem right!* Maybe. But was it right for me to hinder the primary call on Brenda's life by hunting whenever it pleased me?

Would hunting every Saturday actually prevent her from raising godly kids? That's not the point. If she believes it would, then every time I stepped into the fields, I would be trampling her. That wouldn't be right. The apostle Paul showed by his own example that it's righteous to give in for the sake of unity:

> If we have sown spiritual seed among you, is it too much if we reap a
> material harvest from you? If others have this right of support from
> you, shouldn't we have it all the more?
>
> But we did not use this right. On the contrary, we put up with any-
> thing rather than hinder the gospel of Christ. (1 Corinthians 9:11-12)

Paul lived as if he had no rights rather than hinder the gospel. Would you rather have rights or righteousness? You'll never be a servant as long as your rights are a factor in the decision-making process.

Would it be wrong to hunt every week? It was for me. My wife sets the terms for oneness, remember? On the other hand, your wife may not feel that your absence during pheasant season has any long-term impact on your kids. She may say, "Go for it! Just be careful!" If so, bag a bird for me.

What I'm trying to say is that the "master" defines your rights (And remember again that though we refer to your *wife* as your "master," it's our shorthand for the fact that *becoming one with her essence* is actually your God-given master). Why? Because you're called to oneness, and her essence sets the terms. Defending your rights is not conducive to even *seeing* your wife's convictions and essence, let alone honoring them.

You have few rights of your own besides those granted by the "master." Understanding this ensures that her convictions and essence are considered in decisions. When you go through married life saying, "I have a right to _____," it doesn't matter what you pencil in. You may think you have a right to go out with the guys once a week. You may think you have the right to choose every show the family watches on television. Decide where you go on vacation. Determine the restaurant you go to.

But these aren't rights until your wife agrees they are.

RELAX—IT'S JUST TELEVISION

Jon grew up watching Iowa Hawkeye basketball with his dad and his grandfather. Now married, he still watches the games every Thursday and Saturday on television, as well as the NBA doubleheader on Sunday. This bugs his wife, Marlee, to no end, and all this basketball has hurt their relationship. Jon simply replies, "I have a right to watch those games. I work hard during the week, and I need these games to relax."

Baloney.

For Earl and Karen, the issue was gambling at the Elks Club. Karen told me, "I didn't want him to do it because gambling is wrong and it creates debt. He did as he pleased, though. He also went traveling on weekends without me, and I objected because he was already gone so often during the week on business. He also controlled the checkbook and never gave me enough spending money. He refused to change, doing what he wanted, despite how I felt. I never felt intimacy with Earl."

It's far better to get used to giving our rights away. Soon it will *become a way of life,* and you won't even have to think about it anymore. You become a servant in your mind, and thinking sacrificially becomes a matter of course.

Let me offer an example. A few years back, Brenda and I had been waiting months for the season opener of *Star Trek: The Next Generation.* The previous television season had ended with an evil Borg ship taking aim at Earth. The starship *Enterprise* had one last shot to stop it before it leveled our planet. The last scene of the final episode showed the captain of the *Enterprise* commanding, "Fire!"

We waited months to find out what happened, and now the season opener was upon us. Brenda and I settled into our big family-room couch and became engrossed while the old episode was recapped. The tension mounted with each scene. Now the final half-hour loomed as a real barnburner. Grabbing snacks after a run to the bathroom, we both anticipated the thrilling climax.

Three minutes later, Brenda smelled something nasty. I noticed nothing. Then again, my eyes were glued to the set.

Brenda turned to find our preschooler, Michael, grinning as his training pants leaked fresh ca-ca down his leg and onto the carpet. Brenda groaned, and I turned to second her emotion. One of us had to take Michael upstairs for ten minutes to hose him off. And one of us had to clean the carpet. But at least the lucky carpet cleaner could still watch the show at the same time.

So who would escort Michael for his bath?

I would. I simply swept him up without a word of discussion. That's what servants do. Acting from a servant heart means blessing your wife and giving her a chance to blossom fully. I know Brenda appreciated my doing that, but it was more than that. I was loving her as myself and leading by example.

WHAT ABOUT THE WEIRD STUFF?

Before we leave the topic, do we have a right to our personal idiosyncrasies simply because they add to our "charm"? Not if they trample oneness.

Let's take a closer look. When I wash my face in the morning, I like to splash water around my face—and thus all over the counter. Brenda simply says, "If you want to be a walrus, fine. Just wipe up afterward."

So I take a towel and clean up before I go.

But Nate says, "I like to slurp my soup loudly. It tastes better that way." Slurping sets his wife's nerves on edge. Nate also "reserves" an hour to soak in a warm tub following work every night. His wife feels as though she's doing all the work to get dinner on the table while he soaks in bliss. The bottom line: You don't have a *right* to one-hour hot-tub sessions.

As another example, consider this: You have no right to use the "silent treatment" on your wife, even if it's your preferred method of handling conflict. I remember once talking to Tim, who constantly gave his fiancée the silent treatment. In a conversation they had with me, he crossed his arms and stuck out his chin proudly, grinning, "Sometimes I'm silent for a whole week, and she still doesn't know what I'm mad about."

His fiancée smiled sheepishly then looked painfully at the floor. My first temptation was to call the courthouse and suggest, "When Tim comes down for his marriage license, send him down the hall for his divorce certificate, too. He'll be needing it soon enough, and it'll save him a trip." Instead, I tried to talk some sense into Tim.

At this point, you may be wondering what rights you *do* have. We husbands have a few, but not many. Even our sexual fulfillment and our authority at home must be defined within the context of our wife's convictions and soul essence.

In premarriage class, I often say, "If any of you guys have a problem with giving up your rights for the sake of the one you love, get up and run for the hills."

If I didn't have at least one couple per class call off their marriage, I suspected I wasn't telling the truth clearly enough.

Questions for Reflection and Discussion

1. This chapter says that marriage isn't about the pursuit of happiness. How fully do you agree with that assessment?

2. What are your rights as a husband as you currently understand them?

3. To what extent can you relate to Fred's experience of wanting to go hunting more often than his wife wanted him to? What similar issues have cropped up in your marriage?

4. This chapter also says that your rights as a husband should play no part in your decision-making process at home. Do you agree? Why or why not?

5. What's your reaction at this time to the concept of giving your rights away as a husband? Do you fully buy in to it? Do you have doubts or some other form of resistance to it?

6. This chapter says that giving our rights away as husbands can become a habit, a way of life, so that you don't have to think about it anymore. To what extent have you seen this to be true in your own life?

7. What, if anything, do you believe God wants you to do in your own marriage as a result of reading this chapter?

your time is not your own

A bondservant is always at his master's call. That's fine with him. He lives to love and serve his master anyway. He never says, "I think I'll take a night off." His time is never his own unless his master says so.

When Sandy and I (Steve) discussed what's important to a woman and what every woman desires, we invariably ended up talking about what was important to her and what I was doing (or not doing) to give her what she longed for. One of the most important desires of a woman is time, so Sandy and I discussed what time meant conceptually. She said that without time with her husband, a woman becomes disconnected and feels devalued and very alone.

You see, when a wife feels undernourished, underappreciated, and underloved, she wilts into a bland nothingness instead of blossoming with life and excitement. With nothing to nurture her, her unique beauty and allure can be shrouded.

When men notice this lifelessness, they draw back from the faint, dark image of the woman they married. Sadly, rather than devote more time and reverse the condition, they spend even *less* time at home. The more his wife wilts, the more justified he feels to have his own life. The death of her spirit under his lack of commitment is often the death of the relationship because he cannot stand to be with someone who's so unresponsive.

The other wifely reaction to a lack of time is war. Rather than wilt, the woman begins to fight for what is hers. Her anger spews all over herself and onto her husband. She's ticked, and she wants him to know it and to figure out how to undo the damage. Her war is with him, but what she's fighting for is her own sense of value. After all, she dreamed that marriage would be a place where she would feel supremely treasured.

The reaction of a husband to a wife at war is never pretty. He may withdraw or rage back, but such conflict never leads to connection, intimacy, and a maturing relationship. The dynamic can change when the man decides to be her bondservant by giving freely of his time—just as any servant would. This action will make all the difference in the world.

TIME MAKES ALL THE DIFFERENCE

I (Steve) once worked for a very unhealthy company where almost everyone in management worked six days a week. The expectation was that managers would work until about three o'clock on Saturday afternoons. The joke around the water cooler was this: "Well, if you aren't going to show up on Saturday, pack up and don't even think about showing up with the rest of us on Sunday." This is what happened on Sundays: After a few hours of kickback work, they would break off to go play golf together, nine Sundays out of ten. I tell you, it was a sick place.

I didn't fall in line with the program. I rarely came in on Saturdays, and I never joined the others for a round of golf on Sundays. So, comparing myself to them, I was one fantastic guy to Sandy. But they weren't the standard I should have been comparing myself to. The standard I should have been looking to was a bondservant, not a workaholic from Southern California. While I wasn't wasting my time like my work colleagues were, I certainly wasn't giving my time to Sandy either.

That's why when we discussed what women need in general, time was at the top of her list. For quite a while, I wasn't very good at giving Sandy my time. I would be with her but not really *with* her. Preoccupation and endless activity on my part kept us so far apart that I might as well have been playing golf on Sundays with my work buddies. Thankfully, I wised up in time.

When I asked Sandy what had gotten better about our relationship, she focused on the issue of time. She had noticed how I did little things that showed her I was paying attention to her—like rubbing the muscles in her neck and back that needed a bit of love and attention. I wasn't just there—I was *there*. And being there was so much more enjoyable (and a lot less confusing!) than having my body in one place and my mind in another.

Sandy noticed something else I was doing differently as well. I quit negotiating with her over time. In the old days, whenever she would ask me to do something, I would negotiate to perform the task at some other time, on some other day, or during some other week. Now though, I dropped what I was doing and just did the chore immediately. I became like a computer with a return key: All Sandy had to do was punch in her request and I was on it. This seemed like a small thing, but in her mind it was huge. To Sandy, my action was a visible difference in commitment and acknowledgment.

When I had responded slowly to her requests in the past, it was as though I wasn't making a full commitment to her. My conduct was the opposite of how Christ was committed to the church or a bondservant was committed to the master. When I noticed that difference and changed my behavior, she felt the love I wanted her to feel. No need to wilt, no need to war. Then I started to notice something interesting: Fewer requests started coming my way. Sandy no longer needed to prove to herself that I was committed. She could see it and feel it because she knew I was "really there" when we spent time together.

If you're married to a wilting or warring woman, you might want to consider how much time, and what kind of time, you're giving her. In other words, what's your own approach to time in marriage?

IS ANY OF IT FREE?

Just like a bondservant, all husbands need a humble view of their "free time" (that is, their discretionary time), or they'll readily trample their wives' needs right off the clock. During my (Fred) dating days, Brenda was living in Moline, so I played softball a couple of nights a week to stay busy. I loved it. To me, nothing topped the smell of a freshly mowed field, freshly laid chalk lines on a finely raked infield, and the crack of an aluminum bat.

This was my "Field of Dreams," right here in Iowa. And when we began our married life together, I expected to keep playing ball. Our team had only two games a week, which meant I was gone for a couple of hours each night.

It wasn't long before I noticed something disturbing, however. Every evening, Brenda arrived home from work in a weepy mood; I could tell she'd been crying. The reason? The environment at the local hospital, where she worked as a nurse in the surgery bay, was almost intolerable. Heavy smoking, coarse language, and "Look at that!" jokes about patients' genitals abounded. It had to be awful for her.

To add to her difficulties, Brenda was still grieving the recent death of her father, and life closed in on her after work. If I weren't around the house to take her mind off things, long, lonely hours lay before her. She knew how much I loved to play softball, so she bravely let me go. I don't ever recall a time when she asked me to stop playing. Whenever I returned from a game, however, I could tell she'd been crying. She'd lay her head on my shoulder and shed a few more tears.

I struggled about the use of my time. I didn't fully understand the depth of her pain, and I knew I really couldn't do anything about it anyway. The way I saw things, she was just going to have to grow through it, and it would be good for her in the long run.

I told myself I needed the physical release after a long day of office work. Exercise always helped me keep my sanity. On the other hand, what about *her* sanity? While I had a good half-dozen justifications to keep playing, was my choice loving? We were one flesh. Even if I couldn't literally feel her pain, I had to consider it in my decisions as if I did.

In the end, no matter how I looked at it, I came to this conclusion: Brenda needed me more than I needed softball. I knew she desired that I stay home with her rather than bat cleanup. Under these circumstances, her desire was more important than mine.

How she treasured me for this decision! And it paid off because this act of willing submission helped her give me the benefit of the doubt during times that I trampled her. To Brenda, it was a heroic act of oneness, and she still talks about it to this day.

HOW DO YOU SPELL IT?

To use our time wisely, we must view our wives as our masters, not in any traditional sense that gives them the final say, but in the sense that they've bought us at a price. We return their love by giving up our rights and freedom to be one with them. Oneness is our first commitment, and our wife's essence sets the terms.

With this perspective, our time is not our own, and in a sense, we're at her call. It's not because our wives own us. They have dreams tied up in us, and God's call on their lives can't be accomplished without our time.

As the old saying goes, wives spell love T-I-M-E.

As men, we don't spell love this way, so we husbands and wives will encounter impasses. Can we still have oneness? Yes, but we husbands can't make unilateral decisions regarding our time, or we'll pay a dear price. And although men don't naturally spell love T-I-M-E, we need to learn to do so if we expect to love our wives and kids properly. This proper kind of love requires a servant's heart because it requires sacrifice.

With four kids, Brenda and I don't get much time together during normal waking hours. Yet I've learned over the years that she needs time just to sit and talk with me. She draws interpersonal intimacy from sharing conversation. Trouble is, I'm a morning person, and I'm practically on life support when 10 P.M. rolls around. If I lie down on the bed, I'm fast asleep for the next eight hours.

Yet again, I've had to remind myself that my time is not my own. If Brenda needs to stay up and talk, I have to do everything I can to engage her—and not fall asleep. So I've made a rule for myself that when I retire to the master bedroom at night, I can't lie down on the bed immediately. Instead, I sit down in what I call my "talking chair." I can stay awake and talk with Brenda if that's what she needs. I've learned to spell love T-I-M-E.

It's a small act of oneness that honors her vital need as I would honor one of my own.

IS THERE QUALITY AND QUANTITY?

You've heard parents say this about their kids: *I don't have much time to give them, but what I do give is quality time!* We don't know what that means. Neither do your wife and children. Even if they did, can you really build relationships on so-called quality time? It's not done in business, is it? The best business relationships are built over a significant quantity of time with your coworkers and clients, and you know it.

Besides, how can you predict the quality of "quality time"? What if your vaunted block of quality time at the ballpark gets rained out? Do your children have to wait another month before you can find another free afternoon in your schedule?

How do you make the distinction anyway? Once I bought some tickets to a minor league ballgame for Jasen and me. I planned some real quality time, man to man, where I could pass on a few intricacies of this game I loved. At the bottom of the first inning, he spotted a friend, and the two disappeared to play under the bleachers for the rest of the game. So much for quality time!

But that same week, I was heading to the local grocery store to buy a loaf of bread. Laura was three and a half years old, and I threw her into the car because she loved to take rides. No chance of quality time here, right? On the way there, she asked me from the backseat, "Daddy, what does salvation mean?" Now that's what I call a quality moment.

The only way to ensure quality time is to *make sure there's quantity time— and plenty of it!* God only grants you so many times in your life to go fishing with your kids, and when they're gone, they're gone. Don't miss one of those opportunities! We'll add that God only grants you so many times to throw them in the car to run to the store with you too. Don't miss one of those times, either.

ARE YOU COMPARING SCHEDULES?

Most of us learn pretty quickly that we must check with our wives before planning our schedules. Cheryl says, "I appreciate how Dave always checks with me before committing evenings or weekend time with a friend." That's great, and it should be normal, everyday behavior.

The concern here has less to do with how we view our time and more to do with how we arrogantly view *our wife's* time. It's not so much how we squander our time, but how we trample hers, as this story from Ellen demonstrates:

> Al arranges his work to make time to be with the kids and me, especially on weekends when he isn't working. But timing is a difficult thing for Al. When he feels the need to discuss an issue, or when he needs to address something with the kids, he doesn't seem to be able to wait for an opportune time.
>
> Whenever a thought pops into his head, he addresses it, although it usually isn't a good time—like right before the kids are leaving for school, or I'm leaving for work, or when there isn't sufficient time to respond. Whenever I bring this up, he just doesn't seem to understand that the deep things of the heart need to be discussed in the right atmosphere. As leader, he feels that if he has the time to do something right then, everyone else needs to make time as well.
>
> It's very difficult to respond correctly without resenting his inability to see that he's being wrong. It even makes it hard to respond with the right attitude later. The kids have just written him off, I'm afraid. They don't have the capacity to look past that side of him to see his incredible heart and love for us.

It's in these subtler areas of time where you'll know whether you've developed a servant's heart or whether you're still Chief Tiebreaker. Daily life will reveal whether your time is more important than hers—whether she must stop what she's doing to receive your decrees and announcements. Such disrespect could never flow from a servant's heart. Also, a bondservant would never dream of chiding his master over the use of his time. But as husbands, we do it to our wives far too often. Such behavior is arrogant and trampling, and it breaks oneness every time. I know from experience…

Brenda was a registered nurse and an excellent one because she loved nursing all the way from her head to her toes. When Jasen, our firstborn, came along, she and I decided that she would stay home and give up her career for a while. My business was finally going well enough that we could make ends meet, and we felt that making Brenda a stay-at-home mom was right for our young family. We made other decisions to create a stable home life with as much family time as possible. We chose a time for me to be home after work so Brenda could have supper ready for a regular sit-down family meal. But we also made another rule that could preempt this first one at Brenda's discretion. Whenever a child's emotional tank was running on empty, Brenda had the freedom to drop what she was doing to fill that tank by reading a book or playing for a while. That second rule meant I could work hard to be home on time only to find there was no rush at all.

When our second child was added, then our third and fourth, Brenda invoked this rule more frequently. I remember coming home on time only to find no one in the kitchen, nothing cooking on the stove, lunch dishes still sitting on the table, and the sounds of chaos coming from every room. This irritated me. *What has she been doing with her time all day? If I were in charge, this wouldn't happen!* And sometimes I made the mistake of saying what I was thinking.

But I had no idea how her day went with the four kids. Even if I could get more done in a day than Brenda, how does my telling her so honor her essence? How does that bring us closer together? Being a mom is her role, right? Is she not free to make her own decisions about managing her day? If she doesn't match my standards, so what? God knows her skills, and He had no trouble entrusting her with our four precious little ones. Who do I think I am?

Besides, my arrogance only made it more difficult for her to keep our priorities in place. When I was putting pressure on the Supper by Six rule, how could she freely respond to our Empty Tank decision? I became an obstacle to the very priorities I'd put in place.

No bondservant would chide his master on the use of his time. Respect for the master's wisdom was a given. Respect for our "masters" has to become a given as well. Does it mean we can never discuss time management? Of course not. But it certainly means she has first dibs on how she spends her time in the home with the children.

Questions for Reflection and Discussion

1. How would you describe your approach to time in your marriage, after seeing this issue discussed in this chapter?

2. To what extent can you relate to Steve's or Fred's experiences as mentioned in this chapter?

3. How fully and frequently do you check with your wife when planning your schedule?

making room for her to express her gifts

By nature, most of us guys are hardly Mr. Hospitality. To us, lying down on the couch while pondering the meaning of life—or thrilling to a good college football game—is the best this world has to offer. Who needs people? We've got all the people we need right around us: our family.

Before marriage, I rarely entertained, and if I did invite you over, you'd have to consider yourself honored if I cracked open a fresh jar of honey-roasted peanuts. I was also a bit of a Spartan. When Brenda surveyed my apartment for the first time, she was aghast. My living room furniture consisted of a ten-dollar plastic lawn chair, a thirteen-inch portable television resting on the well-worn carpet, and four cheap pictures leaning against the walls. (Why hang them? They were at eye level when I sat in my chair.)

When we married, Brenda just *had* to decorate our nest, which in those days was a modest apartment in the northeastern suburbs of Des Moines. I soon learned (yes, even someone as obtuse as I was) that Brenda had a gift of hospitality and warmth with friends as well as with people she barely knew. Whenever she invited another couple or family over, however, her preparations challenged my sanity.

"Fred, would you get out the napkins?" she asked from the family room, where she was invariably straightening up the magazines lying about the coffee table.

"You mean the ones in the pantry?" I asked from the kitchen.

"No, not the paper napkins! Use the cloth ones in the china hutch. They'll make everyone feel special," Brenda responded.

"Okay, I'll lay them on the table," I said, slightly befuddled.

"No, no, don't just lay them on the table. Make tents out of them like they do at Elwell's restaurant. Aren't they neat that way?"

"I don't know how to make tents," I called out, then mumbling, "and I don't really want to learn either."

"That's okay, honey! I'll teach you. It's fun!" she said.

She joined me in the dining room, where she took the cloth napkins, folded this way and that way, and—*presto!*—tentlike napkins stood at attention on the table.

"Oh, by the way, we're going to let the kids dip marshmallows in chocolate fondue. Won't that be a blast?" asked Brenda.

"I suppose so," I lied. "I'll go find some toothpicks."

"No, not the toothpicks, silly! I picked up some cute fondue forks at Dillard's today. Gary's kids will like them much better. They'll feel fancy and remember it for days," she gushed.

My mind was spinning that afternoon, but I had no time to gather my senses because Brenda also insists we vacuum and mop and dust and rearrange as if the queen of England were dropping in. And yet, despite a house that's neat as a pin and an attractive table set just so, none of our guests fear plopping down and messing things up. Everyone feels comfortable in our company. I don't know how Brenda does it. As I said, it's a gift. Naturally, I thought she was the silly one, but entertaining seemed to be her thing, so I rarely complained…at first.

Then our four kids started growing up. Napkin tents mean nothing to them. They were demanding and busy and hungry continuously, which cramped Brenda's style, often tightening her preparation time for guests. Sometimes there was another crisis to manage, such as buying new cleats for Little League, which started the next day. Forced into a higher gear, she'd rush around town in the biggest tizzy. When she could finally get to the house, it was at the last minute, and there were carpets to vacuum and rugs to shake—things she "just couldn't get to because of the kids." As I'd arrive home from work, she'd be in a panic, and most of these chores fell on my shoulders during our last-gasp efforts to have everything "just so" when the guests arrived.

So I put my foot down.

"Why do you do all this?" I demanded. "It's ridiculous! No one really cares about the napkin tents, and no one cares if the house is perfect. They're our friends, for heaven's sake! If they can't take a little mess, let them eat elsewhere. Better yet, let them find new friends!"

When that argument failed to carry the day, I took a different tack.

"Look at you!" I bellowed. "You're running around like a nut case, and none of it even matters! You're upsetting the kids, and you're upsetting me. I'm to the point where I don't even want anyone over anymore. Just knock it off!"

I'm sure I hurt Brenda's feelings often, but someone had to step in and say what needed to be said. I knew I was right. Or was I?

THERE'S MINISTRY HERE?

Following one of my sermonettes, Brenda told me through tears, "I just can't invite people over anymore until the kids get older. If I can't do it the right way, I don't want to do it at all."

This was crazier yet. I didn't mean we shouldn't have friends over. I liked having company. "Brenda, are you telling me you'll deprive us and the kids of having their friends over simply because you can't do everything just right? Isn't that a bit extreme?"

"Fred, can't you see?" she said with pleading eyes. "I don't expect you to care about this the way I do, but having it all just right is important. Inviting friends over is a ministry for me."

Ministry? This was the first time I'd heard that word connected with a Saturday night get-together for barbecued ribs and corn on the cob. The word pounded me between my eyes. Brenda saw this as a *ministry?* I finally began to get it, and when I did, I reconsidered how I'd been treating the situation.

Normally, as H-Hour approached, I halfheartedly helped with the kids, picked up around the house, or swept up outside. I dogged it until I could answer the doorbell and welcome our friends to come in. That's when all the "prep" work could finally stop.

I had to put my foot down, all right—on me! I needed to make room for Brenda's gift of hospitality to blossom.

If we were having friends over on a weeknight, I began arriving home from work an hour earlier to help around the house. On the weekends, I made sure I was home *hours* before our guests were scheduled to arrive. I shouldered the menial duties like vacuuming and dusting, freeing Brenda up for her special touches. I washed pots and pans as the recipes moved through their stages. In the winter, I shoveled snow off the sidewalk or swept the walkway in the summer. I started a fire in the fireplace stove and rearranged the couch pillows. In short, I hung out a shingle that said, Cleanups "R" Us.

I noticed that Brenda and I became closer when we worked together toward the common goal of having a spic-and-span house ready for hungry guests who'd enjoy one of my wife's great home-cooked meals.

But it's not just the common goal. It's not even that I now understand Brenda's gift or feel the same urgency that drives her to do it all. I don't. It's just that I started to recognize that she has a valid ministry right in our home, and I began honoring it alongside my own ministries.

Thus she feels oneness with me. Brenda's essence sets the terms for oneness. If I trampled her gift of hospitality, there would be no oneness.

Let's reason this out for a minute. No master purchased a slave hoping this servant would make it more difficult for him to express his gifts and ministries. And no bondservant ever laid his earlobe to the post in a desire to make things tougher for the master. He loved his master, and he gave up everything to ensure his master could fully live, to ensure his gifts and ministries could fully blossom.

What about your wife? Are you making it easy for her to please God?

Imagine your wife's freedom to serve God before marriage. When God touched her heart to do anything, she simply did it. When God asked her to give money for a missionary in need, she obeyed. She honored the Spirit's convictions without any interference. She could rest when she needed to and pray when she desired. Now everything must pass through you, right?

But she expected even more freedom after marriage. Did she get it? Have you made room and shouldered burdens so she can really blossom?

DISCOVER WHO SHE IS

Fred isn't the only offender in this area of refusing to allow a wife to blossom. My (Steve's) wife, Sandy, is one of the most creative women in the world. When she puts a lamp next to a chair, you can be sure that's where it should go. Everything she touches feels right and looks great. God gave her many creative talents.

But when we got married, I could have cared less. I just wanted her to look like females I'd been used to. I wanted to be comfortable, and I didn't even consider what she might feel if I had my way with her. Sandy's creativity applied even to the great clothes she bought. Although she had a taste and a style that other women envied, I didn't care. I wanted her to dress like an Ivy League preppy princess. I bought her tartan pleated shorts, knee socks, and stiff blouses with big bows around the neck. Boy, was I proud when she dressed like I wanted her to dress. Oh sure, she was lifeless, irritable, and angry, but she sure looked good to me.

I have a picture of her in one of those tacky tartan outfits I bought her, and it breaks my heart to see it. What an idiot I was to expect her to look so plain, dull, and boring, instead of letting her really express herself. Why did it take so long for me to see her unique gifts and my own responsibility to help her develop those wonderful gifts rather than stomp all over them? Like so many other Christian men, I thought that my job was to be boss and that what I said was the most important thing. My wife's feelings meant nothing compared to the way I felt things had to be.

This heart attitude is destructive to any relationship and to women in general. Just today I was meeting with Rich Stearns, the head of World Vision, and we were discussing the plight of women around the world. The poverty they experience has many causes, but he and I agreed on one big one: the sin of men. It's men who sinfully mistreat these women, treat them as second-class citizens, use them, and either throw them out or abandon them with no thoughts for what's good or best for them. Some men are literally more thoughtful of pets than they are of their wives! And this treatment keeps women down, totally disconnected from the person God intended them to be.

What a far cry from God's ideal of a woman's being cherished by a man! So evaluate your treatment of your wife. If it's unkind and uncaring, confess this to her, ask her to forgive you, and begin the journey of finally discovering who God intended her to be.

LISTEN UP!

You may find it difficult to recognize your wife's ministry, but you'll always be able to *hear* its urgency if you keep your antennas up. Here's an example.

A two-mile ribbon of concrete encircles my (Fred's) neighborhood, and Brenda and I love to exercise on it with a five-lap bike ride on warm summer evenings. One twilight evening, as we circled toward our house on our fourth lap, we noticed our friend Jack talking in his driveway with Jose, an acquaintance from church. Anxious to complete our five laps before stopping, we offered a friendly wave and kept pedaling. When we swung back around following our final lap, we found Jose's car gone, and Jack had gone inside.

Worried that Jack might have felt we were rude by not stopping earlier, Brenda said, "Maybe you should go in and explain to Jack that we wanted to complete our laps before stopping to talk to him and Jose."

Yeah, right. First, I had better things to do. I'd been taping some music for our music director, and I wanted to finish the job before bedtime. Second, it was getting dark. I never knock on a neighbor's door after dark in summertime. Maybe it's a guy thing, but a man's home is his castle, and a knock on the door after dark is an assault on the peace of the realm. Third, I knew Jack was all guy. He wouldn't have given this a second thought because guys don't give such things second thoughts. I didn't want to make something out of nothing. Fourth, only sissies run around making sure everyone's feelings are okay. Fifth, Jack clearly was in a friendly, neighborly mood when he was talking to Jose, but I was not. I just knew if I knocked on his door, he'd get me talking for thirty or forty minutes.

"There's no way on the planet that this is necessary, Brenda," I said. "Jack has already forgotten we rode by. Trust me."

"Yes, but there have been a number of nights lately when we've passed him on our bikes, and he has seemed to want to say something. I just want him to know our bike rides are workouts, not pleasure rides. We're not stopping because we need to complete the workout, not because we're unfriendly."

My irritation level rose two notches. My music project was waiting, and it would be bedtime before I knew it. Closing the garage door, I pushed past her into the family room, saying, "Look, I'm not going to be owned by his perceptions. If he thinks I'm rude just because I don't stop every time I pass his house on a bike, that's his problem. I have my own house and my own life, and I don't have to explain my decisions to every neighbor along the way. Besides, I know he hasn't given this a second thought. Men aren't like that."

Sitting down, I inserted a CD. Brenda dogged my steps, sitting down for the long haul. "I really think it's the right thing to do," she offered.

"Then you go talk to Jack. I've got things to do here, like tape some music."

"Now you know I can't do that. I can't knock on the door and say to Tonya, 'Hi, can I speak to Jack?' That's too weird!"

By now, I'd reached the known limits of patience. "It always has to be your way on this stuff, doesn't it? You think you're the only person in the family who knows anything about relationships."

Not so gently, she reminded me, "You know I have a stronger sense for these things than you do."

Countering, I replied, "That doesn't mean you're never wrong and I'm never right. He's a guy. I know guys. He hasn't given this a second thought."

"Well, I still think you should go," said Brenda. Though I had my heels dug in plenty deep, I suddenly knew I'd soon be riding back up the street. While I couldn't see why this was so important to her, I could *hear* that it was. She just couldn't let go. She hadn't given me a decent reason, but there had to be one. I decided I'd go, but I'd take my time. I was in no hurry to make a fool of myself with Jack.

Unable to read my thoughts, she assumed I'd launched the silent treatment. "Okay, fine! Be that way," said Brenda crabbily. "I've got to go upstairs and wash up for bed."

I wasn't going to let that shot go unanswered. "Well, that's sure nice for you to say. You go off to sleep after sending me off for who knows how long? Don't wait up for me. I may never get back." Yes, I was being a big baby, but I had reason to be.

Climbing aboard my bike, I pedaled over to Jack's house. By now, it was plenty dark, and I felt like a major knucklehead knocking at Jack's castle door. When it swung open, Jack appeared genuinely surprised. With a huge smile, he pumped my hand. "Hey, Fred, come on in and sit down," he grinned. "Let's talk a while!"

I knew it.

I decided to regale him with a blow-by-blow description of the last twenty minutes, figuring we could share a good laugh at how women think.

Jack understood where I was going. "Hey, when you and Brenda pedaled off, I never gave it a second thought. It never crossed my mind."

"I thought so," I said, while thinking to myself, *Wait until Brenda hears this!*

We sat and chatted for…I was right—forty minutes.

In fact, I was gone so long that Brenda thought she had to rescue me by riding her bike over to Jack's. As we headed home together, she warily asked, "Well, what did he say?"

"He said he hadn't given it a second thought."

"Oh, he was just saying that to be nice."

Shrugging, I said, "I doubt it. Men aren't that complex. Besides, I could truly tell he hadn't given it a thought." We rode the rest of the way in silence. She knew I'd been right.

Preparing for bed, I sat down in my chair and said, "Brenda, you've got to tell me something. I went to Jack's though *I* knew it really wasn't necessary. I did it just for you, and for you alone, simply because it seemed important to you. Does that mean anything to you?"

I expected a simple, understated response. I was amazed by her animation as she exclaimed, "Oh, yes, it meant everything! I've been on this push to be neighborly. I don't feel we do enough that way, and as Christians, we should do a better job. I thought you were doing something important along those lines, and it meant the world to me."

You could have knocked me over with a feather. Our intimacy meter registered higher that evening, and such a simple thing like going over to my neighbor's at Brenda's behest seemed to speak volumes to her heart.

Sure, I'd been right all along. If there were ever a job for Chief Tiebreaker, this was it. I could have cast the tie-breaking vote and stayed home—and been in bed on time with my music project finished. But would I have been righteous? I would have shut down her voice before I'd heard that urgency in her heart, burying her ministry.

A bondservant always made room for his master's gifts and ministries so his master might fully live and blossom. That's why we must keep talking with our wife, not so much to understand, but to hear her feelings. We must make room for what God places on her heart and respect her gifts, although those gifts may be tough to recognize. Yet our effort to make room for her gifts frees her essence to find its place in the marriage.

Questions for Reflection and Discussion

1. What opportunities do you and your wife have to work together toward common goals?

2. In what significant ways are you making it easy for your wife to serve and please God?

3. In what significant ways have you allowed your wife's gifts to blossom?

4. How would you evaluate your wife's gifts? And in what opportunities for ministry does she feel most fulfilled?

making room
for her weaknesses

The bondservant loved his master fully. And why not? Though his master had his weaknesses, he was still full of mercy and grace and was certainly worthy of the servant's love. *Look at all my master does for me, despite his frailties!* Rather than resent those weaknesses, the servant embraced them in love. Whenever he could, the servant sought to make up for his master's weakness with his own strength.

A servant's heart allows us to do the same for our wives. Yes, your wife has weaknesses that can make her hard to appreciate, just as your weaknesses can make it hard at times for her to appreciate you. Nevertheless, she's a gift from God, and He picked this particular gift for you for a reason. And love is a reason behind most gifts.

Let's take Father's Day, for example. There's no telling how love will translate into gifts on this occasion. I have four children, so I receive four loving gifts. On a typical Father's Day, I might receive a sharp new jacket, a superb CD from my favorite Christian artist, another tie, and a painted rock.

What am I supposed to say? "Wow, I really appreciate the CD, and the jacket knocks me out, but you other two better get a life. Get your gifts out of here!" No, when it comes to gifts, you take the good with the bad, and you're only too happy to do so for the sake of your children's feelings, because love was the purpose of their hearts.

Similarly, while your wife is the most precious earthly gift God has given you, let's face it—the package has a few painted rocks strewn into the mix. Why would God do this? Love was the purpose of God's heart. These "bad" qualities are meant to make you better, not bitter. We mustn't resent them.

A TRANSFORMING PURPOSE

When I (Steve) married Sandy, I couldn't believe all the stuff I hadn't known about her earlier. I started seeing all these things I didn't like, things that made me feel uncomfortable. I embarked on a mission to change her so I could have the freedom to be me. Actually, what I was looking for was an excuse not to grow. Over time I discovered something you can discover also: *The things that irritated me the most were the things God was using to transform me.*

Sandy, for example, wanted tasks done now and put out of the way and that was a real challenge for a procrastinator like me. And I couldn't get over how confrontational she was (at least that's what I thought it was). Actually her "confrontation" was pure and loving honesty. If someone crossed a boundary, she addressed it rather than acting as if it didn't happen, the passive course I would have taken.

Everything in Sandy that was different from me was God's challenging me to grow. Sandy's differences have made me who I am today. If she had naively worshiped me and allowed me to stay the same, God would not have worked on me the way He has, and that work would not be happening now. Thankfully, I'm no longer thinking about how "difficult" Sandy is; instead, I'm looking at areas I need to change in response to the ways we're different. The transformation in me is neither easy nor painless, but I'm so grateful it's occurring every day—thanks to her. .

God wants marriage to be a transforming agent in your life, and you need to embrace that divine purpose. He wants marriage to grind away your rough edges, and He chose your wife—this particular package, with just these flaws—because she was best suited for this job in you. She'll force you to grow up, so that you will learn to love when you don't feel like loving. More important, God wants you to be a transforming agent in *her* life. A bondservant always knows his place because God has defined it for him:

> For by the grace given me I say to every one of you: Do not think of yourself more highly than you ought, but rather think of yourself with sober judgment, in accordance with the measure of faith God has given you. (Romans 12:3)

In other words, don't forget that you have weaknesses too, weaknesses you hope she'll handle with grace even though they'll grind hard at her edges. As Chief Servant, you can teach her how to love someone despite his weaknesses.

In my marriage, I (Fred) will have to admit that Brenda learned that lesson first. My temper was more than a weakness: It was sin—and boy, was it ugly! But while she *did* stick her finger in my face on occasion, she never demeaned me. Neither did she verbally pound me every time I slipped up. She never failed to grant forgiveness when I asked for it. She never failed to hold me when I apologized after yet another failure. She even cried with me when I confessed how my childhood wrapped such tight cords around me. Through it all, she never took away our sexual intimacy, although I must have seemed repulsive in her eyes at times. She knew how to allow her strengths to make up for my weaknesses and to be a purifying salt in my life.

This, too, is God's intention for marriage. We must not only embrace our wives' weaknesses with mercy and grace, but our strengths and loving commitment must serve as a purifying salt in her life. You and your wife are sprouting a new branch on your family tree. As His leader, God intends for you to grow the strongest, purest branch possible:

> As for man, his days are like grass.... But from everlasting to everlasting the LORD's love is with those who fear him, and his righteousness with their children's children. (Psalm 103:15,17)

God is interested in us as individuals, and make no mistake about that. Through Jesus, God came for us as individuals, and He died for us as individuals. But He's also interested in us as links in a very important chain. He knows the power of heritage as it's passed from generation to generation and how easily the message of salvation can be passed to our children in a purified home.

Jehonadab is a relatively obscure man in the Bible, but he's a priceless role model to husbands (read his story beginning at 2 Kings 10:15). We first find him walking the streets of Samaria during Jehu's overthrow of Ahab.

Jehu had a mandate from God's prophet to overthrow this wicked king, and he approached it with zeal. As he raced around Samaria butchering Ahab's seventy sons and destroying every sign of Baal worship he could find, he spotted Jehonadab, son of Recab, and invited him into his chariot. He probably wanted to show off his zeal before Jehonadab, who was known by all as one of the godliest men of his day, staunchly opposed to Baal worship and anything else that stood against God.

Jehonadab isn't mentioned again until the book of Jeremiah (where his name is spelled *Jonadab*)—

This is the word that came to Jeremiah from the LORD:... "Go to the Recabite family and invite them to come to one of the side rooms of the house of the LORD and give them wine to drink."

So, I went to get...all his sons—the whole family of the Recabites. I brought them into the house of the LORD.... Then I set bowls full of wine and some cups before the men of the Recabite family and said to them, "Drink some wine."

But they replied, "We do not drink wine, because our forefather Jonadab son of Recab gave us this command: 'Neither you nor your descendants must ever drink wine.'... We have obeyed everything our forefather Jonadab son of Recab commanded us." (Jeremiah 35:1-6,8)

God's people had once again strayed and were ignoring Him. God wanted to show Jeremiah an important truth to speak against the children of Israel:

> Then the word of the LORD came to Jeremiah, saying: "This is what the LORD Almighty, the God of Israel, says: Go and tell the men of Judah and the people of Jerusalem, 'Will you not learn a lesson and obey my words?' declares the LORD. 'Jonadab son of Recab ordered his sons not to drink wine and this command has been kept. To this day they do not drink wine, because they obey their forefather's command. But I have spoken to you again and again, yet you have not obeyed me.'" (Jeremiah 35:12-14)

The term *sons* likely refers to all disciples but surely included descendants as well. Do you know how much time had passed since Jehonadab had set his example? Two hundred years! The purifying work he began in his family tree had such an impact that it was felt ten to fifteen generations later.

Jehonadab reminds me (Fred) of the great-great-grandmother of my pastor, John Palmer. In the late 1800s this woman turned to Christ from a godless background. She was so true to Christ, and her example was so powerful, that in the hundred years since, every single descendant has been either a pastor or pastor's wife or a missionary or a missionary's wife. Would you say she was a strong limb in her family tree?

By contrast, my family tree is rife with sin. In its branches you'll find adultery, pornography, incest, sexual abuse, physical abuse, and many examples of hatred, discord, jealousy, fits of rage, selfish ambition, carousing, drunkenness, and the like. Some of those characteristics were rooted in me as well.

At some point, every man must decide: Will I purify my branch of the tree, or will I allow this poison to seep through the generations, leaving the job for a better man down the line? If you desire to purify your branch, adopting a selfless attitude like Abraham did will surely help you. He was chosen to be the father of many nations because God knew he would cause his family to follow Him. Does God know that about you? On what evidence?

A STAKE IN THE GROUND

Purifying your branch of your family tree begins with stopping the flow of generational poison by ramming a stake into the ground and declaring before God that you'll cause your family to follow Him.

When you do this, you create for all time the transitional generation in your family heritage. You transition your family from a pattern of sickness to a repeated experience of living for God. For generations to come, people will look at your family tree and see that once your branch sprouted, the family was never the same. They'll see that under your leadership, life for generations to come was influenced for good rather than for bad. Going against the trends of past generations like this isn't easy to do. But it's worth the effort to set a new course.

You set that new course by studying God's standards and committing to live by them yourself without mixing in all your gray areas. An example would be the approach to purity taken in our book *Every Man's Battle*. We clearly declare God's standard of sexual purity, using His own words: "But among you there must not be even a hint of sexual immorality" (Ephesians 5:3). God's intent is clear, and we spent the book showing men how to train their eyes and mind to "bounce away" from sensual images that result in impure sexual gratification.

Sexual sin was practically a family birthright for me (Fred), and I lived up to it. To purify my branch of the tree and to kill this legacy, I had to commit myself—without compromise—to God's standard of sexual purity.

Of course, it's far easier to simply allow this poison to seep on down through the generations. One person we know responds to God's standard by saying, "God couldn't possibly expect us to live that way." Another writes, "I am amazed by the conclusions you've drawn from this verse. As for men diverting their eyes, you're expecting far too much from what is the 'breeding' nature of every man. I'm not sure how realistic it is to expect men to comply."

When God's standards seem too difficult, we simply stir in some of our gray with His black and white to create something new, something comfortable, something mediocre. Although comfortable, we remain as ensnared by our sin as our forefathers were, and our conscience dims until we can't quite tell what's right or wrong anymore.

Ramming the stake in the ground and making the commitment to follow God's standards without compromise halts the flow of old poison into our new branch. Completing the purification process means pouring mercy and grace into our homes throughout the years, and we do this by following the principles of mutual submission and by loving in the midst of weaknesses. As we've seen, this way of behaving is not a one-way street. Through love and mercy, Christ used Brenda to help purge my character and prune away that nasty temper so common in my family tree.

As husbands, we all must do the same, loving our wives for who they are today and allowing Christ to use us to help build up her character (according to His plan, not ours). It's unlikely your wife will begin her married life any lovelier than you are. True, she's married and "a big girl" now, as her mother promised she'd someday be. But she doesn't always *feel* like a big girl, and she certainly won't always *act* like a big girl. We all come to marriage with differing levels of immaturity.

A SHOULDER FOR HER WEAKNESS

What baggage does your wife carry? She's surely not immune. Your wife may carry the baggage of traumatic events, like the crushing blow of her parents' divorce or her father's heavy verbal abuse. Countless girls are fondled and raped through the years by cousins, uncles, and fathers. I know of one lay leader who regularly raped a friend's young daughter, quoting Scriptures as he did.

I (Steve) will never forget the night I was listening to Chuck Swindoll address about ten thousand Christians, and right in the middle of his admonition for everyone to get their act together, I heard a statement that stopped all of us from even breathing. Not only could you have heard a pin drop in that huge arena, but you could have heard it start to fall. He proclaimed, "I know some of you are having sex with your children. And I'm telling you to stop it. I'm asking you to stop it. You must consider the impact on your child. You must stop having sex with your children." Why did he say that? Because he was the pastor of a church and he heard the confessions of members and leaders who had been involved in incestuous relationships. If that's you, I repeat what Chuck said that night, which I hope was a turning point for many who heard him: "You must stop having sex with your children."

The journal *Cerebrum* recently reported that the trauma of child abuse actually rewires parts of the brain in both function and structure. The effects include poorer development of the left hemisphere, a reduction in transmission points in the corpus callosum, and electrical impulse disturbances in various parts of the brain. The abnormalities can last right through adulthood, leaving the victim with such problems as aggression, poor emotional control, memory and attention disorders, and serious mood and personality disorders.

Even if divorce or sin didn't traumatize your wife, the struggles of adult life can lay her low for a long time. We're all living east of Eden, under the curse of sin. Life is like a steamroller, easily mashing our flimsy dreams of companionship and oneness. We often have to work long hours by the sweat of our brows to pay the bills, and we don't always see each other as much as we wish. We're sometimes beaten up and used up by bosses, leaving our minds so numb that we just don't want to talk when we get home. And the pain of childbirth brings whining babies as cursed by sin as we are.

As you know, I brought plenty of baggage to marriage. While Brenda brought only a handbag's worth, she was certainly no day at the beach. Life's steamroller had flattened her, and she was hurting. She was less than lovable at times.

Coming from a peaceful home where all was stable, her new world was collapsing on every side during those early months of marriage. I needn't recount the reasons again, but she was wobbling under the pressure of it all.

Then Jasen was born, and he was a difficult baby who just wouldn't sleep. Brenda's discouragement nearly debilitated both of us. Confused, she couldn't take another blow. She didn't look the same to me. She wasn't at all what I expected in a wife.

Gratefully, I had just made my "eat gravel" stand with God. Reading about Uriah for the first time, I began to see Brenda in a new way. Rather than despise her and her weaknesses, I began to shoulder those weaknesses as if they were my own. For instance, I have a very strong will, and I can handle tough physical situations. I decided to get up with my son every time he awoke at night, though Brenda didn't work outside the home after Jasen was born. Logically, since she didn't "work" and could rest at different times during the day, she should have been the one to get up. I could have said, "C'mon, you're a big girl now. Pull yourself up by the bootstraps and get tough!" But she couldn't act like a big girl yet. So I had to love her as she was.

Brenda was married to me, and she was my little ewe lamb. It's true she was no longer the person I thought I married, and I didn't always feel tender toward her. But I still carried her because it was right.

During that period, I noticed a peculiar thing. The physical drain of nursing, the unsettled sleep at night (she would get up to nurse then hand Jasen to me), and the psychological exhaustion wasted Brenda. If she awoke in the morning and stumbled down to a dirty kitchen, she would immediately be discouraged and have difficulty starting her day. With her courage melting like a snowman in May, she found it easier to stay in her pajamas all day.

I didn't like my beloved starting her day like this. Yes, I could have asked her to shape up, grit her teeth, and push harder. I could have reminded her she wasn't living up to my expectations. Instead, I made a promise to her that I would never, ever go to bed again with the kitchen dirty.

I knew what this promise would cost me. Because of Brenda's exhaustion, my promise meant she would often head off to bed and leave me alone to do all the dishes and scrub all the pans. My promise meant that she would often be asleep when I got to bed, and I would miss out on sex. It meant I would forfeit nearly an hour of precious sleep, but I also knew my promise would help me cherish my ewe lamb in ways she never thought possible. I never broke that kitchen promise.

Eventually, in Christ's hands, Brenda grew to who she is today. She's *everything* I knew she would be. But guess what? She's also more because of our oneness. She saw my mercy in the face of her weakness, even in the unloveliest of times.

A WIFE FOR THIS DAY

Are you allowing for your "master's" weakness, loving your wife for whom she is *this day*, not for who she might be at some other future date down the line? Sure, you may be shocked and dismayed at the weaknesses in your wife that were hidden until this life spun you both in its new direction. Still, your spouse has a heart that beats like a little lamb's heart, a heart that still skips through meadows of hope and desire, longing for your love. This part of her may be difficult to see. Maybe her father was an alcoholic or an abuser who didn't protect her. Maybe she isn't much of a Christian. Maybe she was promiscuous before she met you.

All these things may be true. But some other things are also true. Your wife *did* forsake her individual freedom in clinging to you, believing you would provide love and strength. Your wife is *still* God's little ewe lamb, regardless of the pain and sin she's been through and the character wounds she carries. Don't forget: God *has* entrusted her to you. Will you resent her, or help restore her? Does your heart warm to the task of restoration? Is there any nobler act than pouring out your mercy on your precious one?

Deal with your spouse based upon who she is today, not upon what you want her to be. So what if she isn't who she should be today? Are you? Besides, it's not important that she becomes everything you expect. It's important that she becomes like Christ. Your mercy and your strength help carry her there.

One more thing. It's not human nature to want to do a job that isn't ours, especially when it looks as if our wife is a sissy and we have no idea how long we'll have to carry her. But rise above your nature. Be like Christ for a change: "Blessed are they whose transgressions are forgiven, whose sins are covered. Blessed is the man whose sin the Lord will never count against him" (Romans 4:7-8). Blessed, too, is his wife. She needs someone to understand, someone to fill the gaps until she can recover.

You can become your wife's hero:

My Dad was always very bossy and domineering, and it got very old being told what to do by him, especially after I became a Christian. It is wonderful to be under Lee's covering instead of my dad's domination.

Be merciful as your wife recovers from her childhood:

My husband took the lead in housework, though he didn't like it. I was not good at cleaning floors and not at all concerned about neatness, even though I grew up in a home that always had to look perfect. Then, when Mom left us, we went to the other extreme and lived in a pigsty. Jim knew what it was like at my dad's, and so he was very good to encourage me and help me keep the house clean.

Be merciful as your wife's weaknesses or mere differences press in on you:

If Michael does something that totally irritates me, there are times when I have trouble expressing it with the right spirit. So I made a rule for myself, and I decided that I wouldn't say anything at all until I could tactfully say it without tearing him down. Sometimes it would work, and I would later be able to talk about it in a caring way. But when it didn't, I would walk around and pout. It's a horrible habit, but in the process of trying to hold back words until I can think of a kind way to say it, I sometimes just start pouting. Of course, by the time I've reached the pouting stage, I can't think of a kind word at all.

Michael not only chooses to ignore this weakness, but he actually will come to me kindly and pull me out of my shell. He will insist on hearing my views and frustrations. He may already know what I'm going to say, but to snap me out of my mood, he will insist on some communication. The conversation will usually turn to smiles, tears, laughing, and making up—sometimes even making out! My husband is awesome.

Your wife's weaknesses will create impasses and threaten oneness. What will you do to bring oneness from such impasses? By demanding, as her leader, that she straighten up and fly right? Surely you can find a more effective way to help her when she needs guidance. Why not lay down your rights as the leader and graciously love her through these impasses?

Your wife's weaknesses are as much a part of her soul essence as her gifts are, and neither should be trampled. You love yourself and handle your own weaknesses with mercy and grace, hoping others will make allowances and work around them as you do. So allow your wife's weaknesses to be expressed as freely as yours are. Then, in grace, work together in kindness and diligence to purify your legacy for those who will follow.

I (Steve) want to challenge you to do what I finally started doing. Stop evaluating your wife and resenting her because she doesn't perfectly measure up to your standards. Instead, start accepting and appreciating her—and showing it to her in practical ways. When you demand that she change, or manipulate her into changing, you actually cause her to dig in her heels in order to defend her ground and the person she is. But when you accept her and love her no matter what, she drops her guard. She stops digging in her heels because she feels free to be the best she can be. Free to change. Free to be the wife you need.

So if your approach has been to crow like a rooster over every one of your wife's imperfections, eat some crow, confess your unloving attitude to God and to her, and watch what happens. If she's like 98 percent of all women, she'll draw closer to you, and your relationship will continue to grow for as long as you appreciate and accept her, imperfections and all.

Questions for Reflection and Discussion

1. In what significant ways can you lovingly make up for your wife's weaknesses with your own strength?

2. In what ways has God used the differences between you and your wife to cause you to mature and improve?

3. In practical, everyday terms, what can you do in your marriage and family to strengthen and purify your branch of your family tree?

4. In practical, everyday terms, what can you do to be merciful to your wife in regard to her weaknesses?

making room for her thoughts

No bondservant would dream of stripping his master of the right to voice his opinions. After all, he was the master. That fact alone made his opinions worthy to be heard. Isn't the voice of your "master" also worthy to be heard?

When courting, our wives were worthy of speaking to us about any topic on every level. Think back to those heady days of dating, when you couldn't drink in enough conversation from the young woman you knew you were going to marry. You loved listening to every thought, every wide-open hope, and all of her deepest dreams as you shared a bowl of nacho chips at the local eatery. Every opinion was a lovely thread in the tapestry she wove around your heart. But then things changed...

SNUFFING HER OUT?

When the honeymoon is over and our differences follow us home, our wife's opinions feel more like binding cords threatening to choke our freedom and disrupt the peace. No guy would ever envision tuning out his lover before the wedding day, but in apartments, townhomes, condos, and starter homes across the fruited plain, countless men are snuffing out the voices of their wives seeking to express their views. What that does to oneness is not pretty, says Jerri:

> My husband usually gets mad because I'm not on the same wavelength that he is. This leads to a fight, and he'll say degrading, belittling things

to me. There's no compassion or consideration for my feelings. I've found that to be very hurtful.

To snuff out your wife's voice is to sin against her. It's also a sin against God because it blocks His purposes for your wife's voice in His kingdom.

Rene says she's an open person who finds it easy to share her feelings. Her husband, Paul, is a more private individual who shares few thoughts with other people, especially in Sunday school. Once when the couple was traveling home from church, the conversation went like this:

"Why did you have to bring up our kids again in our couples' class?" he asked. "And while we're at it, why do you have to talk so much?"

"I have experiences and insights that I just have to express," she replied.

Telling Rene to not exhale her thoughts would be like telling a whale not to spray water through its blowhole. Inwardly, each time Paul told Rene to keep a lid on it, she felt as though she were an embarrassment to him. It wasn't as if she were giving away family secrets about the boys; they were a handful, that's all. *It must be something about me as a person that he doesn't like*, she thought. *Openness is who I am, and he was attracted to that quality when we were dating.*

The couple talked about it, but this impasse wasn't overcome in a day or even in several months. Over the years, however, after several people in their Sunday school class commented to Paul about how much Rene's sharing had helped them in their own lives, he slowly began to appreciate her transparency. He finally stopped telling Rene what she should or shouldn't say.

RELEASE HER VOICE

Most of your wife's gifts will be expressed through her thoughts and opinions. Her voice is the vehicle through which we husbands will be blessed, so stripping her of her voice by demanding that she clam up in public renders many of her God-given gifts useless. In addition, when you keep her from voicing opinions at home, the damage is infinitely greater.

The Women of Faith conferences have been a phenomenal success because God has chosen to use them to give some dedicated and brilliant people a voice in the Christian community. The speakers have gone from speaking to two hundred or two thousand women at a time to twenty thousand. These speakers have found their voices and are using them to deliver encouragement to women all over the country. That's really the intent of Women of Faith to begin with—to encourage women.

After a few years of working with this ministry, I (Steve) felt a growing need not just to encourage women, but also to equip them. I wanted to help them find the skills and talents they needed to survive and succeed in a very tough world. From focus groups, surveys, and brainstorming sessions, we began to recognize several critical areas in which women felt they needed help in becoming all God wants them to become. One of the most frequently mentioned areas was the need to "find my voice." This is a strange phrase, but of course it means more than learning to talk. It means discovering who you really are and expressing it in a way that honors God. As a result of our research, we developed a conference called Breakthrough in which one of the key elements is helping a woman find her voice.

The reason so many women need this kind of help is that so many men pressure and push a woman to be silent and to reflect him rather than be herself. A woman often senses that her role is perceived as being so low that she has no right to have a voice or to feel complete in the eyes of God. Men secure their own position by stifling or ignoring the personhood, the identity, and the unique gifts of women. But many women are resisting this and are demanding a place and a voice at the table with men.

If you think this kind of trampling is a problem limited to the poor or uneducated, you're mistaken. Just last week I spoke to a group of people who all give over two hundred thousand dollars a year to ministries around the world. The biggest problem they asked me to address was the reluctance of traditional husbands to allow their wives to be involved in decision making, specifically in decisions about how the family's income should be used. These wise and wealthy men hadn't found a way to comfortably include their wives in the mission of allocation. But the women were demanding a voice. The problem is universal, and it's the challenge of every man to help a woman find her voice and to respond respectfully to it.

As a former stockbroker, I (Fred) love investing. Wall Street has fascinated me ever since I started reading the stock pages at age twelve. By age thirteen, I began buying stock with earnings from my newspaper route.

Since then I've continued to dabble here and dabble there in the New York Stock Exchange. I'm far from being a day-trader, but I like finding unique investments. On occasion I've talked about those investment ideas with Brenda.

Brenda knows nothing about investments. She wouldn't know a stock from a bond, and she couldn't figure an ROI if it bit her on the ankle. She does, however, have an intuitive female brain that thinks globally. Translation: Brenda possesses an uncanny ability for spotting investments that, in her words, "seem silly." Because she uses intuition and feelings, however, she can never tell me *why* they seem silly.

Early in our marriage, before I learned my lesson, I introduced a hot stock pick to Brenda that I thought would be a sure winner. I explained the company's history, the type of product it produced, and why I thought the company was poised for explosive growth.

"Why would you want to invest in that?" she said at the time.

"Because the price earnings per share…" I knew it was no use. "Because I think it's a good stock!"

"That one seems silly to me," she said.

"Silly? Why do you say that? This is a cold dollar-and-cents decision. Don't you think I've researched this company?"

"You can do what you want, but I wouldn't invest in that company."

I shrugged my shoulders. It bugged me to comply with someone whose best analysis tool was intuition. "I might as well use a Ouija board," I fumed.

I passed on a number of beauties, but then my broker brought me a wonderful little opportunity to invest in a real estate limited partnership. I loved this one. I considered showing it to Brenda, but I was tired of consulting someone who failed to give financial investments a cold, hard eye. Since I was the head of the family, it didn't matter what she said. I would do what I wanted. At least that's what I told myself.

Shortly after my investment (this was in the mid-1980s), the U.S. Congress passed a law that severely changed the rules regarding real estate limited partnerships. Result: I lost nearly all my money in a lousy investment.

When it was time to come clean, I carefully laid out my tale of woe to Brenda. "I would have advised against it," she said.

I knew that.

"From what you've shown me," she continued, "this investment seemed a bit silly to me."

I didn't say anything.

Brenda took pity on me. "But if I were handling our finances, I would probably do much worse."

She was being kind, but I'm not so sure anymore! I learned an expensive lesson about trampling my wife's role. She simply desired a voice in our marriage so she could express this intuitive gift. When I shut down her voice, though, I shut down her gift. Obviously, I would have more money in the bank if I had listened to Brenda's intuitive thoughts.

Since our wives have gifts we don't have, releasing their voice in our homes can bring incredible blessings. Case in point: As Melissa and Kevin's two children reached school age, Melissa started thinking about how her boys should be educated. Their options, as she saw them, were to send them to the same public elementary school that her husband had attended or to homeschool the children with a Christian-based curriculum. Melissa researched the neighborhood public school, sought out opinions from friends who sent their children there, and discussed with homeschooling parents the pros and cons of teaching her children herself.

Then Melissa prayed for guidance. When she brought up the home-schooling issue with Kevin, he was clearly disappointed because a part of him wanted his boys to walk the same halls and even have some of the same teachers he'd had.

But the more Kevin listened to his wife's heart and the more he prayed about it, the more he realized this decision was very dear to her. He agreed to give this "adventure," as he called it, a worthy try. He and Melissa were not disappointed.

VIEW HER AS A TRUE HELPMATE

It's especially critical to hear your wife's voice when she's speaking from the very center of her gifts. Our wives are fellow heirs of grace, every bit as worthy to lead our homes as we are, except for God's grace in granting us that role. This ability to lead is especially evident in the areas of their strengths.

I (Fred) am the quarterback type. In fact, I played quarterback in high school. My high-school aptitude tests pointed me toward a career as an air force officer, a good fit for an on-the-field football general. I have never been the nurturing type; my family can attest to that. I believe in discipline and getting things done—now! So when the two oldest children turned six and four, I thought it was time for a little Christian boot camp. They were the wet-eared recruits, and I, as their D.I., would drill Christianity deep into their hearts.

Every single night I lined them up against the headboard in the master bedroom. "Time to memorize the hymns of our faith," I'd command.

"Yes sir," they responded in pipsqueak voices. They could be kids all day, but when they toed the line in boot camp, I tolerated no goofing off. (Please, I'm exaggerating here. I never made them drop and give me twenty if they flubbed up a verse.) I had high standards of performance. They needed to be armed with God's truth and prepared to defend their beliefs.

I never required that my children wear camouflage or anything, but in retrospect even sitting at attention was a bit much. When one of them started to cry, I commanded him or her to be quiet—now! "We have to focus on God's Word," I announced in a strict tone of voice. Actually, I didn't mind if one of them started crying—the discipline it prompted made them focus and get tougher. Applying focused discipline lies right in the heart of my waters.

However, when my D.I. routine all got to be a bit much and they'd both start crying, I knew I was rowing into Brenda's waters. Remember, she's the nurturer, and I'm not. She wanted to be heard on these matters.

"I don't like how you drill them," she said. "They're getting scared of you, and they'll hate the very songs you're wanting them to love. Besides, you're keeping them up too late. They need their sleep."

My reply, as I recall, was something lofty, something along the lines of: "Listen, I'm responsible for teaching my children all about God, so I'm going to do it my way. In God's eyes, the buck stops with me, so I don't think you have a right to say anything. I'm glad they lose a little sleep over it. I don't think that's such a big sacrifice for the work of God!"

One night Brenda tucked the kids into bed after another tear-filled session. She came to our bedroom, where I was reading in bed. Sitting down on the edge of the mattress, she softly looked into my eyes. "Every night the last image in their minds is their father speaking sharply to them," she said. She patted my hand, kissed me, and walked into the bathroom to wash up.

My response? I pulled myself out of bed and traipsed down to the family room, where I sat down in the dark and thought things through. There the Lord reminded me that nurturing was Brenda's best strength and that she could keep me from becoming like my domineering father if I would let her.

I dismissed my charges from boot camp. My kids eventually passed Christian basic training anyway. Through the years I've elevated Brenda's voice even higher. In the areas of her greatest gifts, I not only allow her essence to be expressed with mine, but I allow it to dominate.

One recent Saturday she called and said, "I don't think I'll take the kids to swimming practice this morning. I'm going to take the girls shopping instead because I think they need to have a little fun with their mom today. I'm also keeping Michael home with a sinus infection."

Now she always passes these things by me because she knows how I feel about the kids' wimping out. *Michael's going to stay home because he has a little sinus infection? Give me a break! He's got to be a man! He won't win any championships this way,* I thought to myself.

Yet she heard me saying, "Okay, sweetheart. Sounds good." Why? Because I know her gifts. I know that if she thinks she and the girls need some fun together, it means she must've seen some small thing I wouldn't have seen in a million years—and I wouldn't have understood it if I *had* seen it anyway. When it comes to nurturing the kids, I don't just consider Brenda's opinion. Her opinion is the *only* one necessary for me.

Please view your wife as your helpmate. When she accepts this role, she commits her gifts to supporting you and lifting you to Christian greatness as a husband and father. You've got to admit, she can be a big help. Her very presence is an encouragement, especially during those dark days when you have many dragons to slay.

LET HER GIFTS SURFACE

Remember that your marriage is *her* call too. She simply has a differing role. Your leadership means allowing her to play her role freely. It doesn't mean you have to be out in front all the time, making all the decisions. *It means allowing the right gifts to surface at the right time in your marriage.* It may mean allowing your wife's gifts to predominate from time to time, especially if you're married to a go-getter like the "Proverbs 31 woman," as she's often called:

> *A wife of noble character who can find?*
> *She is worth far more than rubies.*
> *Her husband has full confidence in her*
> *and lacks nothing of value.*

She brings him good, not harm,
*   all the days of her life.*
She selects wool and flax
*   and works with eager hands.*
She is like the merchant ships,
*   bringing her food from afar.*
She gets up while it is still dark;
*   she provides food for her family*
*   and portions for her servant girls.*
She considers a field and buys it;
*   out of her earnings she plants a vineyard.*
She sets about her work vigorously;
*   her arms are strong for her tasks.*
She sees that her trading is profitable,
*   and her lamp does not go out at night.*
In her hand she holds the distaff
*   and grasps the spindle with her fingers.*
She opens her arms to the poor
*   and extends her hands to the needy.*
When it snows, she has no fear for her household;
*   for all of them are clothed in scarlet.*
She makes coverings for her bed;
*   she is clothed in fine linen and purple.*
Her husband is respected at the city gate,
*   where he takes his seat among the elders of the land.*
She makes linen garments and sells them,
*   and supplies the merchants with sashes.*
She is clothed with strength and dignity;
*   she can laugh at the days to come.*
She speaks with wisdom,
*   and faithful instruction is on her tongue.*

She watches over the affairs of her household
and does not eat the bread of idleness.
Her children arise and call her blessed;
her husband also, and he praises her. (Proverbs 31:10-28)

Pastors often preach about this hard-working, virtuous woman (who seems too good to be true, one must admit). We've yet to hear anyone preach about the *husband* of the Proverbs 31 woman. That's too bad because we could learn a few things from him. He allowed his wife's gifts to lift him and to bless his home. He granted her the latitude to shop and decorate the home. He encouraged her cottage business of sewing linen garments and sashes. Most of all, he respected her opinions. It sounds as though she had a great deal to say about how the family budget was spent.

To free our wife for her multifaceted role, we must free her voice. If we don't, her gifts are blocked, and she can't answer God's calling as a "suitable helper" (Genesis 2:20). Pressing our rights at the expense of God's purposes is always wrong.

Also, just because we're leaders doesn't mean that we should never be told what to do. Our wife's role of helpmate is her way of complementing *our* weaknesses and God's way of blessing us. She's not trying to lord it over you, though it seems at times that she is.

When Brenda, for example, was making her stand against the harsh treatment she received from my family, she was simply bringing her gifts to bear upon my weaknesses and our circumstances. I didn't recognize it because of my arrogant leadership, which created an impasse.

REMEMBER: SHE'S BLESSING YOU

What do you do to bring oneness out of impasses? You allow the voice that speaks from her areas of giftedness the right to be heard. You honor her as a fellow heir to God's kingdom who's actually a great blessing to you.

Of course, when we *do* free our wife's voice, we must understand something going in. As a helpmate, your wife at times will be the greatest source of antagonism in your life. She'll nag. Scold. Ride you like a bronco. She'll also make you see things you don't want to see, remind you to do things you've forgotten, and help you improve your manners when necessary. All this is what the "blessing" from your wife may feel like at times!

Recently, I was offered a wonderful speaking opportunity. I told Brenda all about it as if I'd already said yes. (In my mind, I already had.)

Fixing her eyes on mine, she simply said, "Who told you that you should go speak?" See what I mean? That irked me, but she was merely pointing out that I shouldn't walk through an open door until God told me to walk. Chastened, I prayed about it and discovered I should *not* accept the speaking opportunity. It turns out Brenda had the right words—a bit irritating, I know—to stop me in my tracks.

Serena told me she's frustrated when her husband, Jeff, doesn't give any merit to anything she has to say. "I can state my viewpoint or opinion, but he just says I'm flat wrong, so I've stopped giving it," said Serena.

Jeff is living in a very dangerous position because a wife's opinions, thoughts, and musings act like a governor on a male's impetuous behavior. One time Brenda threatened to stop giving me her opinions, and I was mature enough to be scared to death. I stopped everything on the spot and asked her to promise right then to never get so frustrated with me that she would stop telling me the truth. You can see the danger of muzzling your helpmate in the following two stories.

Roberta wrote, "My husband Kevin is planning to file for divorce this week. He initiated an adulterous affair with another believer. All this will be a shock to almost everyone because of the positions Kevin has held at the church, but he has never been what he appears to be. Kevin has filled our home with heavy, frightening verbal abuse, and even some substance abuse. He would have lost those church positions long ago *if he hadn't forced me to back down and cover up for him all these years.*"

With her voice silenced, her gifts and insights could not bless her home by challenging her husband's character. He sank deeper and deeper until he drowned in his own sinful hypocrisy.

Singer Annie Chapman's style of helping her husband offers a sharp contrast. In a radio interview before a performance in Des Moines, Annie said of her husband, "If Steve were to live a cesspool life off stage, I would expose him to the world. It would make me sick."

Her husband may not agree, but that's what we call a helpmate! I often encourage Brenda to be vocal in exactly this way, so that her insights and strengths can bless me.

Questions for Reflection and Discussion

1. How do you see your wife's particular gifts expressed through her thoughts and opinions?

2. In what ways might you have been guilty of securing your own position by stifling or ignoring your wife's personhood, identity, and unique gifts?

the source of your prestige

A bondservant didn't draw his prestige from his work, but from his relationship with his master. To some degree, he had no control over his reputation. It was based solely on whose servant he was. Being bondservant to a high priest would have been more prestigious than being servant to a local street merchant, for instance. But by choosing the life of a bondservant, he knew that if he served well and strengthened his master's house, he would strengthen his master's honor in the community as well as his own.

Have you chosen to draw your prestige primarily from your relationship with your wife? Probably not. Truth be told, most of us draw our prestige from our careers. It's our work and what we do five days a week (or more!) that lifts our self-esteem, not whom we're married to. If you must work long hours and nights for six weeks, it may mean some unusual business project came up. Everyone can understand that. But if you work long hours and nights for six months, then you've made a crucial decision about what you value most in life.

CHOOSING THE SOURCE OF PRESTIGE

While it's natural to draw prestige primarily from our careers, we must choose to draw our prestige primarily from our service to our "master," the one to whom we've given our hearts. If we don't, we have little hope of having her convictions and essence represented in the relationship and carrying the same weight as our own.

I valued the prestige of being the "go-to" guy when I was growing up. I was starting quarterback at Cedar Rapids Jefferson High, a traditional power in Iowa large-school football. In my senior year, I was state champion in business management decision making and graduated valedictorian of my class. I applied and was accepted to Stanford University, certainly one of the most prestigious institutions of higher learning in the country and the "Harvard of the West Coast."

When I started my freshman year on "The Farm," I knew I was on my way. But an interesting thing happened as I rubbed shoulders with hundreds, if not thousands, of valedictorians from around the world. We began to believe our press clippings. We really believed we were part of the elite, those set aside to become captains of industry, the greatest innovators, the top researchers, and the leaders of the free world. Our universe revolved around advancement, success, and achievement. We expected to leave a mark high on the wall.

That was all part of the Stanford mystique—or hype, if you take the less flattering view. I felt I had the world at my fingertips. I won't go into too many gory details, but I blew my chance, just like the prodigal son: He "set off for a distant country and there squandered his wealth in wild living" (Luke 15:13). Squandering my wealth of opportunity on a series of sexual relationships and dissipation, I soon found myself back trudging the sod of Iowa, clutching a barely marketable Stanford degree and wondering where my dreams had gone.

My friends had gone on to get their MBAs while I straggled into embarrassing obscurity. One friend was designing artificial hearts. Another was studying New Testament Greek at Cambridge. One was on the fast track at Abbot Laboratories. Another was making millions trading bonds in New York and London.

While I wasn't quite sleeping with the swine and eating their pods, my little company's start-up costs and trickling sales left me living below the official national poverty line for more than a year until Brenda came along with her nursing degree to save the day. That hurt my self-esteem.

Brenda was befuddled by my pain. "I don't understand this status thing," she protested. "You have nothing to be ashamed about. You're a hard worker and a decent man." This helped at times, but the feeling never lasted. I longed to reverse the years the locusts had eaten.

One day the call came. Pete, my best friend from college, made me the offer of a lifetime. His father had founded one of the largest electrical supply companies in America, and the old man had sent his boy to Stanford to be groomed for CEO. Pete offered to train me as his right-hand man. "We're talking executive vice president," said Pete. "I think you're perfectly suited for the job." This was the break I'd been waiting for. All the wasted years would soon be swept away.

I ran into one big roadblock: my wife and kids. Since the job entailed a move that would place Brenda six and a half driving hours from her mother, rather than the current three, the issue was a nonstarter. Quick weekend visits would be history. Furthermore, I'd soon be moving from branch to branch every few years to learn the business from top to bottom. First stop? The great state of Alabama. We loved the South, but we'd be even farther from home.

In addition, Brenda had finally laced together a network of good friends in Des Moines, and she felt she was finally hitting her stride away from Moline.

Another consideration: When I checked out the churches near the new company headquarters, they were small and didn't "feel" right. This would be a problem for my tender little family, which included two toddlers. I'd be risking our family's stability and Christian growth for the sake of business prestige.

In my current position, I worked long, hard hours, but I was my own boss. Though Pete was a close friend, business was business, and I knew I'd have to answer to him instead of myself. That meant my time wouldn't necessarily be my own anymore, and I'd have far less freedom to be with my family.

Despite the downside, Pete's job offer sat there like a crown jewel, the desire of my heart and the answer to my professional dreams. I could choose to draw my primary prestige from my career, or I could put my family first and be satisfied with drawing prestige from my home.

The decision I faced was exactly like the decision facing the Hebrew slave at the end of his six years of service. The slave, formerly independent and free to chase his own dreams, had crashed and burned into the life of slavery. Now came the chance he'd been waiting for. Finally, he could prove he had the right stuff and could earn back the prestige he'd carelessly squandered.

Or…he could turn away and choose to draw his primary prestige from his master. Which would I choose?

RISKING A LITTLE TRUST

As I was weighing my decision, I remembered listening to Chuck Swindoll on his *Insight for Living* radio show. He had spoken of a survey of eighty-five-year-old people as they entered the twilight of life. They were asked what they regretted most about the way they had lived. The seniors said:

1. I would have spent more time reflecting in meditation and contemplation.
2. I would have risked more.
3. I would have done more things that would live on after I die.

It was the second response that captured my attention. Most respondents referred to regrets over forks in their career road, saying things like, "I wish I would have risked starting that small business when I was thirty-five" or "Too bad I never tried living and working in London."

It's a sad thing to look back and say, "I wish I had risked more during my career," but it's positively tragic to look back and say, "I wish I had risked more in trusting God's Word." That's why I was glad I took the risk and wrote *Every Man's Battle* with Steve Arterburn. I didn't want to be sitting in my rocking chair thirty years from now saying, "I wish I had risked opening up my sinful past to the world and writing that book."

I was also thankful I'd already risked trusting God's Word in my time management. I was essentially an independent sales rep working off straight commission, so if I didn't work, we didn't eat. At the time of my marriage, I was working from 6 A.M. to 6 P.M. every day, plus 7 A.M. to noon on Saturdays. Having been in business for only a year, I really had to put in long hours.

After a while, Brenda suggested I was working too hard and should stop working on Saturday mornings. She pointed out relevant Scriptures that suggested I would eventually burn out. She also said that I should trust God and follow His Word. Eventually, I risked working less and gave my sales to the Lord. When Jasen, our firstborn, came into this world, I cut my hours to 6:30 A.M. to 5 P.M. to make time for him. When Laura came, I went to 7 A.M. to 4:30 P.M., which still translated into a forty-five hour workweek.

So what's my point? I wanted to follow the command of Deuteronomy 6:6-7, which said I was responsible for impressing God's commandments upon my children's hearts and that I was to talk to them when I was at home, walking along the road, and any other time I was with them.

How was I going to do this if I were never around? I had to risk trusting God and allowing Him to bring in enough sales during my shortened workday.

Was this really a risk? I certainly felt it was! Each time I cut back, I sweated profusely, suspecting my business would suffer significant reversals or even collapse. I fought these changes like a dog. (You can check Brenda's ankles!) Yet I counted on this promise from God:

> The pagans run after all these things, and your heavenly Father knows
> that you need them. But seek first his kingdom and his righteousness,
> and all these things will be given to you as well. (Matthew 6:32-33)

When we choose God's way, He's intently interested in vindicating our decision before the world. It brings Him glory when we tell others about that decision. It's nothing for Him to give us favor with the boss or to open doors to sales or advancement we hadn't noticed before.

Getting back to my story, I'd been given a huge pop quiz. Did I have a servant's heart? Did I, like the bondservant of Israel, draw my primary prestige from success in the home? If I did, then I should choose the safest, most promising path for my family, the path that would honor my wife's essence as well as mine. If I did not, then I should choose the safest, most promising path for my career.

There was one other thing to consider: Was I going to risk trusting God's Word? Was I going to risk putting God's kingdom first—His priority of oneness with my wife—and trust God to take care of the rest?

All I could see was what I'd lost through my sin and how desperately I wanted to catch up to all the success my friends were enjoying. The temptation to grab the job offer and run with it was enticing, but I was reminded again of the Lord's words: "I will repay you for the years the locusts have eaten" (Joel 2:25).

I had to be willing to trust God's promise and to allow Him to restore things in His own time. If I waited for Him to do it, He'd find a way to restore my losses without destabilizing my family or moving us to a community without a strong church. But my mind played around with this thought: If I waited for Him and He didn't come through, my one chance would be gone. Was I willing to bet my career that God would keep this promise?

That was how my mind was working at the time, but after prayer and reflection, I knew I wouldn't go wrong by making my family the primary source of my prestige. So I stayed in Des Moines because that was the best decision for the family. But I also trusted that God would keep His promise. He did, restoring beyond my wildest imagination the years the locusts had eaten. He blessed me with exciting career twists and advances. Furthermore, my marriage and my relationships with my kids became as solid as an Iowa rock quarry. When I'm eighty-five, I'll be saying, "I'm glad I risked less prestige and achievement in my career for higher achievement in my home."

What good is your Christian faith if you can't lay your career on the line in obedience to God's truth? Thousands of martyrs have done far more, and we'll have to look them in the eye some day. I don't want to have to avert my eyes.

Look, I'm not against corporate advancement, and heavy travel and sacrifice may be part of the mix at times. It's our nature to work hard and *want* to work hard. But what if we chose to make our home our primary source of prestige? What if we risked slowing down our race up the corporate ladder for the sake of oneness with our wives? What if we risked trusting God for our corporate advancement, so we might put Him first and honor her essence, strengthening our marriages and our families? This strength would live on in our children long after we die. Remember, when we're eighty-five, we'll all wish we'd done more things that would live on after we die.

Do you really believe that if you put God's kingdom first He'll give these things to you? Have you laid anything on the line to prove it? Think about it.

BUILDING HER PRESTIGE

As a bondservant leader, we'll not only draw prestige from the success of our marriage relationship, but we'll also build the prestige of our "master" in the community. Of course, we begin in the home, where her prestige is first built through our words.

In Proverbs 31:29-31, the husband grants his wife her proper prestige with these words:

> *"Many women do noble things,*
> *but you surpass them all."*
> *Charm is deceptive, and beauty is fleeting;*
> *but a woman who fears the LORD is to be praised.*
> *Give her the reward she has earned,*
> *and let her works bring her praise at the city gate.*

If Cal's praise has anything to do with it, his wife will be standing next to the Proverbs 31 woman at the city gate. This is what Cal's wife, Joni, had to say:

Cal often tells me that my high standards have helped him keep high standards himself. Before we met, he had heard of my standards, and he was bound and determined to meet me one way or another because he had never known anyone who actually kept high Christian standards. He knew plenty who'd been raised that way, but none who had kept to them. Again and again he tells me how refreshing it was to meet a girl like me. I know Cal feels good about himself because he's married to me.

While our words build prestige in our wife, our actions are to honor her essence as well: "Husbands, in the same way be considerate as you live with your wives, and treat them with respect as...heirs with you" (1 Peter 3:7).

Granting her the rightful place of prestige at home respects your wife as a fellow heir. Robbing her of what you promised to give, and what God promised she'd have, means you're sinning against her and therefore breaking oneness. You have no right to do that. Oneness is built on actions; it's not a feeling. You've either given her the rightful place by your actions or you haven't.

It's often easier, however, to grant our wives prestige in words than in action, especially in the area of finances. Listen to this story from Rebecca:

> I don't know what's going on with him in the area of finances. He doesn't share anything—information or money—with me. I've asked him to show me our finances, and he says that he will, but it never happens. I'm usually uneasy and worried because I'm in the dark. Due to some poor financial choices he's made without me, trust is a big issue too. I walk around expecting to step into financial quicksand.
>
> How can a couple have complete oneness when these issues aren't shared? It feels more like a game of strategy than a marriage. I hate it.

Rebecca's husband didn't honor her essence or treat her as a fellow heir. Can you imagine any bondservant treating his master that way? Remember, oneness lies not in the *sentiment* of loving your wife as yourself, but in the *act* of loving her as yourself.

Outside the home, actions also speak louder than words when building your wife's prestige in the community. If you haven't given her that irrevocable highest place of prestige in your life, you're trampling her. And let us tell you a little secret: If you haven't done so, she knows it.

A bondservant held his master in the highest esteem, and he wouldn't dream of giving that high place of prestige to anyone else. However, as husbands we often do, most often placing our parents ahead of our wives. We won't discipline ourselves to obey God's command in Genesis 2:24, choosing instead to trample our wives, as Bill did with Becky in this case:

> I have always felt second best compared to Bill's mom. I never feel cherished by him when we're in her presence. He often takes her side on issues and, when he has to choose, he inevitably chooses to offend me rather than offend her. We never discuss this—if we do, we have great tension. This goes double for his father, the king of the family who makes us all walk on eggshells whenever he is around.
>
> For instance, we can get pretty picky about whom our kids spend their time with. Bill's mom has mentioned two or three times that she would like to baby-sit our kids and have some of her friend's grandkids over simultaneously. We don't really need another person choosing their playmates, though. When she mentioned this to me, Bill was standing nearby. I told her I didn't know these parents, and I wasn't sure about it. In other words, I was trying to stonewall her while I sought Bill's help.
>
> Bill immediately said, "Oh, I know that family, so it's okay." I was very hurt that there was zero discussion between us and that once more he preferred to offend me rather than his mom. His mother loves our kids, but she is not a believer and doesn't have the same standards we have. Bill and I have never discussed this incident, but I wish we had because it definitely hurt me.

As another example, when we recently ate dinner with Bill's parents, his father told my daughter Alicia to "sit down and shut up." Not only was it 100 percent uncalled for—she wasn't even being loud—but we don't speak to our kids like this. I sat quietly, waiting for Bill to stand up to his dad, but it never happened. I was very upset with his father, but even more so with Bill's silence. About three days later I got up the courage to talk about it. Bill admitted he hated his father's harsh treatment of our sensitive girl. He admitted that he wished he had said something at the time. I hope if this happens again, Bill will stand up to his dad.

Bill's words may have been right, but he failed to take action to assert the prestige of his wife. Here's a similar story from Andra, but this time there is proper action:

Early in our relationship, my husband would put his parents' opinions first. He was controlled by what they might think of his choices, and that caused much friction in our marriage. Jon usually left me to deal with my feelings on my own because he refused to confront the problem.

At one point things got so bad that Jon had to decide whom to stand with—and he chose me. He protected me from his parents' intense interference in our lives, and he would not allow them to communicate directly with me. I gladly took refuge behind him. I finally felt that he was listening to me, and I felt cherished and valued. We were connected on a new level.

We've also seen men give their ex-wives more prestige than their wives. What bondservant of Israel would ever grant a former master higher prestige than his current master? It's ludicrous to imagine, but we do it continually, as Lisa relates:

This is my husband's second marriage and my first. He's had custody of his son, Tim, since he was two, and we married when Tim was five. Over the years, he's left me out of conversations with his ex-wife where his son is concerned. I usually find stuff out later, and by then, I'm hurt and angry. After all, I've been the stay-at-home mom raising the boy.

Even now that Tim is twenty-three, on his own, and making poor choices, I'm not included in the discussions. Frequently his ex-wife knew what was happening in my home before I did. I don't respect my husband for handling it this way, nor do I trust him. I'm certain he's keeping things from me, and there's a part of him that is still connected and loyal to his first wife.

I try to stay emotionally disengaged from issues surrounding Tim now that he's moved out, but it seeps into other areas of our family life. To me, it's unreasonable to expect me to care and take an interest in Tim and then to remind me that I'm still an outsider with no investment. It's an impossible balancing act.

Gentlemen, can we justify placing our wives anywhere but in the highest place of prestige in our lives? In fact, that place should be hers already. How can we rob her like this? We must build our wives' prestige in our homes and the community. We have no right to do anything else.

Questions for Reflection and Discussion

1. In what significant ways have you taken risks to strengthen the one-ness in your marriage?

2. Do your wife and family represent your primary source of prestige?

3. In what significant ways have you worked to build up your wife's prestige in your home and community?

PART IV

igniting your bondservant mind

study your "master" to serve her better

As we stated previously, marital adjustment is simple. Before marriage, you commanded your ship of life based upon the personal convictions and soul essence of one person—you. Now, as skipper of the USS *Matrimony*, you must command based upon the convictions and essence of two people. These convictions will sometimes conflict, and it won't be your love that brings oneness out of the impasse, no matter how sincere your emotions. It's your *decisions* that honor her essence and your *actions* that bring oneness.

If our wife is to live fully in marriage, we must study her essence—what she's all about—until we know it like our own. Without such study, our natural male mind-set makes us reckless commanders. We must ignite within ourselves a new mind because reckless commanders sink ships.

A STUDY IN...STUDY!

Bill and Carol were married two years ago. Shortly after the wedding, Bill was offered a job that paid big money, but it required traveling nearly every week and often weeks at a time without coming home on weekends. When Bill and Carol looked at the income, they calculated that if he had this job for just three years, they could put away a big chunk of money to put toward a down payment on the home of their dreams.

Discussing it as a team, they decided Bill's plan looked good. He took the job, and Carol hunkered down for the three-year stint. But soon the swells of life began breaking over their bow. Loneliness swept into Carol's life. Bill brushed it easily aside, calling it a small price to pay for their financial goals. For Carol, it was too dear a price for any goal. She sensed their marriage taking on water.

When they did see each other, the normal blasts from their incompatibilities hit them broadside, but then he would leave for two weeks with no resolution. Bill simply placed these emotions into a holding cell for processing later. Yet the periods of no resolution took a heavy toll on Carol. Their ship was listing heavily.

From Bill's perspective there was no imminent danger. (Talk about rearranging deck chairs on the *Titanic!*) Carol sounded the alarm and told Bill their plan wasn't working. She begged him to change course and head home so they could chart a new course together. Bill recklessly pushed on, commanding, "Full speed ahead, present course."

Relying on his own logic and instincts, Bill was commanding the USS *Matrimony* as if Carol no longer had anything to say about the course he was taking. He ignored the seriousness of the new information. Rather than studying Carol closely, Bill made reckless assumptions about her emotions. To him, her loneliness was just a sign of temporary weakness. She needed to toughen up on the Seven Seas. When Carol couldn't resolve conflicts, Bill assumed she just needed to grow up and face her difficulties like an adult. She needed to maintain the present heading while she "worked through" her issues.

Bill never understood that Carol was just different, not weak. All things being equal, relationship means something different to women than it means to men. Loneliness and lack of conflict resolution will have a huge impact on women, while guys seem to brush these things off.

Why didn't he understand? Because Bill hadn't studied the differences between men and women, and he was still leading based upon his essence alone. Bottom line: Bill didn't listen to Carol's plea. He maintained his course, and their marriage crashed on the shoals of conflict. Today, they're separated while they await divorce proceedings.

As we've seen before, the differences between men and women create seemingly unresolvable incompatibilities and impasses like this one. How do we bring oneness, not divorce, out of the impasses? We submit to oneness. But we can't do that until we study our wives, and even then, we may still see things only from our own point of view since we aren't used to looking at things through two sets of eyes.

Even now, for instance, Bill's head spins as his grounded ship is pounded apart. *What went wrong? I made the logical choice!* It was and still is logical if we leave Carol's differences out of the discussion. If we're leading solely from our own perspective, disastrous decisions can and will look perfectly logical. If we haven't studied our wives carefully, however, using logic as our reference point can be very dangerous because our own logic excludes her essence and is therefore fatally flawed.

Bill could easily brush loneliness aside. He had no trouble with unresolved conflict. To him, it was perfectly logical to expect that after being separated for weeks at a time they could pick up their marriage right where they left off. Since he could do it, she could too, right?

Wrong.

Those who have studied women know that long separations between a husband and wife rarely enhance a marriage and do nothing to build intimacy, which is her heart's desire. Bill looked at the horizon and thought giving up three years of relationship to financially secure the next ten seemed perfectly logical. But it wasn't, not by a long stretch. Bill's "logical" decision failed to factor in the effects on Carol of loneliness and poor conflict resolution. Simply put, he didn't make allowance for her essence.

COMMANDING WITH SACRIFICIAL THINKING

If we're committed to helping our "master" (our wives) blossom in marriage, we must move beyond a merely logical leadership style. We must seek to be a righteous commander, one who honors her essence always. In other words, we must think sacrificially. Doing so will bring healthy marital adjustment.

To think righteously and sacrificially is to reject our right to lead solely from our point of view. This is far easier said than done, since our bloated male egos practically demand center stage. But without sacrificial thinking, we'll never realize oneness. Real leadership in marriage means allowing her gifts to surface at all the right times. This is necessary to honor our wife's place in the marriage.

For example, over the years I (Fred) have helped many friends move to new homes. I've seen all the different approaches to the task, including the guys who insisted on using complicated numbering systems to make the unloading easier on the other end. They must have all read the same book!

Mark was especially insistent. He refused to let his wife, Gerri, do any of the packing unless she did it his way. Unfortunately, he worked two jobs and couldn't be around much to pack. "This is ridiculous," said Gerri. "His plan doubles the work of packing, and I have so much to do! Besides, he's not here to pack, and he won't be there to unload. What's it to him? I'm just going crazy trying to get it done his way. But if I don't do it the way I've been told, I'll get into trouble!"

I know Mark and Gerri, and it's no secret Mark is the gifted organizer, but it's not like Gerri can't manage to pack up bedrooms and kitchens. Why not let her take over for the sake of unity?

Sheila has wanted to hang pictures of the kids for nine months, but her husband, Erik, refuses to let her because he has a certain way he wants the task completed. Erik is so busy with work during the week and with his car on weekends, he never gets around to hanging those pictures.

Sheila's house is her nest, and she wants to dress it up with pictures of the kids. When he won't allow that, he severely tramples Sheila's heart and essence. "I feel like I have far less freedom than when I was living at home with my parents," she said. "In fact, it feels like I've traded one father for a stricter one, but this one doesn't trust me or care about my feelings as much. Erik makes me so mad. I just want my stupid pictures on the wall!"

We may like pictures hung just so. But that doesn't mean we have to be the final arbitrators of how it's done. There are more important things than exerting our authority in our marriages—things like oneness.

Barb said, "When I discuss changes to make the house prettier, Don can always say something to crush my enthusiasm. Either my plan is unnecessary, or he can come up with something better. If I really want something done, I just don't mention it to him and go and do it anyway. That way I can have it done the way I want it."

If Don keeps leading like this, oneness will suffer further, and he'll deserve his fate. Like most women, Barb feels her house is a reflection of her. Granted, Don may have a strong gift of style, but he needn't use it all the time. Don should care more about oneness than interior decorating, especially when Barb is hiding things and running around behind his back just so she can have a few things in her own house the way she wants them.

The point is, these negative experiences build up in the heart of a woman. If you won't sacrifice your way to let her hang pictures or pack boxes, before long she won't sacrifice to have sex with you when she's not in the mood. She'll find it hard to submit to your spiritual leadership because you seem like a cold, heartless phony. Everything will become hard for her.

So in our attempt to command the USS *Matrimony* in a godly way, we must first reject this leadership style. Our second step in becoming a righteous, sacrificial commander is to study our wives, as we've been saying. If we don't know her essence as well as we know our own, we can't expect her to ever feel one with us.

Here's another simple example:

Margie loves dogs, and she grew up with "inside" dogs that lived in the house and became like members of the family. Her husband, Jess, merely tolerates animals, and while he had "outside" dogs as he grew up on the farm, they were largely ignored. Now living on their own farm, Margie and Jess had a dog named Buster. "Buster was an outside dog," said Margie. "But I grew to love him so. When our son, Gabriel, was born, Buster became extremely jealous and wanted to come inside. When we wouldn't let him, he began running away constantly, and that was tearing me up. I begged Jess to allow Buster to come inside our home.

"Jess wanted no part of it. But he knew how hard this was on me, so eventually, against every last fiber of his being, he agreed to allow Buster inside the home. Jess will always be my hero because of this!"

As commander, what course seemed most logical to Jess? Well, Buster should stay outside since he had always stayed outside. That's the way things were. But Jess found the right answer not by thinking logically, but by thinking sacrificially.

Jess had studied Margie and knew how this problem tore at her soul. The impasse was real, and while the fate of the world didn't hang in the balance, this was a big deal to both of them. He allowed her pain over the dog to carry as much weight in his decision as his disgust at the thought of having an inside dog. He sacrificed his right to choose his way for the sake of oneness. He allowed Margie's essence to take its proper place in the decision-making process.

IS IT EVERYTHING SHE WANTS?

Let's get practical and explore sacrificial thinking within the context of a number of marital adjustments we all face. You'll see how this kind of thinking is far superior to logic in honoring your wife's essence just as you honor your own. Of course, we must understand a couple of things going in. First, sacrificial thinking isn't giving your wife everything she wants. It's making sure her essence is expressed equally with yours, in the same way the white stripe is expressed equally with the red on a candy cane.

Second, sacrificial thinking is more than taking her thoughts into consideration. It's taking those thoughts and putting them into play with as much emphasis and care as you give your own thoughts, although some of her thought processes may not make sense to you as a guy. You must simply understand her essence and act upon it as if you do understand, or there'll be no oneness. She'll feel trampled and always left out, no matter how often you say, "But darling, I listened to you. I just felt my way was better."

Third, you may not agree with our answers in some of the situations laid out below. Fine. The answers aren't important, but the way of coming to those answers is important. Your wife is different from your wife's best friend, and you're different from me. The answers may be different, but the use of the servant mind-set must always be consistent among all of us if we wish to love our wives as ourselves.

1. Working Toward a Career

"I'm in my third year of graduate school," Joanne said. "I couldn't succeed in this challenge if it weren't for my husband's constant support when I'm in class and when I have to barricade myself in my room to do homework. He feeds the kids, helps with their homework, and runs them where they need to go. I can't explain the relief I feel when I know he's stepping in to take over my role. He's so emotionally supportive that I don't have to fret about possibly shirking my duties as wife and mother. He never ever pouts or acts put out that he has to do more. I feel so responsible for my family that if he did these things for me grudgingly, I would feel defeated very quickly. Because he helps me with a cheerful attitude, I feel a lightness inside that helps me get through the day."

Joanne's husband is a wise leader who thinks sacrificially. She says that if she saw a grudging attitude in him, she'd feel defeated and want to quit. He knows that about her, so he makes sure he keeps a perky attitude. That's a real man.

2. Making a Major Purchase

A while back, I (Fred) reached a special point in my life as a homeowner. We'd lived in our house for eleven years, and having made some extra payments over the years on our fifteen-year mortgage, our house was nearly paid off. Riding on cloud nine, I felt quite proud and couldn't wait to burn my mortgage note.

Of course, during those same eleven years a familiar herd of four kids and their friends roamed throughout the house, and it no longer looked the same as it did when we'd moved in. The carpets were worn, and curling seams on the blotchy kitchen linoleum whispered its age. Our dated wallpaper was fading, and our well-worn furniture sagged in all the wrong places.

Our thundering herd had grown to adolescence, which meant they had long outgrown our game room. The upshot: There was nowhere for the modern teen to hang out. While we had a pair of computers, we had no decent study space to go with them. Our house seemed to be shrinking.

As commander of the ship, what should I do? To me, the logical choice was to stay the course. I had a perfectly good house with no mortgage. If I purchased a new one, I'd tack on another $100,000 mortgage. If I stayed put, a major makeover would require a home equity loan of $40,000, by my estimates.

The kids weren't complaining, and they were all doing fine in school. Brenda wasn't complaining, except for the ugly kitchen linoleum that gagged her every morning. As for me, I was the guy who was satisfied with a cheap lawn chair and a portable television back in my apartment days. I already had far more than I'd ever dreamed I would have, and now I was nearly debt-free. With no complaints raining in my direction, why change course? Logically, we could wait four or five years and pay cash for the upgrades.

Just one little matter. I had studied Brenda through the years, and I knew a few things about her. First, she rarely squawked about material things, so her lack of complaint was no guarantee she felt fine about everything. Second, her home was her nest, the place where she lived and raised her children and hosted her friends. Lots of emotions were tied up in those things. Her home was an extension of her personality and self-esteem, as it is for nearly every woman.

I knew I needed to address this topic with Brenda, especially since she was being kind not to push me about the topic of renovation. I knew Brenda was a nurturer, and since the kids had nowhere to bring their friends, this was a problem to her. We also needed a community space for broadband Internet access, especially since Brenda didn't want the kids cooped up in their rooms behind their computers. She preferred having the kids study in a community setting nearer the heart of the home.

I knew something else about Brenda. She has a restful soul that hates clutter and crowded conditions. Since the family room was the only room in the house where everyone could hang out, it didn't take many bodies or much time for the largest room in the house to become overcrowded and messy. We needed more "comfort space," and an updated game room would appeal to teens. Finally, I knew she'd been dreaming of her own office nook to keep her bills and papers organized.

If I decided to apply *my* logic alone to our family dilemma, no changes would be made. Still, I figured I'd try to be fair. While I couldn't see either moving or upgrading every corner of the house, we were in a financial position to at least start a remodeling project that would bring great joy to Brenda and improve our living conditions. So I drew up a reasonable plan and presented it to Brenda. I had about $10,000 in cash, which, I figured, would allow us to get off to a good start. We could finish the remodeling project as the money came in.

"I don't want to do it that way," responded Brenda. "The house will be torn up forever. Plus you know I don't have a gift for decorating. If we do things in a piecemeal fashion, everything will turn out ugly. If we can't do it all immediately, and if I can't use a decorator, I'd rather not do anything because I'd be embarrassed by the results. Besides, the kids really need the computer room now, and the only place we can put it is in the living room. They also need a place to have their friends over, and that would be the basement. Even if we started with just these two rooms, refurbishing them alone will cost more than $10,000. Maybe it would be just as easy to move."

Thinking logically didn't come close to honoring Brenda's essence. To love her as myself, the look of her nest had to carry as much weight with me as a paid-off mortgage. Her nurturing desires had to be represented in the decision-making process as prominently as my financial desires. There had to be oneness.

We ultimately decided to fix up the house. I was prepared to borrow up to $30,000, even though that meant we couldn't redo the family room just yet. Within those parameters, I made plenty of room for Brenda's essence. She could hire a decorator and spruce up the basement with an air hockey table, a pool table, and an entertainment corner for Nintendo madness.

Upstairs, the living room became a combination sitting room and computer room. Coupled with the basement, there were now three comfortable areas in the house to gather and talk, instead of only one. We found room for Brenda's nook in the new living room layout, and new porcelain tile on the kitchen floor did wonders to spruce up that area.

The traffic flow changed dramatically. The living room, which was never used before, was constantly occupied by Net surfers. The basement was a magnet for the teens. The family room had a "new and improved" look. Who needed a new house?

I didn't like the new home-equity payments, but I managed to grin and bear it because I knew the decision reflected the needs and desires of both of us.

Like many decisions, when it comes to major purchases, it's easy for men to ignore important factors that don't affect them directly. Recently our dryer died, and our washing machine, because of its repair record, was on its last legs. I gave Brenda a number to work with, and she went shopping. She returned gushing over Maytag's new Neptune washer and dryer. The Neptune front-loading washer removed tough stains better than conventional washers, handled much larger loads, and conserved water. The Neptune dryer from Maytag, with its IntelliDry Control feature, would finish a load in half the time.

Of course, there was one drawback. Like a Mark McGwire home run, the Neptune washer-dryer combo landed well beyond our budget fence. We're talking more than $1,500 for the pair. Logically, I could have said no because I had just dropped a wad on remodeling the house. I could have asked her to be fair and split the difference with me, asking her to look for something that landed between the original figure and the cost of the Neptune washer and dryer. I felt no pressure. If I had said no, she would have agreed without a peep.

But as I studied her life, I realized she spent the better part of two days every week dealing with laundry—my laundry as well as the clothes belonging to my children. Brenda managed to handle all the laundry by herself, so this decision meant a big deal to her. She'd done her research, and I had done none. Why should I have the greatest say in this decision? After voicing my gentle concerns about overspending, I said she could do whatever she wanted.

She bought the Neptune washer and dryer setup. And I know it sounds silly to say this, but that was one of the best decisions we made in years. She now spends only one day a week in the laundry room versus the two days of drudgery before. One way to look at our purchase was that we were buying not a washer and dryer, but an extra day per week for Brenda to use in more fruitful ways.

Sure, we paid extra, but what we purchased was priceless.

I would have missed out on lightening Brenda's load by being logical or fair. Sure, there are times when you just can't justify a big-ticket expense (like driving a new Suburban off the car lot), but adhering to a strategy of prudent buying decisions with her input honors your wife and says "I love you" in ways you never imagined. She will feel one with you, which enhances intimacy.

3. Determining Where to Live

Should our wives get everything they want? No, but they should get plenty. If we're to set good examples in our home, then as servant leaders we must keep focused on the word *servant*. As Chief Servant, we are to give in more often at impasses than anyone else. No one should choose to inconvenience themselves more often than we do, and no one should have a better attitude in serving than ours.

Jesus taught us submission by laying down His life for the sake of our relationship with Him, even though we were sinners. That being said, we husbands must keep the proper emphasis on the word *leader* as well. Yes, our responsibility as husbands is to command the ship along the course we've set as a couple, and though we must often serve by submitting our rights for the sake of oneness, we must never forget our duty to lead the ship safely into harbor.

We must study our wives carefully so we don't confuse their essence with their emotions as we lead. From the beginning, Brenda dreamed of being a stay-at-home mom when the children arrived. This dream meant two things.

First, we had to locate in an area that would give me the best chance to earn enough money to make that possible. Second, I would have to like my work.

Those early years were difficult because of her father's death and my trampling. As our married life unraveled, Brenda pushed to return to her hometown of Moline. She said I could get a job at one of the large production plants there, and then we could be near her family. She could get her old job back, and we could return to the church she grew up in. To her, everything would be better immediately if we would only move back to Illinois.

While she was probably right in the short term, I couldn't see a Moline move working in the long term. Though my business was no great shakes as yet, it was finally starting to click. I enjoyed my work far better than the suggestions she offered about opportunities in Moline, and I couldn't move my business to that area because of competitive situations. I knew keeping this business was my best hope for supporting her dream of being a stay-at-home mom.

Yet Brenda remained adamant, so I had to study her closely. Was she expressing her deep emotions, or was something deeper transpiring? In her heart of hearts, she wanted to build a new life with her husband, distinct and separate from her extended family. She could do that best in Des Moines. She had dreamed of being a stay-at-home mom since she was a little girl. She didn't have to return to Moline to have that lifestyle. We could eventually find a good church with lots of young friends, and when we did that in Des Moines, we began forming friendships as cochairs of the Young Couples Activities Committee.

There was nothing *in her essence* that wouldn't be met in Des Moines. Her desire to move home was based on pure emotion. As leader, I had to find room for her essence, but in doing so, I knew I couldn't allow her emotions to determine the outcome. I told her I thought we should stay put.

4. Finding a Place of Worship

We should study our wife to make sure her spiritual needs are given full consideration along with our own. Then, even when things can't go her way, we've at least taken her essence into consideration, and oneness remains strong.

Recently, after a few unhappy experiences with his kids, Greg felt unsatisfied with the Sunday school program at his church. He thought it was time to find another church. His wife, Candy, though, was dragging her feet.

Did she disagree with his assessment of things? No, she understood perfectly. Then why was she reluctant to change churches? Candy's temperament resisted any significant changes, and for her, the situation didn't quite warrant a drastic move. Greg, having studied his wife through the years, understood her temperament and expressed his concern for her feelings. Nonetheless, he knew his priority was to have the entire family in a church that met their spiritual needs.

He told Candy, with grace and mercy, that though she was struggling with the move, he felt strongly that they must change churches right away. Seeing how much this meant to him and understanding her role as helpmate, Candy submitted to Greg in leaving their old church. Now they're thrilled with their new spiritual home. Greg played the role of Chief Tiebreaker ever so gently.

Wives don't expect or need to get their way in order to feel one with us. They only need to feel honored as fellow heirs and to genuinely sense that their thoughts and gifts have been put into play with ours. Deena said, "Gary always considers my viewpoint and really listens. He makes it a safe place for me to express my opinions, right or wrong. We'll talk about the issue, and ultimately he will make the decision. But I always know he's listened, and I've truly been heard."

ROMANCING YOUR WIFE

If there's any area in which we need to study our wives to serve them better, it's here. Romance inspires her and brings feelings of intimacy to the surface.

Ask a guy what romance is, however, and he'll mumble something about a candlelight dinner or a bouquet of roses. It's more than that. It's knowing what sparks her romantic motors. For some, it will be stuffed animals. For others, it's the *j* word—jewelry.

Don't ask us why. No man alive really understands the big deal about jewelry. If you tell us you do, we'll call you a liar. The best we can do is shrug our shoulders and ask her which one she likes. She'll squeal like a schoolgirl when you buy her those eighteen-carat gold earrings.

If we can put a guy spin on this, romance is serious business for women. A woman going through marriage without romance feels like a man who goes through life without sex. Much of the color of life disappears, and everything turns to gray. We must study our wives because we need to find out what she thinks is romantic, not what Julia Roberts or Jennifer Lopez thinks is romantic. Once we find out what the "it" is, we should sacrifice for her.

When we make sacrifices for our wives, they find it romantic. Rhonda told us:

Paul hates shopping with a passion. Before we married, I often went to the mall with my mom and sister for leisure and relaxation. We never spent much, but window-shopping relaxed us. We just enjoyed being together and eating a Häagen-Dazs chocolate ice cream cone as we meandered around. Paul couldn't understand our thought process in the least.

Our first few shopping trips together were disastrous, but then something changed in him. He knew that "mall crawling" was an enjoyable pastime for me, so he began to occasionally ask me whether I wanted to go to the mall to look around. He'll even top off our time with a visit to the ice cream store or cookie stand. Häagen-Dazs or two chocolate chip cookies with white cream in the middle. What a choice! We have so much fun.

When we're romancing our wives, we have to do what *they* think is fun and what *they* think is romantic. That shows we know them and care for them. Now, if your wife were to romance you, visiting a cookie stand wouldn't cut it at all, but sitting down on a Friday night on the couch with a bowl of popcorn and watching an old Cary Grant movie? Bingo. It's restful, and it's romantic. You're sharing the moment, sharing laughter, and sharing conversation. You're relating to each other, and that builds intimacy.

Women love it when you prove you know them, spring little surprises on them, and somehow show you're sacrificing to do things she loves.

That's romance.

But it's also romantic when you do things for her that she hates. We had a wife tell us she hates to wash silverware after meals. She would even scrub a crusty pan before tackling the silverware. Her husband knows this about her and will step in to wash silverware for her—even if he doesn't have time to wash the sink full of dishes.

Why is doing for her what she hates romantic to a woman? It proves you know her and have an intimate relationship with her.

Cheryl told us this story: "Sometimes I don't want to do the mundane things like grocery shopping alone. It's not one of Rod's favorite things either. But he goes with me if I ask, and he makes it fun just because we're together. And there's been more than one classical concert he's suffered through with me."

Do you sense the romance here?

We do.

Questions for Reflection and Discussion

1. As fully as you can, how would you describe your wife's essence—what she's all about? How does this compare to your own essence?

2. To what extent can you identify with the experiences of any of the couples mentioned in this chapter?

3. In each of the following arenas in marriage, analyze how well you have allowed for your wife's essence. In what practical and significant ways can you do so even more?
   —your wife's career development
   —making major purchases
   —determining where to live
   —finding a place of worship

4. What are the most effective things you can do to keep the flame of romance alive in your marriage?

learning how to make the right pitch

Raising children garners little status in our society. You don't see warm-and-fuzzy films these days about hard-working mothers who are there for the kids, day in and day out. In the last few years, we've heard the term "soccer moms" bandied about, which sounds patronizing at best and derogatory at worst. It's as though these carpooling mothers have nothing better to do than stand on the sidelines and cheer while their kids bunch up around a soccer ball.

Raising the next generation is a draining pastime and not a "career" many aspire to. When Brenda left the medical field to become a stay-at-home mom, she went from being a registered nurse, which enjoys high social status, to being a caretaker of children, which is about as low on the totem pole as you can go. At first, this change was a bit hard on Brenda's self-esteem. As I watched her bravely adjust, I wondered, *What can I do to lighten her load? If she won't have the respect of the crowd, can I at least make the task of raising our kids less draining?*

TIME TO PITCH IN

To help Brenda, I realized I had to pitch in as Chief Caregiver whenever and wherever possible. I left the house early each weekday, so I wasn't going to be much help there, but on Sunday mornings, there was no reason why I couldn't get Jasen ready for church. This meant feeding him some cereal, cleaning up after him, and accompanying him to his blue-walled bedroom, where I dressed him. Then we marched together to the bathroom, where I watched him brush his teeth while I combed his hair and scrubbed his apple-cheeked face.

Then came our daughter Laura. Little girls may be made of sugar and spice and everything nice, but what they wear isn't nice at all. Dads have problems with buttons and pinafores and buttons and sweaters and buttons and tights and buttons and shoes and buttons and necklaces.

And did I mention all the buttons?

On top of that, everything had to match. No exceptions, Brenda informed me. I got with the program.

Sure, picking up the slack for Brenda on weekend mornings was a good start, but I knew I had to do more than that. I had to become her equal as a caregiver. She had to *know* I was able to slip equally into her role at a moment's notice, or she'd feel uncomfortable depending on me. If she were sick, I wanted her to lie restfully in bed and get better without worrying that her world was collapsing around her.

If she wanted to leave town with a friend for the weekend, Brenda had to know she wasn't risking our children's health and safety with her decision. She's a nurturer, remember? She had to know they'd be dressed right, fed right, and loved right. It wasn't long before I had the basics down cold.

Those basics served me well until the day little Laura did the unthinkable—she grew hair. Hair as straight as a string. To a mother that translates to only one thing: curling irons. I took one look at the curling iron and knew it was time to drop out of servant school. "A man's got to know his limitations," I said to myself. To Brenda, I simply said, "I don't do hair."

But soon Sunday mornings were a mess again. To arrive at church on time, we had to leave the house by 9:45 A.M. I'd work my tail off to meet our EDT, bathing and feeding and dressing everything in sight. Invariably, I'd have us ready to go at the appointed time. Brenda, however, was not a morning person, especially on Sundays, which she viewed as her one day of the week to take her time getting out of bed. No matter how early we set the alarm, we'd come to 9:45 with Brenda just getting around to curling Laura's hair. I'd stand in the kitchen with my arms crossed and foot tapping, glancing at my watch and glaring at Brenda as she curled and twirled.

We've all been there, right? All too often, we left the house fighting, and we were in no mood to worship as we entered the church.

I knew I'd reached a fork in the road: I could either pray for patience…or learn to curl hair. Finding the necessary patience would be a stretch, even for God. So I went with the irons.

With big hands and clunky knuckles, I knew I was in over my head from day one. Laura liked the new arrangement even less than I did, since I twisted her hair in unsightly ways *and* burned her ears. Ouch! Whenever I rounded the corner with a curling iron in my hand, she'd scream, "I want Mommy to do it! I want Mommy to do it!"

I singed some skin on Laura's ears over the months, but I felt pretty pleased with my developing skills. After all, I was a guy used to hammers and wrenches in my hands, not curling irons. Brenda mentioned a few times that my efforts weren't up to her standards, but I shrugged it off. I noticed that many parents didn't even bother to drag a comb through their daughter's hair before church. On my worst days, my meager skills still easily placed Laura in the upper fiftieth percentile.

An annoying pattern soon developed at 9:45, however. Jasen, Laura, and I would be standing in the kitchen, fully dressed down to our shoes and jackets, waiting for Brenda to finish so we could step into the garage and get in the car. Sweeping into the kitchen at 9:47, Brenda would take one look at Laura and gasp. Then she'd rush her back upstairs to start all over on her hair.

I was ticked! "What are you doing?" I demanded. "She looks good enough! You're being picky. You *know* how much it means to me to get to church on time."

After a couple events like this, I got so angry I stopped curling for a while. I told myself there were only a handful of fathers in this world who knew how to curl hair, but Brenda didn't appreciate it one bit.

We went round and round on this stupid hair curling for a number of weeks. Then something Brenda said clicked for me. "I want my kids to look the best they can possibly look," she said. "It honors God, and it honors them. That's important to me."

It honors God.

Uh-oh. She was dragging God into the conversation. What else could I do but honor this conviction? I had to set the bar higher, and while I hated the thought, I challenged myself. "If every fourteen-year-old girl in America can curl her own hair and make it look great, then there's no reason a thirty-year-old man can't do the same."

To upgrade my curling-iron skills, I enrolled in Brenda's College of Beauty. Practice makes perfect. In a few weeks under Brenda's close supervision, I upped my skill level to the point where I could nominally meet her standards. I knew I'd finally arrived one fine Sunday when we ran into a friend named Jeannie in the church foyer, who exclaimed, "Laura, your hair looks so good! Your mommy must have spent hours on it this morning."

Proud Papa just beamed.

SHE SAYS, SHE SAYS

Is it fair that our wives set the performance standards when we've already traveled the extra mile and pitched in around the house? Shouldn't she just count her blessings and be thankful for what she has?

We need to step inside our wives' Nikes for a moment. Why did they choose these standards in the first place? Because what they view as "the right way" is rooted in their essence. This is how Lisa explains it:

Tom has learned to put diapers on the same way I like to see diapers put on. I know this sounds funny, but I'm very picky about the way I diaper Bethany. I don't want the diaper tabs cutting into her legs. The diaper also needs to be pulled up high enough so it covers her tummy but doesn't cut under her tummy. After watching me several times, Tom does it just the way I do it for her.

Clearly, nurturing is one of Lisa's gifts, and that particular gift is revealed in the details of putting on a Pampers. Whether it's curling hair, changing a diaper, or washing fragile glasses by hand in extra hot water, you respect your wife when you perform these chores to her satisfaction. Sure, they sound like small things, but they aren't small to your wife. Everything she does to nurture others is part of who she is, part of her essence. If we don't do things her way, we're disrespecting her and trampling oneness.

Lisa added this comment regarding her husband: "Tom has learned that I like towels folded a certain way. He let me show him how to do it, so when he does laundry, the towels come out in the way I like them to look."

Lisa's home is her nest and the center of her universe. This mother wants things just so in order to feel she's doing everything right. Wives universally feel the same way, and they feel this way for reasons we husbands may never objectively understand. That's okay. We need to treat our wives in ways that not only get the job done, but please them as well. (You know, like we handle our own things.) Let us illustrate this point with the following story:

In teaching a young couples' Sunday school class, I (Fred) challenged the fathers of toddlers to give their wives one night off per week. Several weeks later, I asked whether anyone had begun the practice. Bill proudly raised his hand, but he soon wished he hadn't. After I congratulated him, I turned to his wife, Cindy, and asked how she felt having a night off. I figured her response would inspire other husbands to take up the practice.

"Oh, I'm getting a night off each week all right, but it doesn't feel like it," she began. I could tell the topic revved her motors. "When I got back home that first night out, Bill was sitting in his big chair, watching a game on television. The kids were running all over the house. Not only was it already an hour past their bedtime, they weren't even bathed or in their pajamas. The house was a disaster. I could tell I'd be working for another hour to clean up following 'my break'!"

Several couples twittered, but Cindy wasn't finished. "Then Bill gave me a big smile and asked, 'Did you enjoy your night off?' He said it in that sly way that showed he expected to receive his reward later in bed. I wanted to cry because all I really wanted to do was go to bed and sleep. Instead, I had to get the kids bathed, get them into bed, and get the house halfway picked up."

"Did you talk to Bill about how you felt?" I probed.

"Yes, I talked to him about it, but things didn't change in subsequent weeks. I still come home to a messy house with unbathed kids. He thinks I should appreciate what he's doing, but we might as well put a stop to this. I think my life would be easier if I stayed home."

"Thanks, Cindy, for sharing your story," I said. Later that morning, I realized I didn't fully understand Cindy's point. Sure, Bill could spend a little more time off the big couch and with his kids, but he deserved an A for effort. At least the guy was trying.

Then a few months later, Brenda and I hired an unfamiliar baby-sitter. The kids were at least in bed when we returned well past their bedtime, but they were wide awake and talking across the hall to each other. Toys were strewn everywhere, and dirty dishes were scattered about the kitchen. It took half an hour for Brenda and me to put the house back in order, and by that time, I'd lost that "up" feeling that comes with dates. Cindy suddenly made perfect sense to me.

Her husband, Bill, had the mind-set that he was simply doing his job. He agreed to give Cindy a night off because he figured he should do it after hearing about it in our Sunday school class. If Bill had had a bondservant's mindset, bent fully on pleasing his "master," however, he would have had the kids sleeping and the house picked up so Cindy wouldn't have to "pay" for her night off. As a bonus, he could have done a couple loads of laundry to make the next day a bit easier for her.

When you implement this servant mind-set, there's one caution that I (Steve) want to share with you from experience: Be sure your *body* is reflecting the intentions you are setting forth with your words. Women can sense when you're going halfway. My wife, Sandy, pointed out to me that she heard my words of concern for her and my desires to help her and connect with her. She appreciated how I had stopped being in a hurry and started to listen and actually talk with her.

Yet, Sandy added, it was quite some time before my body reflected my words. I might have been there, but I looked as though I was ready for any out, any easy exit. When I finally engaged my body with my mind, she drew closer to me. Our relationship changed for the better.

So don't just say you love your wife; reflect that love with your body. It is always easier to talk a good game than to play a good game. Be sure your love is deeper and richer than your words.

Guys, a bondservant's mind-set may push you beyond learning new skills to gaining *a whole new focus*. Tina told us that though she and Tim don't entertain much, there's one thing Tim does for her when friends come over. "If they're my friends, Tim will serve by doing little things so I can focus on conversation with my friends. He'll offer refills on the drinks, take away the dishes, clean up the kitchen, and fill the dishwasher. This allows me to enjoy times with friends." You can be sure Tina feels closer, more intimate, with Tim when she sees him going out of his way to make her life easier.

How is it with you and your wife? Are you making the right pitch?

Questions for Reflection and Discussion

1. What have you found to be the most significant things you can do to help lighten your wife's workload at home?

2. In what areas do you think you might be needlessly violating your preferences for how she likes things done at home?

enjoy serving with passion

I can truly imagine that a bondservant who loved his master not only served, but he served with a light heart. He knew he was helping the master he loved. He loved to see his master's face brighten when he entered his presence. He lived for the moments when his master said, "My dear brother, I don't know what I would do without you."

And his master was just as irreplaceable in the bondservant's *own* heart. He studied his master, planned for him, and sought to be his great joy. Though he had few rights, he was content nevertheless. His deepest passion was his work, spending six days a week doing what he loved. His service wasn't work; it was his joy.

CAN YOU DELIGHT IN THIS?

Is your marriage a delight to you—or is your career the only thing that charges your engines? Do you exist in marriage for your wife, or does she exist for you? What in life is the focus of your greatest passion?

On the eve of their wedding, Brad told his wife, "I just want to make something very clear between us. My job will always come first, and you need to know that going in." That statement clearly revealed where Brad's passion lies.

The following open-book quiz is meant to give you something to think about over the next few days. Ask yourself:

- Does your wife's face brighten when you enter the room? Does she rise to greet you with a kiss?

- Has your wife said to you lately, "If you die, I could never remarry. Who could replace you? No one could ever match your love for me."
- Does she long for your embrace and love to chat with you?
- When her dreams have been scattered, is it your heart she seeks or does she turn to her closest friends?
- Do you guard her convictions and the treasures of her soul even when she's out of sight?

What kind of answers did you come up with? Is your wife your first love? Is oneness your passion? If I asked your wife, would her answers match yours? For extra credit, take a run at this one. Imagine that God offered you the two options below. Which would you choose?

Option 1: Working twelve hours a day for two years in the business of your dreams, a commitment that would quadruple your income.

Option 2: Working twelve hours a day for two years to passionately live out a bondservant's heart when you're at home, an effort that would quadruple your wife's joy.

Be honest—or at least be willing to consider each option. If you're chasing after the next rung up the corporate ladder, you've misappropriated your passion. If you're willing to become a bondservant to your wife, you are worthy of your Lord's daughter.

Let's face it. If the passion's not there in your marriage, you won't find much oneness. Sure, you're comfortable with your wife, and she's the best friend you have. As a mother, you may think she's matchless. She may still knock your socks off when she slips into a sundress. You can no longer imagine living life without her. Just what do these feelings show? Many men feel these things, but such sentiments don't reveal that you've necessarily done anything more than love *you* in the marriage.

Both your passion for oneness and your passion for serving show that you love *her*. It brings joy to *her* journey. (How exactly does this work? I'm trying to say that you need to love your wife as yourself in a different way from a different angle, from the angle of motives.) If the passion's not there, you need to find it. But if it's there, your motives for serving your wife will be true.

WITHOUT EXPECTING PRAISE?

Barry and I were discussing mutual submission when he admitted, "Fred, I'm trying to build servanthood into my marriage, but I'm having a problem. Yesterday, for instance, I fixed supper, changed a diaper, and cleaned the bathrooms."

"Sounds good."

"But Shelley didn't say anything! When I asked her whether it was too much to say thank you, we ended up having a big fight. What happened?"

What happened is that Barry asked his wife whether she noticed. Sure, we all enjoy a pat on the back, but sometimes that's not going to be forthcoming. Can you do things for your wife without receiving any "extra credit," an appreciative nod, or even a quick "Thanks"?

What's your motive for helping her?

I remember when Rebecca, our third child, was born. I had recently been in a car wreck and had broken my hand. Result: I was in a battle with an insurance company. Rebecca's birth happened to fall during the busiest part of my fiscal year, but I still labored to help Brenda with all of Rebecca's diapers and baths and feedings. I even took on kitchen patrol after dinner while Brenda fed the baby. All this extra work left me tired, very tired. My hand hurt, and the two older kids needed extra attention from me since Mom was busy with Rebecca.

Still, I sucked it up and helped Brenda as much as humanly possible. Problem is, I wore my service like a badge, practically demanding trumpet blasts and salutes from Brenda. As I recall, the Medal of Honor wasn't forthcoming.

I had to remind myself I was helping Brenda *just for the sake of helping her.* I had to tell myself that the bondservant's primary purpose was to release his wife to live life and fully blossom. It was the right thing to do, whether she acknowledged it or not. I was doing all those things out of love, right?

Tom watched his young daughter, Bethany, as his wife, Allison, joined some friends for a Girls' Day Out—shopping and lunch. Allison was gone until the early afternoon.

When she arrived home, she invited a girlfriend to come in. They discovered that Bethany was quietly taking her nap, and upon closer inspection, Allison could smell that Bethany had been given a bath while she was gone. While Bethany continued to sleep, Allison and her girlfriend Paula sat in the living room and chatted. Tom joined them at times and made Allison's friend feel welcome by not turning on the television for the football game.

When Bethany woke up from her nap while Allison and Paula were talking, Tom immediately jumped up and retrieved her. He held her close as he walked into the kitchen to warm up a bottle for her.

"That day was so refreshing for me," said Allison. "Tom gave up his whole Saturday so I could have time with my friends. He went beyond the call of duty when he gave Bethany a bath. I felt so proud in front of Paula that I truly had a husband who loved me and was willing to do many things for me." When love is our motive, going beyond the call of duty becomes our norm.

PAYING THE PRICE FOR SOMETHING GREAT...

As the Labor Day weekend approached one year, Brenda heard that our favorite Christian speaker would be appearing in—of all places—tiny Hazelton, Iowa. She was an undercover missionary in a repressive African state, and she prayed six hours a day. As you'd expect, her stories of God's mercy and grace were always mesmerizing. Brenda loved to hear her speak, and when this lady prayed with you, whole new worlds seemed to open.

We've often crossed state lines and driven many miles to hear this missionary speak, so learning that she was in the Iowa countryside sounded too good to be true. Saturday was a daylong women's seminar; the Sunday schedule included morning and evening services open to everyone.

We mapped out a plan. Since Brenda's mom had been sick, Brenda wanted to attend the Saturday sessions, then return home and grab the two youngest kids before driving to Moline to care for her mom. On Sunday, I planned to take our two oldest children, Jasen and Laura, to hear this great woman. We would reunite at our Des Moines home on Monday evening for the start of the workweek and school. I wouldn't see Brenda during this three-day holiday weekend.

If you imagine an equilateral triangle, Des Moines would be in the lower left, Moline in the lower right, and Hazelton at the top. A two-and-a-half-hour drive lay between each point. Obviously, it would be silly to drive to Moline after the Sunday evening service. I'd get in at 1:00 A.M., only to sleep in and leave in the afternoon for the drive back to Des Moines. Driving an extra five hours just to spend six hours in Moline on Monday wasn't sensible. Besides, it would be harder for the kids to do their homework Monday at Grandma's.

Figuring that was the plan, I still threw the kid's homework in the car on Sunday morning, just in case. I had learned to keep all my options open. I never know what my love for Brenda might compel me to do.

On Sunday afternoon, I called Brenda and told her how well the Sunday morning service went with the African missionary. As for Brenda? She missed me. She loves the holidays and the family. She knew the extra drive from Hazelton to Moline to see her and her ailing mother wasn't sensible, but she sure wished I could be with her on Monday. Hoping against hope, she threw out a feeble argument, saying, "I know it's not much time together, but it's better than nothing. Mom would love to see you, and so would the kids. But mostly, I just miss you."

I missed her, too, but I didn't want to go. Who wanted to drive 150 miles after the Sunday-night church service? And then another 150 miles in holiday traffic on Monday? The more I thought about, the more I liked the idea of sleeping in my own bed until 9 A.M. I'd have the rest of the day to catch up on things around the house. I wanted Jasen and Laura to have a good day with their homework, and I didn't want to spend the extra twenty dollars on gas and another twenty dollars on fast food. I could think of so many reasons…

The Sunday-night service ended late. Then we got to talking and talking and talking with friends, and before I knew it, the time was 11 P.M. Time to go home.

Then I literally approached a fork in the road: One turn would have me home in my comfortable bed in Des Moines, the other turn would take me to Moline in two and a half hours. As Yogi Berra said, "When you come to a fork in the road, take it."

As I came to the fork, I grabbed my cell phone to call Brenda and wish her a good night. She sounded tired and sleepy, but she did say, "Gee, I sure miss you."

I took the fork to Moline. I couldn't help myself, but even then I chided myself for being a fool, even exiting twice to turn back toward Des Moines. What drew me on to Moline? Simply this: How many wives married twenty years still miss their husbands this way? Such love demands more than a sensible response.

It demands a crazy response.

When I rolled into Moline around 1:30 A.M., I was beat, and the kids were crabby. Brenda was long since dead to the world. Somehow, though, my zombielike babe stumbled out into the living room and into my arms for a sighing, "Oh, I've missed you. It's so good to have you back." How I live for these moments! Would I do it again? Oh, yeah!

This is every woman's desire. *You can settle for mediocrity, or you can pay the price for something great.* If you pay the price and meet the terms, a deep intimacy will overflow your lives together.

SOME FORLORN CONCLUDING THOUGHTS

I once received a newsletter from Focus on the Family that touches me to the core each time I read it. In this particular newsletter, James Dobson excerpted portions of his mother's diary. In the following section, Myrtle Dobson reflects upon her aloneness following the death of her husband, also named James Dobson:

One day I realized that he did not exist anymore. His name was removed from the church register. The bank took his name off our checks. Our home address was rewritten to include only my name. His driver's license was invalidated. Then I recognized that my name had changed, too. I had been proud to be Mrs. James C. Dobson, Sr. Now I was simply Myrtle Dobson. I was not *we* any longer. I became me or I. And I am alone. Inside I'm broken, sad, stunned, alone. My house has lost its soul. He is not here.

People have told me the first year is the hardest. It's been one year and three days since you died, and tonight I am *frantic* with longing for you. Oh, dear God! It's more than I can bear. The sobs make my heart skip beats. I cannot see the paper. My head throbs. The house is lonely and still. Visions of you have been as real as if you were here and had not left me. Today, I thanked God for letting an angel watch over me, but how desperately I missed you!

I moved into the smaller bedroom today. I wish you were here to share that room with me. There are precious memories there. When I was ill four years ago, you prayed for me in that bedroom during the midnight hours. You lay on the floor, agonizing in prayer for me. We both knew the Spirit was praying through you. Later, the Lord led us to a doctor who helped me find my way back to health. Oh, how I loved you. I love your memory today.

The first time I read this passage in Sunday school, I said, "I want my heart to be ripped apart and never recover when Brenda dies. Then I will know I was truly passionate for my marriage, and I will know I got everything out of marriage God intended for me to have."

Later that afternoon, a friend from class called to say, "Fred, I got that same letter last week from Focus on the Family. When I read those quotes from Mrs. Dobson, I remember thinking, 'I hope I'm never that close to my spouse that it would leave me that hurt.' Now I see I was wrong."

When I'm gone, I want Brenda to miss our prayers. I want her to miss our laughter. I want her to find no secrets where I had compromised her values in private. I want her to miss our bedtimes and to miss the person who defended her soul. I want her certain that her married years were the happiest years of her life, not the loneliest. I want her to enjoy this journey, and I will give my life away before it's taken.

Questions for Reflection and Discussion

1. At this time in your life, how would you rate your level of joy and passion in your marriage?

2. Make sure to ask yourself the questions mentioned early in the chapter:
   —Does your wife's face brighten when you enter the room? Does she rise to greet you with a kiss?
   —Has your wife said to you lately, "If you die, I could never remarry. Who could replace you? No one could ever match your love for me."
   —Does she long for your embrace, then chat with you?
   —When her dreams have been scattered, is it your heart she seeks or those of her closest friends?
   —Do you guard her convictions and the treasures of her soul, even when she's out of sight?

3. Is your wife truly your first love? Is oneness in marriage your passion?

4. Of the two options presented in this chapter, which would you honestly choose?
   —**Option 1:** Working twelve hours a day for two years on the business of your dreams, which would quadruple your income.
   —**Option 2:** Working twelve hours a day for two years passionately incorporating a bondservant's heart when you're at home (which would quadruple your wife's joy).

5. Are you settling for mediocrity in your marriage, or are you paying the price for something great? What exactly is that price in your marriage?

serving as spiritual leader

A bondservant in Israel was quick to defend his master's faith, the source of his master's strength. How better to show his love than to defend his master's love of God?

We, too, must defend the faith of our "master." As a devoted bondservant, we can provide some practical defenses for our wife's faith. As we've seen, when we serve, our wives can freely exercise their gifts. When we don't, they may not be able to find even ten measly minutes a day to read their Bibles.

As a leader and a bondservant, we believe we can do far more than a servant could ever dream of doing. We're called to set ourselves apart unto God, just as the words to many hymns and praise songs remind us: "I'm Yours," "I'm not my own," "All I am belongs to You."

If we moved our lips to these words (notice, we didn't write *sing*), most of us would be lying. When we set ourselves apart, our lives truly aren't our own. If we live and breathe for God, we should live and breathe for her. Wasn't that the example Jesus set for us to follow?

> [Jesus], being in very nature God, did not consider equality with God
> something to be grasped, but made himself nothing, *taking the very*
> *nature of a servant,* being made in human likeness. And being found in
> appearance as a man, he humbled himself and became obedient to
> death—even death on a cross! (Philippians 2:6-8)

Christ came to do the will of the Father, not His own will. He came in pursuit of righteousness and on behalf of righteousness. We need to lead spiritually, like Christ, in our homes since spiritual oneness with her husband is every woman's desire. Too often, however, we hear women wistfully mourn for the oneness that has never been:

> I am consistent and fervent in my pursuit of God. Brian's lack in this area saddens me. I want him to love the Lord as much or more than I do. I want him to lead. I ache for the moment when he will say, "Let's pray together."

LEADING SPIRITUALLY: WHAT IT TAKES

When we're looking for something to do for our wives, many of us would rather lay a new bathroom floor than lay our hearts before her in prayer. We know how to lay floors. But lead spiritually? We don't even know where to start.

How does a husband go about leading spiritually like Christ in his home? You start by taking these six steps in your life:

1. Develop the Deepest Knowledge of God's Word

On one of our earliest dates, Brenda and I gathered with her cousins for an evening of singing and playing Bible trivia. These weren't your typical cousins. Since Brenda's father and three siblings all settled within a one-mile radius of each other, these nine cousins grew up as brothers and sisters. As little sisters so often do, Brenda's younger cousin Lyni took a keen interest in checking out this new beau.

Lyni giggled herself silly when I stumbled over the lines of the most common songs in the Christian songbook. *He's a real winner!* she was thinking. I guess she was right. I didn't know the words, and to add insult to injury, I couldn't carry a tune across the street in a bucket. As for Bible trivia, I needed a lifeline to get anything right!

As husbands, we can't leave things this way. How would it be if every time your wife wanted to talk about something she read in the Bible, you replied,

"Better ask Pastor Rick"? The most important thing I ever did was read the *One-Year Bible* (a type of Bible that takes a few verses from here and a few verses from there so you can read through the entire Bible in a year). Things didn't start to click for me until midway through the second year, when the windows of understanding suddenly flew open. I was reminded in Hosea 4:6, "My people are destroyed from lack of knowledge." I wasn't going to let that happen to me—or to my marriage.

Biblical knowledge brings security and establishes your leadership in your wife's heart. Patty told me, "Derek's greater knowledge of God's Word makes me feel secure. Derek will bring Scripture into a situation, and it brings a 'peace that passes all understanding.'"

Brenda says my knowledge of Scripture raises her level of respect for me. "I'm glad you have the greater knowledge of the Word because it helps me respect you and your decisions. I know I can trust you to do the best possible thing for the kids and me. The more I think about it, I don't know how a woman could see her husband as a spiritual leader if he isn't reading his Bible. Isn't a leader supposed to be setting an example?"

Yes, Regis, the answer is yes, and that's my final answer. I've talked to women who felt a deep ache in their hearts because of their husband's lack of biblical knowledge. Megan told me, "I guess I'm always the spiritual leader since I know much more about the Bible than Dan. That hurts. I yearn to follow Dan's spiritual lead."

Laziness in the area of Bible study will create a place of separation in your marriage, as this story from Arnette attests:

> For the first eight years of our marriage, we went to a Sunday school class for married couples. Brian and I were growing together spiritually then. We'd come home from church so pumped up about Christ that we'd sit in our driveway talking about what we had learned and forget all about lunch. We don't do that anymore. In fact, we don't go to Sunday school anymore, and I miss that. It seems like our spiritual lives are separate.

Separate spiritual lives make oneness impossible in a marriage.

2. Become the Best at Submitting to Scripture

No one in your home should be better at submitting to Scripture than you are. I once asked a marriage class, "What's the one thing that impresses you most about your husband?"

Betsy responded, "Mark is so good at submitting to Scripture. If he sees he's doing wrong, he gets right to it and changes direction." What could be more fitting? You must lead by example.

Hophni and Phinehas, the two sons of Eli, were priests, but they were also wicked men with no regard for the Lord. Neither would turn from their sin, even when confronted by Scripture. God is not pleased with spiritual leaders, or husbands, who harbor sin:

> At that time I will carry out against Eli everything I spoke against his family—from beginning to end. For I told him that I would judge his family forever because of the sin he knew about; his sons made themselves contemptible, and he failed to restrain them. (1 Samuel 3:12-13)

Jill said, "Allen is much quicker to submit to Scripture than I am. He's quick to fix anything in his life that he feels doesn't line up with Scripture. He has always been submissive to God's ways, and this makes me trust him and feel one with him." Again note the security this submission to Scripture brings to your realm. On the other hand, failing to deal with sin brings disorder, confusion, and fear. It tramples your wife's convictions and puts a stumbling block in the pathway of oneness.

Submitting your character to Scripture builds your wife's trust in you. This trust will return mercy to you. She'll give you the benefit of the doubt whenever your leadership is shaky. "Dan has always been amazingly committed to changing character flaws," said Lisa. "He's much better at this than I am. If there's something about him that I've asked him to fix but he's still making the same mistake, I know he isn't acting that way to bug me. I just assume he doesn't understand the scriptural mandate well enough. He'll always try, if he can understand the scriptural lesson."

After my (Steve) relationship with Sandy began to improve, we felt free to talk about the days when our marriage was anything but a marriage. She told me that through the tough times she was always hopeful for a great future together because of one thing: She knew I was up early reading Scripture and having a quiet time. That assured her that I was attempting to connect with God and would hopefully respond in a godly manner one day. I encourage you to awaken a bit earlier and start off your day with God. He will be waiting for you, and someone here on earth will probably be watching you.

3. Be the Most Comfortable with Worshiping at Home

We were created to worship. Worship and praise bring intimacy with the Lord and usher us quickly into His presence. Some fellows, however, tighten up just saying grace before dinner. Others become tongue-tied when asked to "please close us" following a couple's Bible study. When put on the spot to pray in public, they get as tight as a ballplayer charging a ground ball with the game on the line.

I (Fred) have been there, and I blamed it on my lack of experience praying in public. Yet the real reason I choked was that I didn't have enough practice praying in private! The key to deepening both my private and public prayer life was worship. I began by memorizing a few choruses and hymns. Then I began awaking early each day and walking down to the basement, where I sung softly to the Lord. (No way did I want my wife or kids to hear or see me, however.)

At first, I felt very uncomfortable, even though I knew I was alone. Pressing on, I reminded myself that the Lord loves to hear love songs sung to Him, and before long I found that these songs were opening my heart to deeper prayer. As prayer and songs became more comfortable for me to do in private, I became more comfortable praying anywhere. Eventually I even became leader of our church's intercession ministry. Given my beginnings, I'm amazed at what God has done.

If you're a spiritual leader, then no one in your home should be more comfortable with worship and prayer than you are. I've been known to belt out a song or two throughout the halls of my home. I'm not much of a crooner, but the kids seem to enjoy it. Perhaps that's why they seem to worship very freely. Your family needs you to feel comfortable leading them in prayer and song, which "avails much" in the sight of God. "Feeling funny" about it just doesn't cut it as an excuse.

You may have to start singing in the basement or in the car while you commute, but you can't chicken out when everyone is looking to you for spiritual leadership. The Holy Spirit is waiting for you to step up to the plate, and He'll be there to help you. That's a promise.

4. Be the Most Consistent in Your Prayer and Devotional Life

Not only must you be the most comfortable with prayer, you must be the most consistent. Consistency brings intimacy, and intimacy with the Lord brings life and truth. Without it, you'll have little fresh understanding with which to guide your family.

How consistent are you when it comes to praying? How consistently do you lead your family in a short Bible study and prayer time, called devotions in most households? Sure, no one's busier than you, but you must carve time from your busy day to lead the family in this area.

Your kids are watching your example. If you're not praying together as a family, then all your talk about God's being the center of your marriage and family is just that—talk. Make family prayer a priority. Be disciplined about following through. Model your faith with action steps and give your family someone to respect and something to connect with. As with the steps already mentioned, consistency brings trust, as Deena demonstrates with her story:

> Generally, I'm more regular with devotional times than Gene, but then it's part of my temperament to be driven and disciplined. This area is definitely a significant factor in our oneness, though. When Gene has been making himself available to God's Spirit through prayer, I am more trusting of him and more willing to give of myself to him.

There's a real feeling of security for me when I know that Gene is in touch with the Lord regularly. I don't know if he really understands how vital this is to me, but I'm very thankful!

The desire to form a soul connection with her husband is at the heart of every woman. Women *ache* if their husbands abandon this responsibility. Liza said that after she and Bob became Christians, they were encouraged again and again by their pastor to pray and read the Bible together. Bob refused, saying it was just too touchy-feely for him. She can only remember praying with him a few times in her marriage, and that only happened after she nagged him.

Liza had a hole in her heart, and she filled it by becoming involved in a prayer ministry at church. That's good, but it probably makes things worse at home because she also knows that neither Bob nor she is working on their prayer relationship right now. "This is probably why we've ended up like roommates," she says, "rather than husband and wife. I feel he resents my love for the Lord. At home in the evenings, he always does his own thing, excluding me. I have nothing else to do but learn about Christ on my own."

We interrupt this chapter for a pop quiz: Is there ever a time when prayer with your wife seems more desirable to you than sex? If not, your prayer life with her needs attention. As a leader, the goal is to not just be her *nearest* choice for prayer, but to be her *favorite* choice for prayer, the one who brings her the most strength and comfort.

In the Bible, when Hannah was deeply torn and distressed over her barrenness, where did she most want to pray? At the temple, where she might pray with or be blessed by the high priest:

Once when they had finished eating and drinking in Shiloh, Hannah stood up. Now Eli the priest was sitting on a chair by the doorpost of the LORD's temple. In bitterness of soul Hannah wept much and prayed to the LORD. . . .

Hannah replied, "I am a woman who is deeply troubled.... I have been praying here out of my great anguish and grief."

Eli answered, "Go in peace, and may the God of Israel grant you what you have asked of him."

She said, "May your servant find favor in your eyes." Then she went her way and ate something, and her face was no longer downcast. (1 Samuel 1:9-10,15-18)

Hannah left in faith, deeply satisfied by Eli's encouragement. God calls you to play Eli's role in your home when your wife is deeply distressed. You must be the one she yearns to pray with.

Recently, Brenda and I resigned as leaders of a prayer intercession group after four full years. We were certain God had called us away, yet Brenda became lonely and wracked with self-doubt, feeling estranged and cut adrift from this anchor. In years past, Brenda had always turned to me first, simply because "you're supposed to pray with your husband." But to really seek God and to walk away from prayer satisfied, she'd turn to her mother and her friends. Not anymore. This time, she came to me with her doubts, and that's all she's needed. We found the answer together, and like Hannah, Brenda is "no longer downcast."

5. Be the Quickest in the Family to Forgive and Ask for Forgiveness
No one in the family should be quicker to forgive than you. Forgiveness is the cornerstone of Christianity.

It doesn't come naturally to me, however. I prefer a less subtle policy of Mutual Assured Destruction! If someone launches ten missiles at me, in retaliation, I'll launch thirty just for good measure. Mercy? Forget it! I'd rather hang you on the wall until dawn. If you're like me, we needn't remain this way. Hebrews 5:1-2 says, "Every high priest...is able to deal gently with those who are ignorant and are going astray, since he himself is subject to weakness."

Mary Beth told me that her husband, James, has always been the quickest in the family to forgive. "Many times he doesn't even let me finish asking him for forgiveness," she said. "I've learned to ask for forgiveness by following his example. When James asks forgiveness, it makes me feel humble and immediately crumbles any walls. I feel treasured by him when that happens."

I (Steve) host a weekday call-in radio show called *New Life Live* with Drs. Paul Meier, Henry Cloud, and John Townsend. Since we handle many calls each day, it's easy to spot a common theme that may arise. One theme we've been hearing a lot is the one about blaming and judging a wife who "just is not enough" for a man. It's amazing the mental gyrations that men will go through *not* to take responsibility. One day we commented that the worst-selling T-shirt we could market would say, "It was my fault." No guys would buy it! But a T-shirt like that could have quite an impact if the wearer believed it.

Here's an idea for another T-shirt message: "You are not to blame for my problems." Rather than wait for that T-shirt to land in stores, we need to believe what those shirts would say. When we believe these truths, we're humbled and ready to do what we need to do, which is to ask for forgiveness.

You probably know that every computer has a reboot key that enables you to start all over. Everything cranks up as if it were doing it for the first time. For individuals, the reboot key is called confession. Confession realigns the person with God and removes the stain of denial. The reboot key for a relationship is asking for forgiveness. It places the relationship back at ground zero. It does not mean that the forgiveness will be granted, but at least from the point of forgiveness the relationship has an opportunity to flourish. If you and your marriage are stuck, consider the most humbling thing you can do, which is to ask your wife to forgive you.

6. Set the Spiritual Thermostat in Your Home

Consciously or not, you'll set the spiritual temperature of your marriage. But there's a strange thing about the thermostat: You're only allowed to turn it up. Let me (Fred) explain.

Brenda's Christian heritage was deep, crafted over many generations. Her family lived the Word of God even when it hurt. Me? I went to church and Vacation Bible School as a youngster, so I wasn't thoroughly void of a Christian background, but there wasn't an unequivocal respect for the Most High God in our home. Sometimes, just for kicks, my father sang "Hosanna, Banana, Hosanna in the highest" in church. My parents bought birth-control pills for their daughters, despite their awareness of biblical ethics.

Later, even after professing a solid conversion to Christ, Dad approached me during my courtship days and said, "Son, you can't marry Brenda unless you sleep with her first. Sex is too important in marriage for you to risk getting a frigid girl." No, Dad wasn't going to let the Word of God cramp our lifestyle. Christianity was a philosophy, not a way of life. Our American culture had a far greater impact on where Dad stood regarding the tough moral issues of the day.

So I had a choice to make. I either had to ramp up to Brenda's level or drag her down to mine. I chose to raise my spiritual thermostat.

Here's what happens, however, when you turn the thermostat down. Pete and Mary once stopped me after class to discuss a little problem they were having. It seems that Pete's first wife rented X-rated movies and found it "fun" for them to watch together before they had sex. Upshot: Pete was used to watching sexy movies.

Mary, his fiancée, said this had caused a rift in their relationship. Pete would drop by her apartment to watch a recently released Blockbuster video together, but even the most popular movies had some pretty racy sex scenes. "I'm feeling more and more uncomfortable with this," said Mary. "When it gets steamy, I tell Pete we need to turn it off or fast-forward ahead, but he turns angry, arguing that we've invested good money in the rental and it's a waste of money not to see the whole movie. So I go off into the kitchen to do some work while he finishes watching."

She got a tear in her eye and looked down. "I don't feel these movies are good for us," she said. "I've asked him to stop for my sake, but he won't. We usually make it a practice to pray together before he goes home, but after these movies, I feel dirty and cheap. These movies are coming between us."

Of course, Pete was embarrassed when I asked him for his side of the story. To his credit, Pete asked me what he should do. I told him to follow Mary's lead and not rent the sexy videos, and he agreed to do so. He ramped it up to her level. What if he hadn't? Mary's faith and convictions would have been shelled every time they rented a movie.

It's easy to see why God forbids husbands to lower the spiritual temperature. Doing so tramples oneness. Paul taught that when personal convictions clash, the leader ought to submit his rights for the sake of unity and Christian growth. Pete made the wise choice in this category of their marriage.

Increasing the spiritual thermostat is even more important in a case like mine, where Brenda's spiritual temperature was higher in nearly every category. If I didn't ramp up, every time she'd turn around she'd be forced by my leadership to break her convictions. Oneness would be DOA.

BEWARE THE CHILL!

Setting the thermostat lower puts a chill on your marriage, a chill that can have devastating affects. A number of years ago, my friend Jorge became head chef at a pricey private club in Des Moines. Things were going well. Membership was rising because of his culinary skills, and his family was putting down deeper roots in the church. I noticed that his teens became active in the youth group. But while his family members' spiritual temperatures bubbled, Jorge's remained tepid.

With no warning, Jorge announced he was moving on to another cooking gig. When I asked him why, he answered, "In my field, it's important to move every five years or so. It's just an unwritten rule. I was looking around and was offered a position at the Cloister resort in the Golden Isles off Georgia." My heart sank.

"Jorge, you can't do this. I've vacationed there off and on for fifteen years. There are no churches like ours here in Brunswick for your family. I know.

I've looked. Your kids are connected in this youth group, and they're growing strong in the Lord. Your wife is happier than she's ever been. What about their spiritual lives?"

"They'll be okay," he shrugged. "Besides, as I said, it's important for my career. It doesn't look good to stay in one place too long."

I fought back. "God isn't limited by some silly rule. If you put Him first and stay around here, you'll do just fine. You're doing fine already."

We argued on, but it was no use. Jorge moved on, dropping their thermostat in the process. Within months, his wife called us in tears. She was trapped in a spiritual desert, dying of thirst. They couldn't find a decent youth group, and she feared the kids had fallen in with some questionable characters. Soon thereafter, their son was jailed for a criminal offense. A while later, their daughter died in a car wreck. I surmised she'd been drinking with her friends.

We husbands are leaders, and people are counting on us. Let's keep the heat turned up! After all, it's the lukewarm believer who disgusts our Lord— He said He would spit them out of His mouth (Revelation 3:16). We can be many things, but being lukewarm should never be an option for a man who wants to lead.

Questions for Reflection and Discussion

1. Can you identify any ways in which you do not yet fully belong to God?

2. How would you evaluate your knowledge of God's Word?

3. How would you evaluate your consistent obedience of God's Word?

4. How would you evaluate your consistency in personally worshiping God and in personal prayer?

5. How would you evaluate your ability to forgive and to ask for forgiveness in your family?

6. What commitments can you honestly make that can make you a better spiritual leader in your home?

minding your kids' spiritual growth

These commandments that I give you today are to be upon your hearts. Impress them on your children. Talk about them when you sit at home and when you walk along the road, when you lie down and when you get up.

Deuteronomy 6:6-7

When you get right down it, men and women marry because they want to have children. Sure, some couples marry for companionship and inform friends and relatives that they harbor no desire for crumb-crunchers. Some couples marry for what we call "contribution." Whether it's through time, money, or work, these couples make a joint contribution to this world and to the kingdom of God. But in the end, the vast majority of couples marry because they want to have children, and those of us who are parents cannot imagine life without our sons or daughters around. We wouldn't think of paddling along the river of life without 2.4 kids sitting in our canoe.

As the father in the home, how will you and your wife raise the next generation? What standards will you choose? Dr. Dobson or Dr. Spock?

Of course, there's more than one way to parent a child, so it helps big time when you and your wife are on the same page of James Dobson's *The New Dare to Discipline*. So rather than tell you our answers for raising our children, we'd rather share *how to think* like a servant when choosing the child-rearing standards for your homes. With this mind-set, you'll easily find that same page together.

THE DANGER OF ARROGANCE

Your child-rearing responsibilities are a chief responsibility for you as the family's spiritual leader—and an area very susceptible to arrogance and blindness in part because of its importance. For instance, you may recall my response to Brenda when she questioned the way I drafted Jasen and Laura into my Christian Boot Camp. This is the even-handed way I handled things: "Listen, I'm responsible for teaching my children all about God, so I'm going to do it my way. In God's eyes, the buck stops with me, so I don't think you have a right to say anything."

Let's just agree that while I was moving in the right direction, I was acting like the proverbial bull in the china shop. I shattered a few dishes in my aggressive attempt to instill spiritual values in my children, but I was doing it for the right *reason*. I knew the buck stopped with me when it came to raising my children in the "fear and admonition" of the Lord.

And because the buck stops with us, there's no area in your marriage where you'll feel more confident about casting the deciding vote as Chief Tie-breaker. You probably should do so at times, especially if your spiritual temperature is higher than your wife's. Christ never backed away from the truth for the sake of peace, though He knew His convictions would take Him to the Cross. He came in pursuit of righteousness and on behalf of righteousness. That's our call too.

That said, there's also no area where you'll feel more justified in ignoring your wife or in being less sensitive to her essence. This position is dangerous because, when it comes to deciding how to raise the children, playing Chief Tiebreaker at the wrong time can cripple oneness more severely than anything else can. Why is that?

First, so much is riding on these particular decisions for God. He wants you to raise godly children, and He knows the message of salvation passes down to them most easily when the parents are one. Speaking of husbands and wives through His prophet Malachi, God says, "Has not the Lord made them one? In flesh and spirit they are his. And why one? Because he was seeking godly offspring. So guard yourself in your spirit, and do not break faith with the wife of your youth. 'I hate divorce,' says the LORD God"(Malachi 2:15-16).

It's difficult to pass the baton of God's truth after a divorce in the family. While I loved Dad and idolized him in many ways, deep down I knew he'd traded his family life for a mistress. He had betrayed me.

Later, after he was saved, Dad attempted to talk to me about the Lord. Do you think I had any time for him or his God? He'd crushed me and left my heart for dead. He had forfeited his right to be heard, and he might as well have taken ice picks to my ears and gouged out my eardrums. That was how strongly his divorce affected me.

Second, there's so much riding on these decisions for your wife. Raising and nurturing godly children is something very close to her heart, which means any arrogance here on your part will result in the severest trampling. As a spiritual leader, you're both a servant to God and a servant to your wife. God's holy essence sets the terms of oneness with Him. Your wife's essence sets the terms of oneness with her. You should never be more diligent in seeking out the terms, and meeting them, than when choosing how to raise your children.

NO LONE RANGERS!

Men often feel they have the authority to make these child-rearing decisions alone. We don't. The terms of oneness must constrain our rights. Listen to Susie as she shares this story:

> When my son Jimmie was three years old, I came home late one
> evening after running errands and purchasing a trunk-load of groceries
> at Albertson's. My son rushed to the door to greet me and to tell me all
> about the movie *Rambo.* He had spent the previous two hours with his
> father (my husband, Rick) watching Sylvester Stallone shoot up people.
>
> I frowned. Then the next week I came home from errands to learn
> that Jimmie had been watching *Die Hard.* A few months later, Rick

asked me point-blank why Jimmie clearly had a problem with violence! Then he blamed me because I had let him watch *Peter Pan*.

Hello? Rick was giving me a hard time about *Peter Pan* and he was letting Jimmie watch these violent R-rated movies? I overheard Rick tell Jimmie, "It doesn't matter what you watch because it has no effect on your relationship with God."

Becoming nine years old turned out to be a particularly hard time for Jimmie. Sometimes in tears, he would tell me how he struggles "to be good, but it is very hard to be a Christian with Dad, because he wants me to watch television with him, and it's always the stuff you don't like, Mom. He always gets mad at me if I won't watch these shows with him."

Rick, for his part, would tease him and pressure him to "be normal." If I ask Rick about these things, he simply makes it harder on Jimmie the next time they are alone together. With Jimmie on the brink of adolescence, I'm finding it harder and harder for him to follow my rules, especially because Rick doesn't have any.

Clearly, Rick doesn't believe that watching violent R-rated movies is harmful to his own Christian belief system. He feels he has the right to set his spiritual standard anywhere he chooses to set it.

But Rick doesn't have that right. Watching violent R-rated movies might not have been any big deal to him before marriage (although it should have been), but that practice became sin in the context of his relationship with Susie. Remember what the apostle Paul said:

> Instead, make up your mind not to put any stumbling block or obstacle in your brother's way. As one who is in the Lord Jesus, I am fully convinced that no food is unclean in itself. But...if your brother is distressed because of what you eat, you are no longer acting in love. Do not by your eating destroy your brother for whom Christ died....

Let us therefore make every effort to do what leads to peace and to
mutual edification. Do not destroy the work of God for the sake of
food. All food is clean, but it is wrong for a man to eat anything
that causes someone else to stumble. It is better not to eat meat or drink
wine or to do anything else that will cause your brother to fall. (Romans
14:13-15,19-21)

In sitting his son down to watch *Rambo* and *Die Hard,* Rick was sinning
against Susie because he was trampling her convictions. He was also sinning against God by flaunting his position of authority at the expense of his
heavenly calling to pursue oneness. For us husbands, there are always more
important things than exerting our authority—things like growth in that tender, fragile relationship called marriage.

And when it comes to children, two things help them flourish and
become the individuals God wants them to be. One is consistency. There
are few things worse than one parent operating off one set of values while the
other sabotages those principles. You must agree on your core values and present them in a unified front to your kids.

The second important concept in raising kids is teamwork. Give up your
individual rights and the blatant exertion of authority and be your wife's
teammate. Help her. Share duties. Pitch in. Never undermine your wife's
position by making yourself look more important. Help your children learn
to honor her as their mother and to appreciate the value of a woman. This
bedrock principle will have a tremendous impact on your kids' futures, especially their marriages.

In my (Steve's) marriage, I've done one thing right. I've never had a secret
with my daughter that I told her not to share with her mother. I've never
asked her not to tell her mom when I allowed her to have candy right after
she consumed a hot fudge sundae at Ruby's. I never allowed her to see me
give my wife a dirty look behind her back. I've tried to honor Sandy and her
position.

You can do the same. If you haven't up to this point, you can start by admitting the problem to your kids and assuring them that, from now on, you and their mom are a solid team. Then allow them to see you live that out in front of them.

WATCH OUT FOR DOUBLE VISION

Brenda and I (Fred) began teaching premarriage classes about fifteen years ago, and Jordan and Kim attended one of our earliest sessions. We weren't quite so busy back then, so we sometimes met with couples outside of class. We took a special interest in Jordan and Kim—for me, because Jordan had been the starting fullback on the University of Kansas football team, and for Brenda, because Kim was the daughter of a respected family in our church.

Kim, as you would expect, was raised with high Christian standards. Her family didn't drink alcohol, watched little television, and was at church whenever the doors opened. When her father spoke, we hung on his every word out of respect for the way he has raised his children.

One evening, Brenda and I went to dinner with Jordan and Kim. Settling into our booth with a plate of nachos and cheese, Jordan regaled me with stories of the good ol' days at KU. He'd been president of his Fellowship of Christian Athletes chapter and one of the people who led other Christian athletes in a Bible study every Tuesday night.

Almost as an aside, he chuckled when he said, "Yeah, playing football helped, but I was even more popular as the organizer of our fraternity's keggers that we held every Saturday night. We'd really get bombed on those nights." He kept talking, but my mind became jammed in a feedback loop as I pondered the contradictory images he'd just painted.

After refills of our drinks and a fresh bowl of chips, we turned the conversation to child rearing. After Brenda and I shared a few of our thoughts about our own kids, Jordan turned to Kim, patted her cheek, and said, "Of course, sweetie, we'll never keep our children as sheltered as you were. I want our kids to be well rounded."

Jordan feels he has the authority to make this decision unilaterally, but he doesn't. The terms of oneness defined by Kim's essence must be met, or she'll have her convictions trampled every day for the rest of their child-raising years. The terms of God's holy essence must also constrain Jordan, or his one-ness with God will suffer as well.

GOD'S WORDS ARE SIMPLE

We have a question for you, the spiritual leader of your family: Since when does well-roundedness trump holiness in the kingdom of God? Have we missed something? Last time we checked, God didn't care a whit about what we view as normal. His words to His leaders are simple, and they're always the same: "'And now this admonition is for you, O priests. If you do not listen, and if you do not set your heart to honor my name,' says the LORD Almighty, 'I will send a curse upon you, and I will curse your blessings'" (Malachi 2:1-2).

So what does God want from us? He wants passion in our service as fathers to the children He has entrusted to us. "I know your deeds, that you are neither cold nor hot. I wish you were either one or the other! So, because you are lukewarm—neither hot nor cold—I am about to spit you out of my mouth" (Revelation 3:15-16). His attitude here is pretty clear, so we can't be lukewarm in our efforts to raise our kids to know and serve the Lord. If we as leaders are to please God, we must lead our families according to this ques-tion: *How holy can we be?* That alone honors God's essence.

Raising our children to be "normal" or "well rounded" shouldn't be our primary concern because such goals aren't God's primary concern. In fact, God told us we're *supposed* to look a little strange to the world:

Therefore, since Christ suffered in his body, arm yourselves also with the same attitude, because he who has suffered in his body is done with sin. As a result, he does not live the rest of his earthly life for evil human desires, but rather for the will of God. For you have spent enough time in the past doing what pagans choose to do—living in debauchery, lust, drunkenness, orgies, carousing and detestable idolatry. They think it strange that you do not plunge with them into the same flood of dissipation, and they heap abuse on you. (1 Peter 4:1-4)

When deciding how to raise the kids, here's a simple rule of thumb. If you have the higher spiritual temperature, your wife must come up to your level. If she has the higher spiritual temperature, you must come up to her level. In doing so, oneness will flourish, and your children will be given a consistent picture of the standards you require.

One final note: Your kids have secret powers they can unleash to battle the things of this world. You have them as well, but they might have been neglected because no one helped you develop them. Even so, help your children develop the secret power of the Holy Spirit in their lives. Help them discover the power in spiritual gifts, talents, skills, and ability. Help them also learn the power available to them in the truth of Scripture.

Don't allow these powers to stay secret. Work as a team with your wife to help your children grow into the incredible kids God intends them to be.

Questions for Reflection and Discussion

1. How closely do you and your wife work together in parenting your children? How well do you practice teamwork?

2. How do you think you could help your children develop the secret power of the Holy Spirit in their lives? How specifically could you help them develop the power of their spiritual gifts? How could you help them learn the secret power available to them through the truth of Scripture?

get rid of those sins

As spiritual leader in your home, what's your attitude toward your position? Countless men think their title of spiritual leader places them above scrutiny, and they refuse any kind of confrontation by their wives. Contrast this with the bondservant's attitude.

The bondservant once stood on the auction block of shame because of his own foolishness and sin. By grace, his master lovingly restored the tattered pieces of his life. Now the bondservant hates sin, especially his own, but when it affects the master who gave up so much for him, he hates it even more. He knows his master has every right to inspect him and confront him, for his sin affects the strength of his master's house and all who live there.

What's your mind-set? What's your attitude toward your sins, including anything that tramples the convictions and soul essence of your wife? We spoke earlier of your wife's freedom to express opinions in general, but let's move closer to home and talk about a different situation. Does your wife have the right to question you about your actions? Or are you above question?

A MATTER OF ACCOUNTABILITY

The apostle Peter said your wife is a fellow heir of grace, suggesting that marriage doesn't eliminate Christian accountability between the two of you. The apostle Paul taught that mutual submission is expected between all Christians, reaching its highest form in marriage. Paul further teaches that Christians not only have a right to inspect their brothers regarding sin, but that they also have the *responsibility* to do so because harbored sin hurts everyone in the fellowship. He says: "What business is it of mine to judge those outside the church? Are you not to judge those inside? God will judge those outside. 'Expel the wicked man from among you'" (1 Corinthians 5:12-13).

The responsibility for holding each other accountable must be especially true in marriage, since the consequences of sin immediately affect the other partner. We're one flesh, so our sin in effect becomes her sin! Yet as leaders in our homes, we often refuse scrutiny. Like the Pharisees, we're less interested in the consequences of our sin than we are with the perks of our position—respect, prestige, and power. We've missed the whole point, as this Scripture points out:

Now then, you Pharisees clean the outside of the cup and dish, but inside you are full of greed and wickedness....

Woe to you Pharisees, because you give God a tenth of your mint, rue and all other kinds of garden herbs, but you neglect justice and the love of God. You should have practiced the latter without leaving the former undone.

Woe to you Pharisees, because you love the most important seats in the synagogues and greetings in the marketplaces.

Woe to you, because you are like unmarked graves, which men walk over without knowing it....

And you experts on the Law, woe to you, because you load people down with burdens they can hardly carry, and you yourselves will not lift one finger to help them. (Luke 11:39,42-44,46)

We love that important seat of leadership in the home, but we—like Amy's husband, Brant—deflect scrutiny like the finest Pharisee. Amy told us of her recent discovery that Brant, her husband of twenty-four years, had visited pornographic Web sites. The news devastated her. Brant assured her this was a one-time occurrence, but he'd lied and revisited those sites at least one other time. He has again promised to stay away from the pornographic sites, but now there's a very thick wall between them.

Oh, another thing: She doesn't want to be physically intimate with him, at least not right now. Amy says she remains committed to the marriage, but it's a lonely road to travel. "The worst thing may be that I don't have anyone with whom to share this burden," says Amy. "Brant is very highly respected in the church and community, and I don't want to destroy his reputation. I don't feel I can share this dark secret with anyone. The Lord has been my strength and my closest friend, but this has been such a burden."

Brant destroyed their intimacy by using the Internet to download pictures of naked women. Whose face does he see as he lies upon his wife? Whose breasts is he caressing? She's frozen by those thoughts. Besides harming Amy's connection with him, Brant also torched her connection to her Christian support. He's such an empty suit in the Christian community that she has nowhere to turn. Meanwhile, Brant is doing his best to make sure no one else finds out. Rather than repent, he has pressured her not to say anything to anyone else, as if whitewashing his life will make everything all right.

If sin had no power when it's hidden away, and if it only affects our social position once known, then Brant's actions would be correct. His sin would simply be an inconsequential foul ball in the much larger public relations game we play. But sin—like raw sewage—pollutes everywhere it flows.

I (Steve) discovered a damaging sin that I was reluctant to give up. It was the sin of nondisclosure. I kept a private little world in my head where fantasy reigned and "what ifs" and "if onlys" ruled. I wasn't on the Internet because I didn't need to be. I had enough downloaded images in my mind to last a lifetime. While sitting in a counselor's office one time, I was confronted with my dishonesty. No, I didn't come out and tell blatant lies, but I lived a lie by not telling the whole story or by conveniently leaving out details I should have shared.

You may think you're a pretty honest guy, but in reality you may be a man of deception because of what you withhold from your wife. One of the hardest challenges for us men is to become open books with our wives. We want to be a locked diary with our secrets unavailable to her. I was that way. And as long as I was, I prevented Sandy and myself from connecting in ways we could. The honest truth is that I'm not completely there yet. I know I have blind spots, but my beginning to live a more transparent life has allowed Sandy and me to connect at a totally different and much richer level.

NOT A PRIVATE MATTER!

More cards on the table: I (Fred) want to share with you a truth about myself that I disclosed when we wrote *Every Man's Battle.* I used to rise early on Sunday mornings to peruse the lingerie sections of the Sunday paper, taking long, long looks and fantasizing about what was underneath those bras and skin-tight panties. Two hours later, everyone esteemed me as a rising young leader of our church. No one knew, not even Brenda, but one quiet morning while I sat in my comfy chair getting an eyeful, Brenda raced down from our room in tears and terror.

"I just had the most awful dream!" she exclaimed. "Satan was chasing me, toying with me, and laughing at me. I was running everywhere, searching through the doors and hallways, screaming for you to protect me. I couldn't find you anywhere." She fell into my arms sobbing.

Whether or not she knew of my sin then, its power was real in her life, having seemed to remove spiritual protection from her. She experienced these frightening dreams regularly until, by God's grace, I crucified this sin. She's not had another since.

And though no one else knew, my Sunday morning sin was hurting the Christian community. I never arrived at church ready to minister because I was always desperate for someone to minister to me. I had no faith in my prayers because I knew I was harboring sin and breaking faith with the wife of my youth.

What fools we are to question whether our wife has a right to confront our sin or to question who should be told of our sin! Our sin hurts everyone around us. From a servant's mind-set, the only questions that matter are questions like these: Is the power of sin still working in my life? Even though I'm a Christian, am I still lying? Am I still angry? Am I still bitter? Do I still have that critical spirit, where everything always seems wrong? Are there areas in my life I won't allow my wife to talk to me about?

And when the power of sin is working in us, what is Christ's advice for us? Tell our wives to shut up? Cross our arms defiantly over our hardened hearts to protect them anytime someone comes near? Tell our wives to get used to it and to join us in covering it all up...for the sake of the kids?

Hardly. Here's God's advice: "Be earnest, and repent" (Revelation 3:19). Has your wife pleaded with you about something six or eight or ten times, but you just keep blowing her off? If so, you're an empty suit.

Tracy's husband, Pete, was overbearing, withering, and unsaved. Her neighbor's husband was just like him, so these two Christian wives made a covenant to quietly pray together for their husbands' salvation. When believers are married to unbelievers, God instructs them to live godly lives and to pray precisely in this way. For Tracy and her friend, their obedience was rewarded thirteen years later when their husbands accepted Christ on the very same day! Tears streamed down my face as I listened to their story from my pew.

Many Christian men feel that their wives shouldn't confront their sin but instead pray for them silently, as Tracy did. But that's God's plan for dealing with the hard hearts of *unsaved* husbands!

Let's be men about this. Are our hearts supposed to be no softer toward our sin—or toward our wives—than an unbeliever's heart? Surely we can do better than that!

THE EFFECTS DO MATTER!

What damage results if we Christian husbands don't do better? When I heard Tracy's story, Jasen was five years old. Crunching the numbers, I thought, *Man, if I made Brenda suffer through thirteen years of prayer, Jasen would be eighteen and leaving home. It would be too late for him!*

Then again, you may think, *Well, my wife has no right to try to change me!* Are you crazy? She has every right to change you when the hard edges of your sin are cutting up her and the kids. You're the sinner, for heaven's sake! You're not in a position to dictate anything. Besides, is that really what you want? When I was trampling Brenda every which way, she was advised repeatedly by well-meaning friends to "be still and let Fred lead." Christians of every stripe told her to button up and pray. It gives me nightmares to think where we'd be today had she listened to them, and I would still be trampling all over my house in my blindness.

Many people (believers and nonbelievers alike) claim that wives shouldn't try to change their husbands. That's understandable because one person can't change another person. In fact, the more you try changing your partner, the more that person will dig in his or her heels and defend the territory. While a woman can't change a man, she does need to feel free to point out problems and problem areas. If your wife isn't free to do that, you need to give her permission.

When Sandy has something she wants me (Steve) to work on, she always starts by saying, "Now I just want to be sure you want to be told about a problem I might be seeing."

"Sure," I reply, but then I start repeating over and over in my head, "Don't be defensive. Don't be defensive." By giving Sandy the chance to "improve" me, I've eliminated some bad habits and even forfeited some Texan slang. I'm better for what she does for me. You will be too, if you give your wife freedom.

While it is *technically* impossible for your wife to change you, let us also remind you of something. When it comes to sinful, trampling behaviors, it is flat out unbiblical for a husband to declare, "My wife has no right to try to change me." It's more accurate to say, "I married my mate, for better or worse, and she traded her freedoms to marry me. I have a responsibility before God and my wife to be conformed to Christ. I will not rest until my sins are under control. I won't be a quitter, and I won't dog it."

But it's her attitude! Maybe I could take a finger in my face, but I can't take her attitude. I understand. But look carefully at the other side, as Heather counters: "I have a zero-tolerance policy toward Andy's temper explosions.

Not so much for me, but for the kids. These explosions create permanent damage, deeply affecting the kids' self-esteem. I used to think I just had to take it, but I can't when it's this destructive. Andy complains that I'm not discussing the matter with the right attitude. Maybe so, but neither is he. I think he still needs to listen no matter how I say it."

Can we really argue her point? I can't. I have to agree with Heather. Andy can skirt the issue while hiding behind his "indignation" at Heather's "disrespectful" attitudes. While there's no question that a respectful attitude is preferable, does a wife's delivery render our own sin any less heinous? Does her style reduce the urgency we must have in addressing the issue? We're trampling oneness, and God isn't pleased.

Regardless of your wife's attitude, she has every right to expect you to repent in earnest. If you're hesitating, Jesus has a question for you: "Why do you call me, 'Lord, Lord,' and do not do what I say?" (Luke 6:46).

We're offended when our wives confront us, often responding, "Who are you to point fingers? You aren't perfect, either!" Yet I know that when Brenda points out my failings, she's not looking down her long, ecclesiastical nose at me. She knows she's a sinner too. It's not so much the sin, but the break in oneness. She's not so much pointing a finger at my failings but pointing to a wound on us.

That's why when your wife has confronted you six times about the same thing, and you still haven't done anything, she feels you don't care about her. You aren't fixing something that's hurting the relationship.

When his master confronted a bondservant, that bondservant would fix things right away because of his deep love for his master. So what's wrong with us husbands? What's wrong with our love?

HOW MUCH DOES IT MATTER TO YOU?

Is there something hurtful in your past that you just won't give up? Is there something for which your wife and kids have to pay the same price today that you had to pay years ago? Did your father, for instance, never really accept you, so you just keep on hurting and hurting and never deal with it? Did you get abused and now your home life or sex life isn't where it should be because of what some creep did way back when?

Fine, I've been there. But just when are you going to get over it? Does the problem matter enough for you to make a significant change?

When I reached age thirty-five, the lack of my father's acceptance suddenly rocked me deeply. The pain prompted a return to my harsh ways, which severely affected my relationship with my family. Brenda tried to explain away my behavior to the kids, but after a year she became frustrated. One day she told me, "All right, then! Fine. Just tell us how long you plan to stay like this, so we can all prepare for it!" Then she stormed out of the room.

I sat there speechless for quite some time. How long was I going to stay like this? Ten years? Why ten? Why not five? If I could decide to change at the end of five years, why not after one? And if after one, why not...*today?*

After her single stiletto question pointed into my heart, I knew it was time:

> The hour has come for you to wake up from your slumber, because
> our salvation is nearer now than when we first believed. The night is
> nearly over; the day is almost here. So let us put aside the deeds of dark-
> ness and put on the armor of light. Let us behave decently, as in the
> daytime, not in orgies and drunkenness, not in sexual immorality and
> debauchery, not in dissension and jealousy. (Romans 13:11-13)

Starting immediately, I found a counselor. Shortly after that, I attended a Promise Keepers conference in Boulder, Colorado. That first night God spoke to me through the speaker and revealed an aspect of His love I'd never understood. Sitting that evening in the bleachers at the University of Colorado's Folsom Field, I felt the pain from my dad begin to disperse. I had acted decisively, and I was being healed.

You are God's son-in-law, as you've married His beloved daughter. He wants to help you, and she wants to help you. Don't block their inspections by hiding behind the precious title "Man of the House." Let them both speak freely to you. Be earnest and repent. Get rid of your sin.

FOUR PATHS TO CHOOSE FROM

There are four separate paths you can take to make needed changes. The first path is the easiest (though it always winds up the hardest): *Simply make a decision and do the hard work to change.*

The second path is intervention. Either you don't see the problem or are unwilling to admit it until a third party points it out to you. If such a confrontation ever happens to you, don't defend yourself or shrug it off.

The third path is even more painful: the path of desperation. On this path, you lose the ability to deny your problem any longer, usually because you've done something to embarrass yourself or your family (wrecking a car after spending the evening in a bar or getting arrested for tax fraud). If you're on this road, you can always jump back to path number one and decide that your bad behavior has to stop.

The final path to change is—death. Your death! While the third path (desperation) may have resulted in your killing someone else, on this fourth path you lead yourself down the road of no return. Like it or not, you *will* change. Dust will return to dust. As you leave this world, you leave behind all of the consequences of your behavior. The people you supposedly loved are left holding a bag full of pain, emptiness, and despair. Don't do that to them.

In this life it's never too late to take that first path to change. It's also never too early. Make the decision, and when you do, you take one giant step to fulfilling the heart desires of your wife.

Questions for Reflection and Discussion

1. This chapter asks whether your wife has the right to question you about your actions—or are you above question? How would you answer that?

2. What secrets, if any, are you withholding from your wife?

3. Is there something hurtful from your past that you may be reluctant to give up?

4. In what areas of life do you think the Spirit of God may be calling you to repent? What specifically do you need to do in order to repent and change?

PART V

enjoying a resurrected relationship

vive la difference!

Most Christian couples pray their hearts out before marriage, believing God has brought them together. We expect our "unique" love to guarantee marital oneness. Because of that, we confidently stride into marriage, expecting our sexual fantasies to be fulfilled and possibly exceeded simply because we deeply love one another. We expect sex to be so good our wives will want everything our hearts and minds desire in the marriage bed.

In premarriage class, Brenda and I always circle the room asking, "What do you hope to get out of marriage that you couldn't get if you remained single?" The answers should give every man an inkling of what's coming just around the bend in his new marriage. Most men begin by speaking loftily about companionship and working on dreams together. The more honest ones cite sex as a great reason to get hitched. In the twelve years of leading these classes, we can't ever remember a woman answering this way, yet many guys anticipate their wives being as excited about sex as they are. Al, who has never been married, said, "I used to feel cheated when I'd meet a married couple that looked like everything was perfect between them, only to find out later from friends that there had been no sex for months. I can't even begin to understand that."

Singles can't understand, but married men can. While most married men expect sexual oneness to be a slam dunk, it's more like a half-court shot. Sexual incompatibility is as common as two-week paydays. Mark said, "I don't want to seem like a sex addict or anything, but I probably have as many unmet sexual desires now as I did before marriage. On top of that, any sexual exploration seems embarrassing or immodest to her. Sometimes she even calls my attempts 'kinky.' I think she's rather prudish, but what do I say?"

Then there's the frequency bugaboo. This letter was sent to advice columnist Ann Landers regarding her statement that couples should have sex three times a week:

> Thanks a lot. My husband read that and announced triumphantly,
> "Ann Landers says we should have sex three times a week." I looked
> him in the eye and said, "How nice of Ann. When is she coming over?"
> If you think my husband should have sex three times a week, you
> had better come by twice a week because once a week is plenty for me.

We can all laugh (probably because we've been there), but for many of us, the merriment seems a little forced. Let me emphasize the point by repeating a story I shared earlier. After a recent speaking engagement regarding *Every Man's Battle,* I noticed a man who remained behind. Once everyone else had left, he approached me and said, "My wife came up to me this week and said, 'Jim, I have something to tell you, but I don't really know how to bring it up. I'll just say it straight out. I just don't like sex, and I really wish I didn't have to do it anymore.'" Jim then asked her if it was something he was doing wrong. His wife replied no, that every one of her friends feels the same way.

Marveling, I passed this story to one of my pastors as we chatted in his office. "See that chair over there?" he asked. "That's my counseling chair. Do you know what complaint I hear most often from married men?"

"No, what is it?"

"'I'm just not getting any sex anymore.' It's overwhelming!"

A SPECIAL STATUS

Christian marriages should have sexual oneness. How have we gotten from that design to this? It's not as if God hasn't made Himself perfectly clear on this issue:

The husband should fulfill his marital duty to his wife, and likewise the wife to her husband. The wife's body does not belong to her alone but also to her husband. In the same way, the husband's body does not belong to him alone but also to his wife. Do not deprive each other except by mutual consent and for a time, so that you may devote your-selves to prayer. Then come together again so that Satan will not tempt you because of your lack of self-control. (1 Corinthians 7:3-5)

God gave sexual relations in marriage a special status. He made it one of the few marital rights specifically granted in Scripture. We have no more right to withhold sex from our spouse than we have to withhold praise and wor-ship from Jesus Christ. The original Greek translated here as "fulfill" actually means "pay your debts." We could say that our spouse owes it to us. Similarly, the command "stop depriving one another" actually means "defraud not," reinforcing the debt concept.

God is serious about rights. In Malachi 3:8, God declared that the Jews were robbing Him. When they asked Him what He meant, He told them they weren't paying their tithe (giving 10 percent) of their income. In para-phrase, God said, "Look, the tithe isn't a gift you give at your own discretion. It's mine by right. It's mine already. When you keep it for yourself, you're stealing what's rightfully mine."

This principle is also true regarding marital sexuality. Neither spouse has a right to withhold sexual fulfillment from the other. Of course, the real key to this verse lies in this question: What does "sexual fulfillment" mean? The 1 Corinthians passage doesn't define it, and because it doesn't, we're required— as the spiritual leaders in our homes—to properly divide the rest of God's Word to find out what He meant. Do you suppose our verses relating to male submission, sacrifice, and honoring our wife's sexual essence have a place in this discussion? That thought might make you uneasy.

Most of us care more about our sex than we do about God's Word and our wives, so we're purposefully sloppy in handling God's Word in our bedrooms. When God writes, "Her body is not her own," we read, "She's my sex toy. I'll serve her everywhere else, but here she'll serve me!" We treat our wife like some call girl on retainer, a love machine at our beck and call.

But your wife isn't your sex toy. This twisted spiritual leadership in our master bedrooms is the main reason why sexual oneness has died in Christian marriages. Too many demeaned wives have been forced to draw back sexually because God never intended them to carry the burden of sexual fulfillment that their husbands laid on them. (We'll discuss this in depth in the next chapter. For now, we'll leave sexual fulfillment undefined, so, you female readers, know that we'll get to your husbands later.)

Still, the truth remains. A wife has no right to hold back sexual fulfillment from her husband. If yours does, she's robbing you. As you know, that can be frustrating and demoralizing because it crushes your spirit and pounds at the walls of your sexual purity. Your wife isn't just robbing a little recreation from you, she's trampling you in an important area of your personhood, which puts a darker twist to these common statements from wives:

- "Okay, you think you're so perfect! Well, we'll just see how perfect you feel going without sex for the next two weeks!"
- "I'm so tired. Let's hurry up, okay?"
- "Oh, I'll bet you're going to want sex again tonight! I'm going to bed before you get home, so don't wake me up and ask for it."
- "It's not that I don't love you or find you attractive, I just don't get interested that often. I guess that's the way God made me."

God desires sexual purity in His men. It's crucial for His work in them. God made marriage a way of escape for those struggling with purity, and He expects wives to play the role of helpmate in the sexual arena: "If they cannot control themselves, they should marry, for it is better to marry than to burn with passion" (1 Corinthians 7:9).

SEXUAL ONENESS—THROUGH PERSONAL SACRIFICE

A wife is the only legitimate vessel on the face of the earth for a man's sexual satisfaction. She's God's stream of mercy and grace on her husband's path to sexual purity. When she dams the stream, she has forever doomed him to the same struggle he so desperately tried to escape. Before marriage he at least had the hope that marriage would free him. Now God's only way of escape is blocked. In some ways, he may be even worse off than before marriage. As a single, he could at least flee sexual temptation. Now he has a wife showering in front of him, prancing around in partial nudity, and lying next to him in silky negligees within his very reach. She ignites his engine in a million ways, and yet she never helps.

Robert wrote this letter (the italics are ours):

Please help! I am a thirty-seven-year-old man, married for thirteen years, a father of two boys, and a pastor for twelve years. I have read your book *Every Man's Battle,* and it has been used by God to set me free. I have battled pornography since I was about thirteen years old. The shame, guilt, and darkness of my sin are overwhelming, and it affects my marriage, though my wife doesn't know all the details. My ministry has also suffered greatly as a result. I am finally on the road to recovery and could share some of my struggles with my wife, Marissa.

I need your help. Marissa is very attractive and very sexually stimulating to me. She's aware that I need a regular sexual release, but she does very little to help me in this area. I don't blame her for my lack of sexual purity, but she can go for weeks without making love to me or providing release for me. Recently, I went for almost one month without masturbating, which had once been a daily habit, but now I'm beginning to justify why I should resume the practice.

She says, "I'm sorry. I know you need release," *but it doesn't happen.* I'm lucky if we make love two to three times a month. For the first time since I was a teenager, I feel as if God may be delivering me from this wicked grip of sin, but I feel that I may slip back if I can't find a better balance with my wife. It actually brings physical pain to me after five to six days without release, and she is aware of this. Because of the pain, I can't sleep at night, as was the case last night. I was tempted again to watch the scrambled screen of the porn channel or even come to the office in the middle of the night to return to the computer chat rooms as I once did.

I don't want to go back to who I was, or to lose the battle. I love Marissa with all my being. I'm just very confused, discouraged, and *even angry with her* at times over this issue. I am so afraid of being in bondage longer, losing my wife, hurting my wonderful boys, losing my witness, and destroying this wonderful church of over one thousand members.

Two months later I (Fred) received a second e-mail from Robert, stating that he'd fallen back into sexual sin. Before I say anything else, I want to remind you that Robert is still ultimately responsible for his sexual purity before God, regardless of Marissa's actions. We made that very clear in *Every Man's Battle*.

But because of that ultimate responsibility, it's all too easy for some to give wives a pass, saying, "God can give a man in Robert's position the grace to handle it." That's true. God can. He can do a lot of things. He can make all humans asexual with the snap of His fingers. He can stop time dead in its tracks. He can even turn the moon blue if He wants.

But none of that is His perfect will, His plan, or even His vague preference. God's plan is for a wife to lay down her body for her friend. His plan is for her to learn sexual oneness through sacrifice and love, just as the church learns spiritual oneness with Christ through sacrifice and love. His goal is to grow both the husband and wife under this plan. The other plans wither us, and if you don't believe me, ask Robert.

As husband and wife, we're one flesh. Our own impurity affects the other. Granted, Robert's sexual purity is ultimately his responsibility, but Marissa is a pastor's wife, a leader in God's kingdom. She has consciously chosen hypocrisy over obedience to God's Word regarding sexual fulfillment.

Is it fair for Robert to be angry and confused in the face of Marissa's stone wall? You bet. Does he feel fulfilled as a man and as a Christian? Not even close. Marissa is in sin, and there's no other way around it.

When our wives withdraw sexually to this extreme, it can be devastating to us. We received this letter from a reader of *Every Man's Battle:*

> I am a Christian brother who is praying to get victory over my need for regular intercourse. My wife just isn't available for me, so I masturbate. When I do this, my thoughts are directed to my wife. At least this seems to be the right focus, but I'm not sure. What's your opinion?

Our opinion is that Christians have strayed so far away from Scripture that it boggles the mind. God's standard is clear. A wife's body isn't her own, and she's the only legitimate vessel of sexual satisfaction for her husband on the earth. As usual, when God's standards get tough, we choose to mix in our own standards of sexual conduct to create a more comfortable mixture— something new, something mediocre. No wonder we lead mediocre lives where women take control of their own bodies and husbands are "forced" to masturbate.

Our wives can even stir up enough gall to openly ask their husbands to find sexual release elsewhere:

> My wife would like me to masturbate regularly so I will leave her alone sexually. I don't think I should masturbate, because I believe it's wrong. She thinks it's okay. I am struggling with this, but mainly I'm wrestling with the pain of why she wants me to do this. We've been married for twenty-one years and have a good marriage, but this really hurts. How should I address this?

Why ask us? God has already addressed this in 1 Corinthians. It's not your hand's duty to fulfill you sexually! It's your wife's duty. Sex plays the same role of deep, interpersonal intimacy in human marriage that worship plays in Christ's marriage with His bride. When a wife asks her husband to masturbate so she can be left alone, it's the same as the church asking Christ to set up a mirror in front of His throne and to praise Himself.

Men like Justin are left gasping:

> I have to admit I'm losing all hope. I feel as if God made me a sexual
> being and is now asking me to be nonsexual. I know that is no excuse
> for sexual impurity, but I really don't know what to do. I know my
> sexual sin is preventing me from being a godly husband and father.
> Because I feel defeated, I rarely spend time reading the Bible or praying.

Justin is in a state of confusion and anger. His wife, whose role as helpmate is intended to lift him to Christian greatness, has instead relegated him to mediocrity and defeat.

This should be shocking, but we've mixed our standards for so long we don't even notice it anymore. A fresh pair of eyes will still be shocked, however. When I first turned to Christ, I was amazed so few Christians seemed to live any differently than their neighbors lived. Today, Christian men are generally no different from unchurched men in their practice of sexual impurity. That's why we wrote *Every Man's Battle.*

QUESTIONS AND DIFFERENCES

Similarly, Christian women look little different from unchurched women when it comes to fulfilling their husbands sexually. God asks today's Christian wives this question: "Why do you call me, 'Lord, Lord,' and do not do what I say?" (Luke 6:46).

As frustrated and angry husbands, we stand behind Jesus as He asks this question, pointing rigid fingers at our wives, gritting our teeth and exclaiming, "Yeah, we're with Jesus! He's right! Why don't you answer Him, hmmm?"

But then Jesus calmly turns around and levels a steady, piercing gaze our way, saying, "Brothers, why do you call me, 'Lord, Lord,' and do not do what I say?"

Riveted and stunned, we each reply, "What do you mean? I haven't withheld anything from her!"

With precision, Jesus says, "I ask a lot from wives in marriage, but submitting sexually is one of the most difficult of all. Have you made it easy for her to help you in this way? My friend, look to the log in your own eye before you point a finger at your cherished one."

Maybe it's time to look in the mirror and ask an entirely different question, in mercy: *Why are so many otherwise godly women sinning against their husbands this way?* Sex is as natural as breathing, so it isn't natural for them to withdraw this way. Why is sexual submission so hard for our wives? For one reason, it's because we're poor spiritual leaders, but it's also hard because they aren't like us. Let's briefly consider three of the most significant differences.

Difference 1: Men Primarily Give Intimacy During Foreplay and Receive Intimacy During Intercourse

In contrast, women experience intimacy through touching, sharing, hugging, and communicating, but they don't need intercourse to receive intimacy. Is it any wonder that the frequency of sex is less important to women than to men? In fact, women often view sex as a vastly inferior form of interpersonal communication. They resent that we always run to this form of communication. When we want to express our love, we're automatically in the mood for intercourse. That's how we're made. When our wives want to express love, they want to sit and share their feelings.

Difference 2: Men's Sexual Ignitions Are Wired to Visual Stimulation

It's that blue silk nightgown with the bare shoulders that cups her breasts just so. It's that tantalizing bend at the waist as she brushes her teeth, revealing an upper thigh disappearing beneath the lace of her panties. It's that look in her eye when you return from a four-day business trip and she presses her hips softly but firmly against yours.

Women don't understand this in the least because their ignitions are tied to touch and relationship. They often view the visual aspect of our sexuality as shallow and dirty, even detestable. Any effort from husbands to put a positive spin on this "vision factor" by suggesting to our wives that they use it to their advantage in the bedroom is met with disdainful scorn. Lisa, for instance, said, "So I suppose I have to buy one of those cheap teddies and prance around like some saloon girl!"

Since it seems so weird to them, they resent being part of "the way of escape." Soon after Brenda and I married, evangelist Rich Wilkerson visited our church and, during his message, described what it's like to try to remain pure while traveling without his wife. He said, "Sometimes at night I lay flat on my back, staring wide-eyed at the ceiling, and I can feel wave after wave of the enemy bombarding me with sexual temptation."

When Brenda and I discussed this later, she responded sharply. "So now I suppose *your* purity all rests on *my* shoulders! I suppose I have to have sex anytime you want."

Difference 3: Men Have a Biological Need for Regular Sexual Release

This third difference—our regular need for physical release—is the one that really tests our wives. It's well documented that because of sperm production and related hormonal factors, the human male naturally desires a sexual release every forty-eight to seventy-two hours. Imagine how unromantic this seems to women, whose ignitions are tied so strongly to relationship! In marriage class, one young wife scornfully blustered, "Oh, they're just like dogs in heat." Another once blurted, "Oh, what a cross to bear!" And truly, it is a cross to bear because wives rarely have this matching desire for regular intercourse, and yet somehow they must follow through as if they do.

When we put these three differences together, it can stretch our credibility with our wives: "Oh, so you really feel love for me tonight and you really want to make love, huh? Well, what do you know? It's been seventy-two hours since our last go at it. Hmmm. It doesn't sound much like love to me. Sounds more like some kind of hormone bath! Go fly a kite!" They don't see this kind of sex as having even a whiff of relationship to it, so our wives, who want sex to be inseparably swirled with relationship and mutual desire, suddenly find they're required to engage regularly in sex even when they're not in the mood.

Submitting to sex when you aren't in the mood isn't easy—even for guys. Quite awhile ago, Brenda and I had been trying to conceive one of our children. I knew it was to be a lovely time of creation and joy. Yet after a week of trying, Brenda snuggled up to me one night and whispered, "Are you ready?" I groaned in misery. It was as if she'd said, "Are you ready for that plate of raw fish eyes?" In my mind, I just couldn't, and it took awhile to get my engine to turn over.

IN THE MOOD

There's the rub, isn't it? Because of our differences, wives typically won't be in the mood as often as their husbands. How do we get their engines to turn over even when they aren't in the mood? Part of the responsibility rests on their shoulders—wives must have the will to obey God—but part rests on our shoulders. We husbands have to at least be sexually attractive.

And this phrase probably means exactly the opposite of what you're thinking. A woman's sexual attraction to a man is based on relationship, not sight. *One thing that always makes you sexually desirable to her is oneness.*

Why do so many women avoid sex with their husbands? Remember the statistics we quoted earlier:

- Eighty-four percent of women feel they don't have intimacy (oneness) in their marriages.
- Eighty-three percent of women feel their husbands don't even know the basic needs of a woman for intimacy (oneness) or how to provide intimacy for them.

We're simply not sexually attractive to them, and it's not because we've failed to lift weights or wear leopard-skin bikini briefs. It's because there's no oneness. We haven't allowed our wives' soul essences to be honored, loved, and expressed with our own. We haven't provided them with every woman's desire. When we ignore male submission *outside* the bedroom, our wives have little or no sexual attraction to us *inside* the bedroom. Raymond's letter gives us a start in understanding this problem:

> I'm wondering if you have any advice for me, as my wife isn't interested in fulfilling my needs. I believe the sexual needs of a man are very real, but my wife disagrees. She sort of thinks that men are all just perverts.
>
> This situation makes it more difficult to resist sexual temptation. With God's help, I have managed to avoid much sexual sin at this point, but as the situation between my wife and me continues to deteriorate, it becomes increasingly more difficult.
>
> We are both active and involved in church. I play the guitar in church and am a member of the board. I feel God's presence in my life daily and depend on Him for everything. My wife is involved in children's ministry. She's a wonderful mother and has really dedicated her life to our children.
>
> The real problem here is our marriage. We've been married for sixteen years, and I love my wife very much. She repeatedly tells me that she *doesn't* love me and would leave me if it weren't for the children. I've tried to get her to listen to Christian radio programs when they have topics about marriage, but she just isn't interested. She tells me I am not a good husband and that I don't try hard enough, but that is simply not true.

Raymond is confused. His marriage seems good to him. He has obedient kids and a wife dedicated to his kids and his church. He's supporting his family well, and as Chief Tiebreaker, he has peace in his realm.

While they have the image, they don't have oneness. Clearly, this wife has been stifled, kept from fully living in this marriage, and it has left her bitter and angry. And while she can submit to her husband for the sake of Christ and for the sake of appearances, she can't quite find the strength to submit her body to him too. Chief Tiebreakers are just not sexually attractive. Let's look at this verse again: "The wife's body does not belong to her alone but also to her husband. In the same way, the husband's body does not belong to him alone but also to his wife. Do not deprive each other."

For us men, this verse is a comfort. To our wives, this verse seems more like the point of a gun forcing her to have sex when she's not in the mood with someone who isn't sexually attractive. She must open her most intimate, private place to a man who not only has kept her from blossoming in marriage, but who has picked on her weaknesses and selfishly asserted his rights at every turn. This person sounds more like a prison guard than a husband, which means sex can feel disturbingly close to being raped by a prison guard. After all, she has no right to say no, and the guard enters frequently at his whim and pleasure. So when our wives are asked to submit their bodies to us, God knows He's calling them to do something that may be brutally difficult for them. As a husband, it's your job to make sex easier for her by building oneness with a bondservant's heart.

Hold everything right there! It's her responsibility to fulfill me sexually, despite how I act. I'm her husband.

In other words, you want her to fulfill this brutal calling from God without your help, huh? Fine. But let's first look at another brutal calling from God: "But among you there must not be even a hint of sexual immorality" (Ephesians 5:3).

Since you're so anxious to have your wife answer *her* calling by herself, I'm sure you won't mind handling *your own* calling to sexual purity by yourself. After all, God says it's your responsibility to be pure whether she helps you or not. That shouldn't be a problem, right?

It's arrogant for you to think God's decree to women should ensure sexual oneness between you and your wife. Do you really think God's command will make it any easier for her to give her body to you when your relationship is so weak? God commands you to be sexually pure. Has His decree made that any easier for you? How can you expect any more from your wife than you expect of yourself?

You expect her to lead you both into sexual oneness by fulfilling your wildest dreams, right down to the last gasp and groan. What about her wildest dreams? And why are you expecting her to lead your sexual relationship into oneness? We thought God gave that job to you!

The bottom line is this: If you aren't willing to submit to oneness outside the bedroom, how can you expect her to submit sexually inside the bedroom? Take care of the log in your own eye first, then you'll be able to see clearly to help her.

OF THE SAME MIND

Allow me (Steve) to close this chapter with a personal account of my first years of marriage with Sandy. This isn't a story I want people to go around telling, but I want to relay it here because I want you to know you're not alone if you struggle with sexual differences between you and your wife.

When Sandy and I were dating, I attempted to hold her hand one night. She jerked back and said that the thought of holding my hand kind of made her sick. She said it in the nicest way possible, but for whatever reason, I simply wasn't appealing to her. My temptation was to lick my wounds and walk away. Instead, I told her that I wasn't in this relationship to hold hands or do anything else but be with her. Well, that obviously had an impact on her because we eventually did hold hands. Furthermore, we eventually got married.

It is amazing how God lays things out in our lives that make sense only years later. This was one of those weird things. Sandy was probably the most sexually appealing woman I'd ever met. I desired her from the moment I saw her. Having had a promiscuous past, however, I was on a crash course to repeat my relational disasters.

Something was different about Sandy, and I wanted to make the relationship something better than what I'd had before. Add to that the fact that she was also committed to God's standard, and you can understand how a man like me could date someone like her and not have sex before we were married. I was out of the pattern, thanks to her strength and my newfound desires to do right.

When we finally married, I was shocked to find that sex was a painful experience for her. She wanted no part of it. I was humiliated, felt like a failure, and had no idea what to do. Then I remembered the hand-holding incident. I went back to that place and realized that I had to be of the same mind now that I was then. I could not be in this marriage just for the sex. I tried to understand, tried to be patient, and tried to do the best I could in the situation.

It would take years to work out the problems, but the end of the story is that we've had some wonderful sexual experiences in recent years that we never had in our earlier years. It was worth the wait and worth my learning some new things about her—that sex could be something she would actually want versus dread.

If you're in a long, drawn-out struggle, know that you aren't alone. You're not the first person to face this issue. God is there with you, and you can win the battle.

There are many other reasons a man may not be able to have sex with his wife. A few are illness, distance, emotional problems, and even sexual clumsiness on his part. If you're in one of those situations, you aren't justified to do anything except work on yourself, ask for God's help, support your wife with love and acceptance, and patiently wait for her to come around. If you both are willing, you might want to talk with a specialist in this area. If being apart sexually strains the relationship to the point of wanting to get out, you must get some help before the relationship deteriorates further.

In closing, if you're married, you're called to make your body a living sacrifice and to lay it down for your wife. I don't think it could be any clearer than to say *you* must be there for her even if she can't be there for you sexually. Even if her lack of availability is the result of sin on her part, that's never a justification for sin or compromise on your part.

The expression may sound trite at times like this, but it's true: "Just do the right thing."

Questions for Reflection and Discussion

1. What do you understand about the Bible's teaching on sexual one-ness? What is God most concerned about in this aspect of marriage?

2. In what ways, if any, have you ever misunderstood the Bible's teaching on sexual oneness in marriage?

3. What sacrifices do you believe God may be asking from you for the sake of sexual oneness in your marriage?

4. In what way does sexual oneness in your marriage require your own sexual purity? How do you see this taught in Scripture?

don't leave sex to your feelings

At first glance, talking about rights and debts in relation to sex might seem a bit unromantic and even totally out of line. We would expect some women to chafe when told that they're "robbing" their husbands when they withhold sex because they "owe" it to them. On the other hand, we can expect husbands to chafe—and chomp at the bit—when told they shouldn't expect regular sex if they don't consistently honor their wives as fellow heirs in God's kingdom.

All this leads to a question that husbands and wives on both sides of the bed might ask: "What do rules and obedience have to do with great sex?"

Everything. After all, why did God give us these commands? To torture us? To test us?

No, He gave them to complete us.

God knew our desire for intimacy—and how we could attain it—from the beginning. He knew that women give and receive intimacy through sharing, talking, hugging, and touching. After all, He created her so that men might not be lonely. These traits are perfectly fitted to that purpose.

But God also knew that men would be too hardhearted to appreciate these subtleties and that they would ignore their wives' needs. When they do this, their wives wither emotionally or they become embittered and independent. Oneness never grows. God couldn't leave something this important to the whims of mood.

God also knew that husbands would give and receive interpersonal intimacy through intercourse and that His daughters would have difficulty understanding or respecting this difference. Was God surprised the first time He heard a wife rudely compare her husband to a dog in heat? Nope. Did He think it amusing? Not at all because He knew that soon thereafter she'd begin to withdraw sexually without realizing that this withers her husband in the exact same way he withers her with his silence.

READY FOR "UNROMANTIC" OBEDIENCE?

Knowing we wouldn't love our *spouses* enough to soften our hard hearts and seek oneness, God hoped that we might love *Him* enough to follow a few commands. Obedience can move us toward complete sexual oneness despite our hard hearts. We don't even have to understand the differences between men and women. We only have to obey our Creator's instructions. If we do, we meet the terms of sexual oneness and we blossom *emotionally* and *spiritually.*

Let's return to what we know about oneness. We learned earlier that achieving emotional closeness has little to do with emotions; it has everything to do with actions. Oneness has terms, set by your wife's personal convictions and her soul essence. Comply with the terms, and emotional closeness follows. If not, her emotions will die. We need to act right or, more precisely, act righteously. If we do, your wife's feelings of intimacy follow.

Remember how Brenda's feelings for me had died because of my trampling leadership? When it came time to revive those feelings, I had to do more than buy a bouquet and invite her to a darkly lit steakhouse. I had to do what I was called to do from the beginning: I had to love her as myself and to *act as if* we were one. When I did that, her feelings of intimacy returned.

(Not to one-up my buddy Fred here, but for me [Steve], things got so bad with Sandy at one point that she stopped wearing her wedding ring. What's even sadder is that the ring was probably off her finger for over a month before I noticed it. The bottom line was that if I wasn't going to treat her as if

I was married to her, she wasn't going to act as if she was married to me. When the wedding ring came off, the walls went up, and both of those were important events that finally led me to make the changes necessary to meet the terms of oneness.)

Sexual oneness is no different than other kinds of oneness. It has terms as well. Comply with the terms, and sexual oneness lives. Ignore those terms, and it dies. We need to act righteously in the marriage bed. If we do, the right feelings follow.

These truths may seem quite unromantic on the surface. Because of the "chick flick" movies we've seen through the years and because of our own premarital sexual experiences, we naturally believe that emotional desire must come before sex can happen. Conversely, when the emotional desire isn't there, we naturally believe that it's okay either to withdraw sexually or to move on to the next partner with whom it *does* feel right.

But in marriage, waiting for the right moods and emotions to happen doesn't build sexual oneness. Indeed, it shatters oneness.

Let's return to our earlier discussion. Men need regular intercourse to share intimacy. This is an important term of oneness. What if his wife insists on waiting for her moods to kick in before having sex? For many wives, this happenstance occurs two or three times a month. She, of course, thinks this is okay. He doesn't.

Her actions crush oneness because he needs to give and receive intimacy for his emotional health. If she takes that away, she's stolen his primary means of expressing his love and meeting his terms of sexual oneness.

Remember Robert and Marissa's story? Marissa wasn't meeting the terms of sexual oneness. In kindness, she said, "I'm sorry. I know you need release," but she rarely followed through. Robert battled shame, guilt, and frustration because oneness doesn't come with mere kind words. Oneness comes instead in the actions that should have backed up those words. Again, we cannot leave oneness to our feelings.

Brenda and I *do* have sexual oneness. It's not because we're more romantic or sexually charged than the average couple. It's certainly not because we're more compatible than Robert and Marissa. We have sexual oneness because we decided to meet each other's needs. For instance, I'm a typical male. By nature, I simply don't need much talking or sharing in my relationships. But I do have a healthy sex drive, and I do need to share love and compassion for Brenda through intercourse.

Brenda is typical too. She needs a lot of talking and sharing, or our relationship weakens for her. Her natural sex drive? Not too strong. Our love didn't bring oneness, but our actions do. We submitted and met these terms of oneness. On my part, I made a rule that I couldn't crawl into bed at night without first taking a seat in the "talking chair" in our master bedroom. I did this because Brenda needed it, not because I was in the mood to talk. I really didn't understand why conversation after 10 P.M. was even necessary. Didn't we have the rest of the day for that? No, we didn't, which is why I made room for her needs as if they were my own. Brenda did the same for me through regular intercourse, though she didn't particularly desire it at times.

What happened? I got my emotional needs met in bed, as God intended. When I connected with Brenda on a conversational level from the "talking chair," this met her emotional needs as well. But something unexpected also happened. Where once I needed very little conversation and sharing, I have now learned to appreciate—even value—our tête-à-têtes. Something new blossomed in this jock's heart, and I actually looked forward to my time in the chair.

As for Brenda, the regular sex also meant regular times of touching, snuggling, and a nonverbal physical communication that she cherishes. I'm even confident enough to say she now looks forward to intercourse as much as I do. Through obedience, we've both been changed, and we're one. We now have a romantic, sexually charged relationship that's not at all robotic.

Bottom line? "Unromantic" obedience has its place in the marriage bed. You needn't start with the right feelings. The right feelings will always follow right actions. If we plan to love our wife as we love ourselves, we must make room for her essence, and that has nothing to do with emotions. As we pointed out in the previous chapter, attaining sexual oneness calls for personal sacrifice. And you either sacrifice for her essence, or you don't.

The other day I (Steve) had a discussion with my daughter about a little problem with reading. She's an excellent reader and very bright, but one week she decided not to read or do her classwork. Result—an F on a test.

I knew I had to come up with something to motivate Madeline. I wanted this to be a one-time event, not a pattern. I locked the door of our house behind us and held a shiny key in my hand.

"How are we going to get back in?" I asked.

Madeline pointed to the key.

"Correct, Madeline. The key to having all the things you want and not being locked out of college, playing soccer, and enjoying a good life is reading. Reading unlocks it all. You have to read and come to a place where you come to love it."

Obedience is not the point of sex or intimacy, but obedience is the key that will unlock the intimacy you long for. You have to use the key over and over, and then you'll finally unlock the experiences you have waited for.

EXPECTATIONS ABOUND

The simple magnetism of love and physical attraction won't build the emotional and spiritual communion necessary for a satisfactory sex life. Mutual submission will, however: "The wife's body does not belong to her alone but also to her husband. In the same way, the husband's body does not belong to him alone but also to his wife" (1 Corinthians 7:4).

You can't mistake it: Mutual submission is embedded in this verse. God expects mutual submission to be perfected in the marriage bed.

You mean I have to sacrifice for sexual oneness? What else did you expect? Did you really expect oneness to be snap-your-fingers automatic when it isn't automatic anywhere else in your marriage? How were you expecting to make room for her sexual essence without making sacrifices?

Whether we like it our not, there's a distinct place for male submission in the marriage bed. Chances are we may not like it because no sacrifice seems more costly than sexual sacrifice. It's one thing to submit to *her* essence and to let her buy the more expensive washing machine. It's quite another to allow her sexual essence to set the terms of oneness and define *our* sexual fulfill-ment. Still, her essence must play a huge role in defining the term. Failing to make room for our wife's sexual essence will force her to withdraw sexually.

Let's return to Richard, the fellow who complained that his wife was unwilling to French kiss with him. As a husband, Richard felt justified in demanding that she submit her body to him as he saw fit, based upon his incorrect interpretation of 1 Corinthians 7:4. Remember what his wife said? "Richard is so selfish. It's so demeaning when he pushes his tongue into my mouth because he knows I hate it. Is that all I'm worth to him?" The very act of forcing his own way physically breaks their emotional connection.

Herein lies the place for male submission. Paul taught that we must submit our rights as leaders in such circumstances. To paraphrase Romans 14:15-21, "If your wife is distressed because of French kissing, you're no longer acting in love when you push it. Don't destroy the work of God [one-ness in your marriage] for the sake of French kissing. It's better to never French kiss again than to break oneness in your marriage."

We can't make our decisions based solely upon sexual zing. We must honor the essence of our wife and do what's right, but this is difficult when it comes to sex. Sex is personal, and your wife is your only vessel of sexual satis-faction. If she doesn't French kiss with you, you're not going to get French kissed.

Because of my (Fred's) promiscuous background, when it came to my sexual tastes, it was anything goes! You name the game, and I was willing to play. Not so for Brenda. She had her limits. In those early months of mar-riage, questions nagged at me under the surface. Why did Brenda have the right to define my sexual limits? Couldn't I order her to expand her horizons? Didn't I have the right to ignore her limits?

No. And, thankfully, it didn't take long to realize it. Most of us have faced this same conundrum, the very thing we most feared before boarding the USS *Matrimony*. Al, a bachelor, recently wrote this:

> I have a great fear of not being sexually fulfilled in marriage. It's unfair to cop out on marriage just because of that, but what if almost every aspect of sex is unpleasing to her and you are fueled by trying out new things? I think this is more often the norm than the exception, hence the problems in many relationships. How do you convince a guy that his creative sexual desires are unimportant?

Al speaks from his assumption—a false one—that a husband and wife are either compatible or they aren't. To him, marriage is like pulling the arm on the sexual slot machine. If the fruit fails to line up, he must either accept it or divorce her, so he can give the slots another yank with someone else. In truth, sexual fulfillment isn't at all a fixed thing and can only be defined in the context of two. When we attempt to define it on our own, we force our wives to carry a sexual burden God never intended them to carry.

God said a wife should fulfill her marital duty to her husband. This assignment isn't a heavy load as long as "fulfill" is defined by the terms of her sexual essence. When the husband defines sexual fulfillment on other terms, however, oneness quickly crumbles under the weight.

More often than not, these other terms are woven from his own fantasies and past sins. For instance, who taught Al that "trying out new things" is what sexually fuels him? Was this genetically fixed in him at conception, or was it learned during the hours fantasizing over his coworker Sally, who once whispered that she loves to be massaged with warm herbal oil before intercourse?

As we've noted, Richard once stormed, "My wife hates French kissing. She says it makes her feel nauseous and totally ruins the whole sexual experience for her. She's nuts! French kissing really turns me on, and I feel cheated and downright furious when she won't do it." Which girlfriend taught Richard that French kissing turns him on? The one who's been defining sexual fulfill-ment in Richard's marriage for years, even though they haven't spoken since college?

And who's defining sexual fulfillment for you? Who told you oral sex is a must in marriage? Was it Barbara "B. J." Jacobs, the girl the team passed around at the parties after football games? Where did you learn that black thong underwear and black lace teddies were necessary to "spice things up"? At Lacy Edward's apartment—you know, the girl you're still dreaming about all these married years later?

Who taught you to view pornography before disrobing your wife? Was it the countless hours you spent alone in the darkness making love to your computer monitor?

These sorts of things aren't fixed requirements for sexual fulfillment, but you're so twisted by sin that you believe they are. If you allowed your wife's sexual essence to set the terms of sexual fulfillment, she'd be able to answer God's call for you. But you've forced her to meet your false terms defined by past sexual experiences and what the world says is fun.

PURE AS PRAYER

As the spiritual leader of our home, we're responsible for protecting our wives, not withering them. We're to honor their essence, not feed our lust. Sex with us should be as pure as prayer. We aren't to bring impurity from our past into the marriage bed: "Marriage should be honored by all, and the marriage bed kept pure, for God will judge the adulterer and all the sexually immoral" (Hebrews 13:4).

In our role as spiritual leaders, we'll find no other place in our marriage where it's more important for us to think Christianly—for *her* sake. Yet there's no place where we're more willing to stretch Scripture for *our* sake.

We aren't the first spiritual leaders willing to bend Scriptures to get what we want. The spiritual leaders of Jesus' day were twisting the truth to control God's people. They didn't start this way. The earliest Pharisees had pure hearts and a deep commitment to God and His Word. They committed their lives to the study and protection of His Law, and they were honored by the people for their devotion to God. Over time, the situation changed because the Pharisees found things they really, really wanted: "Woe to you Pharisees, because you love the most important seats in the synagogues and greetings in the marketplaces" (Luke 11:43).

Everything they did was calculated to impress the onlooker: "Everything they do is done for men to see: They make their phylacteries wide and the tassels on their garments long; they love the place of honor at banquets" (Matthew 23:5-6). Thus, neglecting the love and spirit behind the law, they controlled the people by adding to the burden of the law:

> Woe to you Pharisees, because you give God a tenth of your mint, rue and all other kinds of garden herbs, but you neglect justice and the love of God. You should have practiced the latter without leaving the former undone....
>
> And you experts in the law, woe to you, because you load people down with burdens they can hardly carry, and you yourselves will not lift one finger to help them. (Luke 11:42,46)

What we've done as husbands is typical of the most misguided Pharisee. We've found something we really, really wanted—specifically sexual practices we learned from previous relationships or from movies and the Internet. And haven't we done exactly what the Pharisees did, controlling our wives by twisting Scripture and laying a guilt trip on them? We *could* honor their sexual essence through male submission, but we don't.

So when the Scriptures say that "the wife's body does not belong to her alone but also to her husband," we turn this Scripture on its head to mean: (1) my wife must submit to sex any time I desire it, and (2) my wife must submit and perform any sexual act I desire.

This verse means nothing of the sort, and the context is plain. Paul had been asked whether celibacy was a valid spiritual virtue. Paul simply said there should be some frequency as opposed to no frequency, so Satan wouldn't tempt us through our lack of sexual self-control.

What was God's intent? Answer: Neither party would have total control of their yes or no in the marriage bed. Sex under the total control of the husband isn't God's plan. If the wife is being consistently forced to have sex against her will, then something is wrong with the relationship. Simultaneously, the wife can't have full control of her no, always waiting until she's in the mood. If the husband is being consistently forced against his will *not to have sex,* then something is wrong with the relationship here as well.

But while God simply intended to remove *some* control of our no, we've twisted it to mean our wives have *no* control over their no. Since her body is now ours, we claim that anything goes as often as we want—as if she's our warm, interactive, inflatable doll. Our spiritual authority, designed to protect her faith and strengthen her, is used instead for our own selfish ends.

What happened to the Pharisees when they turned Scripture on its head? Let's take a look:

> You say, "If anyone swears by the temple, it means nothing; but if anyone swears by the gold of the temple, he is bound by his oath." You blind fools! Which is greater: the gold, or the temple that makes the gold sacred? You also say, "If anyone swears by the altar, it means nothing; but if anyone swears by the gift on it, he is bound by his oath." You blind men! Which is greater: the gift, or the altar that makes the gift sacred? (Matthew 23:16-19)

The Pharisees' traditions replaced God's truth, and the Pharisees became so twisted themselves that Jesus called them a dangerous brood of vipers. Too often, we've become twisted as well. When our wives fail to live according to this new "truth" we've created, we may feel justified in stepping outside marriage to reclaim our "rights" to sexual fulfillment. We honor our own "truth" above God's true call to fidelity. Might Jesus aptly call us vipers as well?

Remember Eli's sons, Hophni and Phinehas, who were priests of the Lord at Shiloh? Here's their awful biography:

> Eli's sons were wicked men; they had no regard for the LORD....
>   Now Eli, who was very old, heard about everything his sons were doing to all Israel and how they slept with the women who served at the entrance to the Tent of Meeting. (1 Samuel 2:12,22)

God wanted His priests to be holy as an example to the people. Hophni and Phinehas chose instead to force themselves sexually upon even the servant girls, right in the temple.

What about you? Have you been an example of holiness in the marriage bed? Is your wife your only vessel of sexual satisfaction? Or do you absolve any means to your orgasmic end, no matter how dark or demeaning?

WHAT ARE YOU CHASING?

The priests in Ezekiel's days looked righteous enough on the surface. But God gave Ezekiel a vision to reveal what was really going on behind the temple walls:

> He said to me, "Son of man, have you seen what the elders of the house of Israel are doing in the darkness, each at the shrine of his own idol? They say, 'The LORD does not see us; the LORD has forsaken the land.'" (Ezekiel 8:12)

Let me pull back the curtains of our master bedrooms for a moment. What do we worship before our shrines, where the orgasm reigns supreme?

Albert and Linda met in elementary school and attended the same church. Somewhere during their eleventh year of marriage, Albert convinced Linda that pornography would perk up their sex life. It started with some entry-level soft-core porn videos. When it finally sunk to a level at which Linda said, "No more," Albert had reached the point of laying pornographic picture spreads across the headboard so he could view them while he had his way with Linda. He knew this wasn't making love to his cherished wife; he was just using her as a kind of sexual appliance. Linda was so traumatized by the cumulative effects of this chronic sexual abuse that she had to leave him in order to heal.

Another Christian man, Alan, has a fantasy partner he calls his Silver Woman. She's perfect in every way, kind of like the mysterious blonde in the white Corvette in *American Graffiti*. She looks great and, most important, she always wants him in bed. According to Alan, a wife is designed by God to fulfill this role for a husband, and he's angry with his wife for not cooperating.

The glazed-over look on Alan's face as he imagines his Silver Woman while having intercourse with his wife has created, shall we say, a few problems for Sherry. She often thinks, "I don't know what's wrong with this, but something just isn't right. I should feel intimate, but somehow I feel dirty." This is as it should be because Alan certainly wasn't making love to his wife.

Maybe you don't have a Silver Woman, and you think Alan is pretty sick. But there are countless Christians who tune in to old *Baywatch* reruns and fantasize about Pamela Anderson while lying upon their wives. Is that any less evil or sick? No wife should be made to share the intimacy of her marriage bed with someone whose surgically perfected breasts supposedly set the standard for feminine allure.

Have you wondered why your sex life isn't more satisfying? You've noticed that there's an empty spot. To fill it, you've asked for more variety, more frequency, and more foldouts on the headboard. But what you really need is the emotional and spiritual communion that comes with sexual oneness. Consider this e-mail from a reader of *Every Man's Battle,* a guy we'll call Matt:

> I went to a frat dance with a buddy of mine. Neither of us were frat
> guys, and we really weren't sure why we went to the dance. But my
> buddy found a girl early on and disappeared onto the dance floor,

leaving me by the wall staring aimlessly at strangers or snickering at his comical antics with this girl. The night was dragging, and I was about to leave when someone said, "Would you like to dance?"

I really didn't, but I was tired of standing around and, while she wasn't a knockout, she did have a sultry little smile. We danced for a while, but one thing led to another, and soon we were alone in her room. When she had finished with me, I could feel nothing in my toes, fingers, hands, or ankles. They were completely numb, as if she'd blown every breaker in my nervous system. We dated for four months, and she blew my circuits every single time we were alone like this.

I've never experienced this since, even with my wife. Our sex life is pretty tame by comparison. But I wouldn't dream of trading what I have now for that. Because of the purity I've gained through following God's principles in *Every Man's Battle*, I have a new spiritual communion with my wife in bed. I can't really define it, but it's so emotionally powerful that it leaps beyond anything I've ever known physically. And it plunges deep into my soul to ignite something truly wonderful. Trading what I now have for that circuit-breaker sex would be like trading gold for straw.

While you've chased fantasies and sought circuit-breaking sex, Matt has chased after oneness with his wife. He's allowed her sexual essence, rather than his own, to set the terms of his fulfillment.

Does Matt have something you don't have? If so, don't despair. Read on…

Questions for Reflection and Discussion

1. This chapter speaks of the wife's setting the terms for sexual one-ness in a marriage. What are those terms in your marriage?

2. This chapter also says that the concept of mutual submission is embedded in the words of 1 Corinthians 7:4. What truths do you discover about this statement as you look closely at this verse?

3. What does your role as spiritual leader in the home have to do with sexual oneness?

no trampling this bed!

If we're to begin to build sexual oneness and enjoy the emotional and spiritual communion it brings, we need to stop trampling the marriage bed. But if most of our sexual problems are caused by the incompatibilities of sexual tastes, how do we bring oneness out of those incompatibilities and overcome the impasses in the master bedroom?

We can do it just as we do in every other room: by honoring the convictions and essence of our wives.

Let's review what Paul said about conflicts among Christians. He said that unity must not require everyone's agreement over disputable questions. Christians will not agree on all matters pertaining to the Christian life because God didn't address every matter in Scripture. Regarding disputable matters of conduct, recognizing the importance of personal conviction is critical. Paul went on to say: "As one who is in the Lord Jesus, I am fully convinced that no food is unclean in itself. But if anyone regards something as unclean, then for him it is unclean" (Romans 14:14).

This statement acknowledges that personal convictions will result in impasses between believers, including husbands and wives, but such disagreements needn't break unity. So how do we overcome impasses lovingly? As we said earlier, traditionally the leader calls for a vote and breaks any ties in his favor. As you recall, that's not what Paul says a Christian leader should do:

Instead, make up your mind not to put any stumbling block or obstacle in your brother's way. As one who is in the Lord Jesus, I am fully convinced that no food is unclean in itself. But...if your brother is distressed because of what you eat, you are no longer acting in love. Do not by your eating destroy your brother for whom Christ died....

Let us therefore make every effort to do what leads to peace and to mutual edification. Do not destroy *the work of God* for the sake of food. All food is clean, but *it is wrong* for a man to eat anything that causes someone else to stumble. *It is better not to eat meat* or drink wine or to do anything else that will cause your brother to fall. (Romans 14:13-15,19-21)

Paul could have demanded that everyone fall in behind him, but he didn't. Instead, Paul submitted to his brother in Christ. In other words, he yielded his right to assert his authority in order to make room for the beliefs of his weaker brother.

Paul understood that pressing his rights at the expense of God's purposes would be wrong, so he wouldn't sin against God by eating meat and causing a brother to stumble. Following this principle will be especially important in the sexual realm because everything is so personal there. When it comes to sex in marriage, you must be a leader with a soft heart, a man who can submit his own rights for the sake of oneness.

Early in my marriage, I struggled with this idea. Many things that I felt were the basic staples of sex seemed kinky to Brenda. And some practices seemed flat out wrong to her. I was perplexed. Why did she have the right to declare that making love on a sand dune under a nighttime sky was kinky? Making love under the stars didn't seem kinky to me at all.

I thought about playing Chief Tiebreaker, but something told me tiebreaking wouldn't work very well (if it was at all possible anyway). Should I force my way with Brenda and get my wish even though it would demean her to the core of her soul? No. Even if I won, I lost.

Yet I still wished we could give the sand dunes a shot. So I took the matter to God. I remember exactly where I was when I turned to the Lord in prayer, saying, "Lord, I don't want to be wrong in the way I approach my sex life. You know I've got enough sexual sins in my past for any four men, and I don't want to sin anymore. Tell me what I'm supposed to do with these things that Brenda finds weird."

I was driving westbound on Interstate 80 between the Iowa towns of Atlantic and Harlan. Why do I remember so clearly? Because God answered me immediately with this

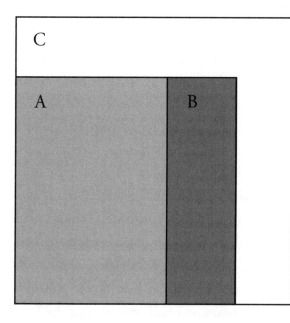

diagram, which I quickly wrote down. I also felt He gave me an understanding of what the diagram was all about.

From that day forward, Brenda and I have had complete oneness in our marriage bed, thanks to this diagram. This little graphic shows how I can honor her convictions and essence within the marriage bed.

Area A: Sexual practices the wife is comfortable with.

Area B: Sexual practices the wife views as sin.

Area C: Sexual practices the husband is comfortable with.

Looking at this chart with sets and subsets, do you feel as though you're back in school? Well, I needed to be sent to school, and I was willing to let God be my teacher. Through this diagram, God conveyed four principles for me to follow if I were going to honor Brenda's convictions and sexual essence always. Here they are:

1. The Husband Should Never Nag or Force Things That Are Outside Areas A and B

This is the white area of the diagram. What was in this area for me? Sex on the sand dunes. For Richard, it was French kissing. Maybe it's having oral sex in your marriage or making love on the kitchen floor ten minutes after you've said good-bye to your last Saturday evening guest. Maybe it's sex with the lights on when she wants the lights off.

These are the things that aren't wrong or sinful per se, because the Bible doesn't address them directly as wrong. But does your wife need a block of Scripture to back up her case? No, because any stumbling block we place in the way of sexual oneness is sin. It weakens God's purpose for marriage and flaunts our position of authority at the expense of God's work. It tramples her sexual essence.

I recently talked with Jim, who asked a question I hear a lot: "What does the Bible say about oral sex? Is it wrong?" Jim told me he constantly argued with his wife about this practice. He felt justified in asking—demanding—that she comply, incorrectly interpreting 1 Corinthians 7:4 as so many of us do. But an interesting thing was happening, and Jim was starting to get worried. When their marriage began, Jim's wife, Calley, loved sex as much as he did. She was raring to go on most nights when he returned home from work (Jim was a pastor).

That enthusiasm waned as Jim demanded that their foreplay include you-know-what. Calley blanched. "Jim knows I find oral sex repulsive," she said. "But all he cares about is his own excitement. I just can't stand it anymore because it's so demeaning. It makes me furious.

"Now I go to bed early, hoping he won't wake me up when he gets home from work. I avoid sex at all costs. It isn't worth being demeaned like that."

Would you say that oral sex is a stumbling block to sexual oneness between Jim and Calley? We'd say so! Paul taught that we must submit our rights as leaders in such circumstances. To paraphrase Romans 14:15-21, "If your wife is distressed by oral sex, you're no longer acting in love when you push it. Don't destroy the work of God [oneness in your marriage] for the sake of oral sex. Oral sex is 'clean,' but it has become sin for you if it causes your wife to stumble in oneness with you. It's better to never have oral sex again than to break oneness in your marriage."

When I was in second grade, a lunchroom rule forced us to eat something from every serving of food on our plates. I have a stomach of steel, so this caused no problem until one fateful spring day. On my tray that day was a dry white biscuit glopped with smelly white gravy and thin slices of reddish "meat." It gagged me to look at it, and it gagged me to sniff it. My tummy flopped wildly as I dawdled, eating everything else and hoping to be saved by the bell.

Suddenly, a substitute teacher loomed over me and demanded, "Take a bite of your biscuit." A hush fell over the table as my friends stared. "You have to take a bite. You know the rules."

"I can't. I'll throw up."

"Quit making excuses," she said icily. "You won't throw up. Take a bite."

"I can't. I'll throw up." Tears were starting to well.

She became very angry, snapping, "No, you won't. Take a bite this instant."

The principal's office was around the corner, and in those days, he wielded a good-sized paddle. I picked up the spoon. The moment the gravy hit my tongue, vomit splashed across the table.

How did I feel toward that teacher? I hated her. I told her I would gag, and she made me do it anyway. Can gagging and intimacy coexist following oral sex? We don't think so.

As with the other areas of marriage, you need to study your wife's sexual essence. Peter knows that his wife just cannot respond to sex in the morning. She's a night person, and if they try a little "eye-opener" in the morning, she absolutely cannot have an orgasm no matter how long he tries. While morning is his favorite time, he doesn't push it because it doesn't honor her essence, and he wouldn't be loving her as himself. Now he waits until nighttime.

2. In Submission to Oneness, the Husband Must Sacrifice What Is Outside A but Inside C

Said another way, the husband must adjust his sexual borders to align with his wife's borders. Then together they can search out and enjoy every corner within A.

Hold it! That's unfair. We aren't called to fairness. We're called to oneness, and this is right to do. Christ calls us "to do what leads to peace and to mutual edification" (Romans 14:19). Surely a husband should be willing to adjust his sexual behavior for the sake of his wife. Paul said:

> Do not allow what you consider good to be spoken of as evil. For the kingdom of God is not a matter of eating and drinking [or oral sex or sex on the dunes], but of *righteousness, peace and joy* in the Holy Spirit, because anyone who serves Christ in this way is pleasing to God and approved by men. (Romans 14:16-18)

Paul teaches here that strong leaders should submit their rights for the sake of oneness. This kind of sacrifice fosters peace, joy, and righteousness. When they demand their way, however, there's no joy or righteousness.

Let's return to Jim and Calley's story. What would happen if Jim forces Calley to submit? Jim gets his wonderful moment, but Calley gags, seething in resentment. But what if Jim gives up his drive for oral sex? Jim merely forgoes one type of pleasure for another, while Calley can happily provide and enjoy a regular sex life.

But how can cutting back on variety improve my sexual fulfillment? It seems paradoxical because of our media and culture, but it's true. When you drop back within her borders, you're essentially taking your trampling feet off her sexual essence. The boost in your emotional and spiritual communion more than makes up for the physical loss.

Here's another point: You're likely overrating the effects on the physical side. In a song made popular during my senior year in college, the singer mourned about how it used to feel when a kiss was something special. The lyrics resonated sadly with me because, at that point in my life, a kiss meant nothing. It was a joyless prerequisite on the path to intercourse.

After college when I became a Christian, I had to cut way back on my sexual boundaries in obedience to Christ. I wasn't married, so most sexual things were off-limits for me. But now the simple kiss became thrilling again simply because it was all I had available. This was totally unexpected, but it taught me that it isn't necessarily the acts that matter, but the emotion and spirit behind them.

I call this the Paradox of Obedience. We often think that obedience shuts down all fun, but the opposite happens. The Paradox of Obedience is clear in Christ's Sermon on the Mount: "Blessed are the meek, for they will inherit the earth.... Blessed are the merciful, for they will be shown mercy" (Matthew 5:5,7).

This seems crazy! The meek get nothing—only the strong survive! But for those who obey, the Paradox of Obedience pours blessings throughout their lives. We've talked with people married ten and fifteen years who are frustrated with their sex lives. How can this happen? Because they haven't applied biblical principles.

Many say that total sexual fulfillment comes from total freedom, exploration of new things, and tons of creativity. But just as political freedom flourishes within the context of moral restraint and borders, sexual freedom and fulfillment can exist within the context of loving restraints and borders.

Why are the borders so important? When we stay within the borders, we're meeting the terms of sexual oneness. When we cross the borders, we aren't. Let's return one last time to Richard and his demand for French kissing. He said, "She just won't give in. From time to time, we'll be in bed and things will be going along so well that I'll give it another try. Every single time she gets rigid and loses all interest." Like Calley, Richard's wife now avoids sex at every turn, simply to skip this battle. Who can blame her?

It's far better to respect the borders. Brenda recognizes that I know exactly where the boundaries lie. Richard knows exactly where the boundaries are with his wife, too, but he chooses to try to cross over them. The difference is that Brenda knows I will never push over a boundary to get a thrill at her expense. So within her box labeled A, I can get as close to any border I want, and she never worries or gets nervous. She can fully enjoy the territory, and she can freely give herself 100 percent to me within the borders of A.

And this is no small gain. I may have less variety, but within these borders

Brenda can give her full creativity and ingenuity to the task. This is far more important than it appears. After all, people get very good at whatever they practice a lot. Her skills will increase dramatically when she's fully given to the task.

Mike told me, "I gave up asking for oral sex years ago, and I figured I'd really lose out. But in gratitude, my wife has gotten so good in other ways that she's still never run out of ideas. There must be a billion ways she can go with this, and I've not really lost a thing."

3. Over Time, the Wife Should Feel a Responsibility to Expand Her Borders to Where She Can Feel Comfortable

However, there's no hurry on this, and if the borders never expand, that's fine too. Her sexual essence sets the terms.

Brenda has not expanded her borders much in twenty years of marriage. But I don't feel robbed a bit. Let me explain why. First, my wife is a gift from God. With all gifts we must take the good with the bad. You may remember the Father's Day example in which I had to accept the painted rock along with the nice jacket. That's how it is in marriage. God chose Brenda for me. He knew then that she had a smaller comfort area with tighter borders. In a sense, that could seem like a painted rock to me. But it might also be the finest gift God's ever given me. How do I know He didn't pick Brenda for me precisely for that reason?

After all, God knew that because of my sexual past, I had a warped view of sex. Maybe He knew that the discipline of falling back within her tight borders was exactly what I needed to learn the blessings of sacrificial love. Maybe He knew this would free me from my selfish sexuality to experience the abundant life He promised me.

Second, I'm not the only one in the marriage. God wanted Brenda to have a good sex life too. And not just physically, but emotionally and spiritually as well.

Let's take the spiritual first. Trampling her essence is sin, and remember that sin puts something between you and your wife in the spiritual realm. If your sin causes a break in your communion with God, it will surely break your spiritual oneness in bed even if she doesn't know about the sin. If you fantasize over some buxom actress from *Baywatch* while having sex with your wife, that's adultery. Is adultery "considerate to your wife," or do you suppose it might hinder your prayer life and your sex life? You may still be meeting physically in bed, but there's no connection between your spirits in the spiritual realm. There are no secrets there.

We believe that's why we received so many e-mails from readers of *Every Man's Battle* about this. They tell us that when their sexual impurity was gone, their sex lives simply went ballistic! We believe it's because they were meeting their wives spiritually for the first time in the marriage bed.

But God also wanted Brenda to have a good sex life *emotionally*. When you trample her borders, you're putting something between you not only in the spiritual realm, but also in the emotional realm. We've already shared many examples. But you're also putting something between you and God in the emotional realm. You're sleeping with His daughter, and you're trampling her sexually.

Imagine your own daughter coming to you in tears after a few months of marriage, crying because her husband forces her to have sex with handcuffs. It hurts her wrists physically, and it demeans her to the core of her soul. Would your relationship with your son-in-law remain unaffected? Mine wouldn't. When you dishonor your wife's sexual essence, God is just as ticked as you would be with that son-in-law, and He isn't smiling upon your marriage bed.

But if you're honoring your wife's sexual essence, He's smiling. So is she. You've made an emotional connection to go along with the spiritual connection.

4. The Area Labeled B Is Off-Limits Forever to the Husband and Must Never Be Brought Up Again

I earlier shared the story of my attempt to take Brenda "parking" shortly after our wedding. Brenda held a personal conviction that parking was wrong. Paul says that in the face of such impasses, we should give in. In fact, to be concerned with such trivial matters as parking at the expense of Brenda's precious faith is to miss the essence of Christian living.

It turns out I could live without parking, and you can live without oral sex or making love standing up—or whatever else is your fantasy.

Let it go.

Following these four guidelines brings sexual oneness out of our sea of incompatibilities. When I lead this way, Brenda feels one with me. She can easily submit to my stronger sex drive. Sex is never a border fight, but always peaceful, kind, and thrilling.

In no other area in your life will you receive such a large and immediate impact when you apply the principles of servant leadership. It's not slow, like other aspects of the Christian life. You serve the Lord now, and after you die, He'll call you faithful. You serve your kids now, and in thirty years, they'll call you blessed. You serve your wife in the bedroom, and—POW!—you'll receive gratification of the highest degree.

Now that's some instant gratification we can all get behind.

Allow me (Steve) to make just one final observation about Fred and Brenda's story. You may need to reread this, but hang with me because I think it's more important than the concepts presented. The most important thing is that Fred and Brenda are obviously both engaged in the relationship, sexually and nonsexually. These are two people working together to make a marriage work, to make their sex life better, and to make their journey together more fulfilling. They're on each other's team.

Let them serve as a great example to all of us, a reminder that we husbands need to be for our wives, not against them. If we follow that advice, we may find ourselves engaged in a fulfilling and fun relationship just like Fred and Brenda's.

Questions for Reflection and Discussion

1. In this chapter, Fred says that early in his marriage he struggled with the idea that when it came to sex in marriage, he needed to be a leader with a soft heart, a man who could submit his own rights for the sake of oneness. To what extent do you also struggle with this concept?

2. How would you explain the diagram in this chapter as it pertains to your own marriage? What practices are in area B for your wife?

an open letter to wives

(from Brenda Stoeker)

Dear Friend,

One night when Fred wanted to make love, I moaned inside, Not again already! I felt put out, so I managed to say, "Okay, I can put up with a quickie for your sake, but let's hurry. I'm tired and want to go to sleep."

Fred took a deep bow and said, "Thank you, oh great and noble martyr!" As I recall, things slid downhill quickly from there.

That week I wondered if these halfhearted, short experiences with me were fulfilling for him. While women draw intimacy from their mates primarily through sharing, hugging, and talking, I've learned that men draw intimacy from the sex acts themselves.

Mulling this over, I reversed the scene in my mind. What if Fred reacted to my need for sharing and hugging in the way I'd been reacting to him? What if he said, "I'm only in the mood once or twice a month to give you a hug and talk to you in any meaningful way, but I can give you a quickie talk before I fall asleep." The light popped on in my head. These two situations are exactly the same, but because of the gender differences, men aren't nearly as concerned about hugs as they are about sex, and women aren't nearly as concerned about sex as they are about hugs. We can't expect our husbands to get interested in hugs if we don't get interested in intercourse.

Initially, in my early years of marriage, I was shocked by male sexuality, especially by its visual orientation and its regularity. Male sexuality seemed rather shallow and almost weird to me, but I started to wonder about that. I discovered that it really isn't shallow. It's just different. And given the obvious struggle men have with sexual purity when they're without sex, I began to understand why God would tell me, "Your body is not your own." I can see where at times sex is vital to Fred's purity and his emotional intimacy with me. And I can really help him out. In fact, God expects me to do it.

While we're quick to expect our husbands to toe God's line of sexual purity, we're often slow to toe His other line and admit that our bodies aren't our own. We have no right to expect our husbands to stay sexually pure if we constantly pull away. We're his sole vessel of sexual satisfaction, and guys need regular sexual fulfillment two or three times a week.

A friend of mine, Cindy, related her husband's observation that she had all the power in their sexual relationship, every speck of it. Every single time, he was the one who had to lock the door and ask for it. She, on the other hand, was always either freezing or tired.

"I know you have no real interest," he said to her. "But it's tough knowing that 90 percent of the time when we have sex you can't even pretend to find me desirable. All you understand is that I need something you don't need, and you're simply doing it out of duty. When you don't show any true desire or passion on your own, I start feeling like a little boy depending on Mommy to give me my candy."

Mood should have nothing to do with it. We're called to help out, whether we're in the mood or not. Countless times I've initiated sex with Fred when we both knew I wasn't in the mood.

Every night when Fred comes into the bedroom, he sits in his "talking chair" to make sure he doesn't fall asleep before I have the chance to talk with him. That means so much to me, especially since I know Fred is never in the mood for talking at that time of night. He's a morning person, so he's really tired when we go to bed, but he converses with me because he knows I need it, whether he's in the mood or not.

If your husband is like most guys, he goes to work at his job when he isn't in the mood at least 50 percent of the time. I know that if it weren't for the kids and me, Fred would choose a different path for his life. How often am I tired at the end of the day, and Fred cleans the kitchen so I can sit and read a book? How often does he play Nintendo to draw the kids out of my hair for a break? (He hates Nintendo. He doesn't know what he's doing and always gets slaughtered, even by nine-year-old Michael.)

Can't we do the same for our husbands when we aren't in the mood? Besides, moods are a funny thing. Moods change quickly. Remember, part of our own intimacy is based on hugging and touching. I've found that if I submit and go ahead with things for his sake, more often than not all the touching and caressing changes my mood, and soon I'm enjoying things as much as he is. In fact, this happens so often that I've begun to count on it. I'm usually rewarded, right on the spot!

I have come to the point where I regularly ask Fred about his needs. Last night, for example, when he came into the room, I simply asked, "Would you like to lock the door?" He understood!

I chase after four kids all day. On many of these nights, I'm not really in the mood for sexual intercourse because I'm too tired or because my natural drive is just plain weaker than his. On those occasions, I'll say, "I'm not really interested myself, but I'd love to do something for you." I know I'll at least like the snuggling, even if I don't get all fired up.

And while a long-term diet of drive-through sex isn't desirable, there's certainly still a place for the quickie since it defuses the power of a man's seventy-two-hour cycle. Sometimes you just don't have the time or energy for the full package, but if you care about him, you can find just enough energy to get by. Regardless, there's something very fulfilling to a man in knowing his wife cares enough to help like this, even if it's not really "her night."

I don't pretend to understand Fred's sexuality. All I know is that sexual purity is not just every man's battle, but every *couple's* battle as well.

God bless you,

Brenda

a closing word

On a recent Saturday, I stopped by the grocery store to pick up some dough-nuts for the kids. One of the bakery's managers attends the premarriage class I teach each Sunday. "Hey, how's the book coming?" he asked.

Before I could answer, a forty-five-year-old woman behind the counter piped in. "You're writing a book?" she said. "What's it about?"

"It's about male leadership in marriage," I offered.

Her face hardened, and with a narrowed glare, she said, "Yeah, right!"

I just smiled. I was reminded again that most of us men have no idea what marriage should look like, and our clumsy efforts to be a "good hus-band" reflect it. And when it comes to "male leadership," many of us lead simply by taking charge. As you've seen in this book, grabbing the reins didn't work too well for me. My marriage to Brenda withered, and as my love life crumbled, I just knew God had to have a better way. He did.

You've read our discussion at length in this book about God's plan for good marital leadership. This book represents truths from God that I have ached to share for fifteen long years…truths that are the passion of my heart and life…truths that lifted my marriage from the ash heap and helped it prosper beyond my wildest dreams. I wouldn't trade my marriage for any other I know.

Now, in closing, I want to express once more God's plan for good marital leadership, but this time reduce it to a single verse: "Submit to one another out of reverence for Christ." (Ephesians 5:21).

This is God's simple plan for oneness in marriage. May you follow it, and may your marriage be forever changed.

Steve can be reached by e-mail at sarterburn@newlife.com.

Fred can be reached by e-mail at fred@stoekergroup.com
or at www.fredstoeker.com.

acknowledgments

First, thanks to my partner, Stephen Arterburn. I recall hearing him speak on a radio broadcast back in the mid-eighties, and thinking, "I really love this man's heart! I'd love to get to know him." Little did I know that God planned a ministry for us some fifteen years in the future! Steve, I still love your heart.

Second, thanks to my mom and my sisters. We've been through it all and lived to tell about it! I love you very much.

I would also like to acknowledge several people who continue to have a profound influence on my life. Mr. Campbell, you told me to keep writing. I have. I so wish you were here to share it. Ray and Joyce Henderson always believe. My mother-in-law, Gwen, is still my fiercest defender.

To those who shared their stories, thank you. May you share in every blessing, for you were indispensable. To Mark Oberbeck, who is never surprised, and to Ron Strack, who is always surprised…thanks for your unconditional friendship. I reserve my deepest gratitude for my children: Jasen, Laura, Rebecca, and Michael. I love you! God asked much sacrifice of you, and you freely gave. Thanks for listening to God, and thanks for praying for me.

And to Brenda. You've never strayed from His path, and your precious voice is like a gentle song to Him. You are my greatest hero, and always this man's desire.

every man's battle workshops

from New Life Ministries

new Life Ministries receives hundreds of calls every month from Christian men who are struggling to stay pure in the midst of daily challenges to their sexual integrity and from pastors who are looking for guidance in how to keep fragile marriages from falling apart all around them.

As part of our commitment to equip individuals to win these battles, New Life Ministries has developed biblically based workshops directly geared to answer these needs. These workshops are held several times per year around the country.

- Our workshops **for men** are structured to equip men with the tools necessary to maintain sexual integrity and enjoy healthy, productive relationships.

- Our workshops **for church leaders** are targeted to help pastors and men's ministry leaders develop programs to help families being attacked by this destructive addiction.

Some comments from previous workshop attendees:

"An awesome, life-changing experience. Awesome teaching, teacher, content and program." —DAVE

"God has truly worked a great work in me since the EMB workshop. I am fully confident that with God's help, I will be restored in my ministry position. Thank you for your concern. I realize that this is a battle, but I now have the weapons of warfare as mentioned in Ephesians 6:10, and I am using them to gain victory!" —KEN

"It's great to have a workshop you can confidently recommend to anyone without hesitation knowing that it is truly life changing. Your labors are not in vain!"

If sexual temptation is threatening your marriage or your church, please call **1-800-N** with one of our specialists.